MANAGING NONPROFIT ORGANIZATIONS IN THE 21ST CENTURY

BY JAMES P. GELATT

W0010559

ORYX PRESS
1992

The rare Arabian Oryx is believed to have inspired the myth of the unicorn. This desert antelope became virtually extinct in the early 1960s. At that time several groups of international conservationists arranged to have 9 animals sent to the Phoenix Zoo to be the nucleus of a captive breeding herd. Today the Oryx population is nearly 800, and over 400 have been returned to reserves in the Middle East.

Copyright © 1992 by
The Oryx Press
4041 North Central at Indian School Road
Phoenix, AZ 85012-3397

Published simultaneously in Canada

Printed and Bound in the United States of America

The paper used in this publication meets the minimum requirements of American National Standard for Information Science-- Permanence of Paper for Printed Library Materials, ANSI Z39.48, 1984.

Library of Congress Cataloging-in-Publication Data

Gelatt, James P.
   Managing nonprofit organizations in the 21st century / by James P. Gelatt.
       p.   cm.
   Includes bibliographical references and index.
   ISBN 0-89774-654-6
   1. Corporations, Nonprofit—Management.   I. Title.
HD62.6.G44   1992
658'.048—dc20
                                                91-37315
                                                    CIP

For Charlie and Leslie

Contents

Preface:
What You Need to
Know to Manage in the
Decade Ahead

There is one thing that can be said with certainty about the year 2000: it will be anticipated with more attention, with more written and said about it, than was the case for any year in recent memory. The media abound with articles and talk shows about what life will be like.

Why so much attention? In part, it signals a new era (remember the movie *2001?*); in part, because we are in the in an Age of Information, wherein the sheer volume of information on any topic is a multiple of what it might have been a century ago; but also, in large part, because there are some dramatic changes taking place in the United States and worldwide. Nowhere are these changes more dramatic than in the not-for-profit, nonprofit, independent, third sector.

THE NONPROFIT WORLD: SOME PERCEPTIONS

When he visited the United States in the 1830s, Alexis de Tocqueville was struck by the spirit of voluntarism in America, by the unwillingness to have everything managed or controlled by business (the "first sector") or by government (the "second"). As the year 2000 approaches, that spirit is not only alive but spreading. Traditional first sector poets, most notably business and marketing guru Peter Drucker, are coming to recognize the vitality and the professionalism—and the value—of the nonprofit world.

Despite the fact that the value of nonprofits is being increasingly recognized, not everyone acknowledges the skills that many nonprofit executives bring to their jobs. There is a lingering perception among business executives who view their counterparts in the not-for-profit world as "unsophisticated, inefficient, unaccountable, and poorly paid."[1] Ask the average person on the street, and one may get a stereotypical perception which reads along these lines: "If you want to find effective managers and leaders, look to the corporate world, where things get done. Nonprofit organizations for the most part are composed of people who don't have the talent or the drive to make it in the corporate world. They're do-gooders who could benefit from having to live or die by the bottom line."

Unfortunately, this negative view of the capabilities of nonprofit executives is held even by some who have toiled in its fields. One former nonprofit executive wrote that "nonprofit organizations are often run by people who know almost nothing about administration."[2]

To be sure, in many cases that perception is singularly inaccurate. While it may have been the case some years ago, it is today no more correct to argue that those who run nonprofit organizations are incompetent than to suggest that all profit-making companies are effectively managed. (Would that were true; it would certainly reduce the clamor about not being as successful in management as are other countries, most notably Japan.)

WHAT MANAGERS DON'T KNOW

In truth, managers in both for-profit and nonprofit sectors often lack some very basic skills and knowledge. Here are the results of one study reporting on a management "IQ test" given to managers:

- Nearly half of those polled did not understand that people tend to repeat behavior that is rewarded.
- More than 60 percent felt it was not appropriate to "brag" about the accomplishments of their subordinates.
- Nearly 7 of 10 did not believe that the way to resolve a grievance was to look for a mutually satisfactory solution.
- Almost 8 of 10 among those questioned were unaware that performance management reviews should address specific rather than just general observations.[3]

MANAGING FOR THE YEAR 2000

Throughout this book, the emerging issues and trends that will affect how and whom we manage as nonprofit executives in the year 2000 will be addressed. There are dramatic changes in demographics, in values, in health care and education, in science and technology—all of which will alter irrevocably the way in which successful nonprofit organizations will be structured and managed. The image of the manager in the 1970s, or even the 1980s, will not fit the manager of the year 2000. While there are some common characteristics of managers in general, it is safe to say that what worked in the nonprofits of 1980 may not work at all in the twenty-first century.

NONPROFIT/FOR-PROFIT: SOME GUIDING PRINCIPLES

There are three guiding principles underpinning this book:

1. **Nonprofit organizations are fundamentally different from for-profit companies.**

   It is true that some of the lines between the two are blurring; health care, for example, is increasingly being offered by for-profit enterprises, while nonprofits in health care talk of "profit centers." Nonetheless, there are fundamental differences in the way nonprofit and for-profit institutions are organized and function.

   Nonprofit organizations exist to serve a constituency or cause; to do so successfully, they must show a positive bottom line.

   For-profit companies exist to show a positive bottom line; to do so, they must meet the needs or wants of a particular constituency.

2. **Although there are dissimilarities, there is much that nonprofits can learn from for-profit entities.**

   Indeed, those nonprofits that are most able to balance nonprofit mission with for-profit business sense will have the greatest likelihood of success.

3. **The term "nonprofit" covers a wide array of activities.**

   It includes everything from churches to environmental groups, from major national trade and professional associations to small, local, even neighborhood charities.

   Despite the vast differences among nonprofits, there are problems common to all; problems that are, for the most part, unique to nonprofits. Ten problems peculiar to nonprofit organizations are delineated below.

THE TEN PROBLEMS EVERY NONPROFIT EXECUTIVE FACES

If there is comfort in numbers, nonprofit management can gain some security in the probability that virtually every nonprofit institution is facing or has at some time in its organizational development had to confront the following ten problems.

1. Many Nonprofits Go from Crisis to Crisis, Emergency to Emergency

The first problem takes different forms, with different rationales offered:

- "There is no time to plan. We are constantly trying just to keep up with the workload, to keep our heads above water."
- "There's little point in writing a plan; nobody follows it anyway. When the crisis comes along, we drop everything. When the new board president comes in, he [or she] wants to do things his [her] way."
- "Planning is fine, but in the real world you have to deal with the day to day."
- "We're lucky we know where payroll's coming from next month. Plan for the next three years?"

However stated, the problem is essentially the same. The nonprofit is operating without a clear sense of where it wants to be five years from today. It is not necessary to live from crisis to crisis. There is another way. Chapter 1 addresses the importance of knowing and stating the nonprofit's mission; Chapter 2 addresses how to create and put a workable plan in place.

2. There Is a Need to Look at the "Big Picture"

Failure to look at the big picture can take several forms:

- "We don't have a way of considering what might influence our organization a few years from now."
- "We are a collection of programs, with no unifying theme or focus."
- "We act without considering all of the consequences, with the result that we often have to develop unanticipated responses."
- "We need a way to make better decisions."

One of the most interesting dimensions in planning is what is known as "systems management," which allows the organization to consider the potential implications of decisions and courses of action. Chapter 2 gives the reader an introduction to systems management; it may be eye-opening with regard to the decision making process.

In order to have a clear sense of purpose, the nonprofit needs to know whom it serves, what their needs and wants are, and how best to respond to those needs and wants. In other words, the nonprofit of the

1990s must think of itself in marketing terms. Chapter 3 provides the tools to do so.

3. The Community Doesn't Understand What the Organization Is About

People who live within walking distance don't know the kind of programs that we offer, to say nothing of the community at large. One reason why we don't do better in direct mail fund raising is that we're simply not well enough known. People don't really have an idea of the good things going on here, so you can't blame them for not being willing to support us. And the newspapers are no better: getting them to cover an event is virtually impossible. They're too busy pointing out what's wrong with the town—who shot whom, who's up on a morals charge. How do we get their attention?

While it is eminently true that the media seem to prefer "hard news," it is possible to become better known. Chapter 4 provides some pointers.

4. More Money Is Needed

Who doesn't need more money? It is hard to imagine a nonprofit organization deciding to curtail its fund raising efforts because it has all the money it needs. (Actually, there was one: Boys Town, which received so much money every time the movie about it appeared on television that it literally had to develop new programs in order to absorb its assets. It is now fund raising for those new programs just like the rest of us.)

The good news is that, regardless of the economy (short of an all-out depression), there is substantial money to be raised; Chapter 5 will address how to set up and manage an effective fund raising office.

5. The Financial Records Are a Mess

It's hard to get a fix on what our real costs are, how well we're doing in fund raising, where we might be able to trim. Frankly, much of what comes out of our Accounting Department is intelligible only to other accountants. We don't have a good way of reporting to donors on what difference their contributions have made.

If there is one area in which many nonprofit executives feel inadequate, it is in finance. Most executive directors come from a background other than accounting. What knowledge they have of balance sheets and audits has been acquired on-the-job out of necessity. Chapter 6 gives the reader an opportunity to check his or her understanding of finance; and it provides information—in plain English—on how to make improvements in managing and reporting financial information.

6. It Is Difficult to Get and Keep Good Staff

Attracting and keeping talented, hard working staff is a very real challenge for nonprofit organizations. Opportunities (for women and minorities in particular) have opened up in other professions—medicine, law, computer science—and more than one nonprofit has lost out to the for-profit sector. But there are indications that as a country we are somewhat less enamored with making money our top priority, returning to some traditional values, looking to work where we might make a difference.

The nonprofit that thrives in the next decade will understand the changing workforce and changes in individual and family value systems, will realize what motivates top performance, will develop mechanisms to reward achievement. There should be ample information at the ready in this book on the topic of hiring and keeping skilled staff. The reader may wish to see Chapter 7 for starters.

7. There Is Poor Communication among the Members of the Organization

One department doesn't know what the other is doing, even when they're ostensibly working on related projects. We have meetings, but they're either too long or too boring—or too combative—for real communication and change to occur. It's no wonder the public doesn't understand what we're all about.

Maintaining effective staff communication is a problem that often comes with growth, although even among small nonprofit organizations maintaining open and clear communication channels can be problematic. Chapters 8 and 9 provide some practical tools that the nonprofit executive can begin using immediately to improve communications and make meetings more useful.

8. The Board Is Involved Where It Shouldn't Be and Not Where It Ought to Be

Our volunteer board is into everything. They want to make decisions about whether the paint on the walls of the new wing should be beige or light brown. They want to be involved in selecting staff. They want monthly reports on activities, finance, new projects. They want to know why we're buying three new word processors for the executive staff.

What they're not into is helping us to become better known in the community, getting us into the state funding agencies, taking the lead on the building campaign, establishing policy for the organization for the next decade. How do we turn it around with a board like we've got?

The answers won't come overnight, but there are answers; Chapter 10 addresses some of the issues and offers solutions.

9. It's Harder Than Ever to Get Good Volunteers

As will be addressed later in this chapter, under the topic of trends affecting nonprofit organizations, there is some truth to the claim that it is harder to get—and keep—good volunteers. There are several issues involved: nonprofit organizations need to understand the changing nature of volunteering, the changing nature of nonprofits, and what institutions really want and need from volunteers. And successful nonprofit organizations will have to do a better job not only of recruiting, but also of retaining and cultivating volunteers at all levels.

Chapter 11 provides an understanding of the changing nature of volunteering and offers tips on how to create a successful volunteer team in your organization.

10. Even Good Staff Members Are Burning Out

Burnout is an occupational hazard for many nonprofit organizations: too few staff, too much to get done, too many frustrations, too little reward. In some jobs, burnout—working with children with severe, multiple disabilities; or with adults caught in the cycle of poverty—may be virtually inevitable. Yet there are individuals who have remained vigorous and committed to such causes for years on end.

There are some alternatives to burnout, which will be addressed in Chapter 12 . There are some ways to keep the motivation high, so that burnout doesn't settle in. And steps to take when it's time for staff to move on.

WHAT IS MANAGEMENT?

In *The New Realities*, management professor and theorist Peter Drucker detailed a set of essential principles which, in his view, capture management. A number of the principles that he articulated are pertinent to the organization of this book.

1. Management is concerned with human beings.

Specifically, management is involved with how to get human beings to work effectively together, building on strengths, mitigating weaknesses.

2. **When it is effective, management is integrated within the very culture of the society.**

   Said another way, the management style needs to fit the cultural milieu.

3. **As will be addressed in Chapter 2, establishing a commitment to common goals is a first priority for management.**

   Common goals make the difference between a mob and a team.

4. **The environment is dynamic.**

   For the organization to succeed, it must adapt. It is the job of management to continually prepare employees, updating their skills—as will be addressed in the chapter on staff training.

5. **Virtually every organization comprises varied personalities, varying skills, and a variety of jobs.**

   Making it all work requires effective communication.

6. **Success should be measured by more than profit and loss.**

   Nonprofit organizations need to ask themselves:

   - Are we being innovative?
   - Has our position relative to our competitors ascended or declined?
   - Are we meeting our mission?

7. **As will be addressed in Chapter 3, success is best measured by asking: "Have we met the needs of those whom we serve?"**[4]

WHAT MAKES FOR THE BEST: HALLMARKS OF EXCELLENCE

This Preface has described some of the problems virtually every nonprofit organization faces from time to time (if not literally all of the time). There is a growing body of literature describing the factors common among the best nonprofits. Here are five characteristics that the best seem to possess:

A Clear Sense of Mission

According to a study conducted by Independent Sector, a coalition of national nonprofit organizations and major funding organizations, the first characteristic of excellent nonprofit organizations is the presence of "a clearly articulated sense of mission that serves as the focal point of commitment for board and staff."[5] The sense of mission guides the organization, frames the long-range and strategic planning, provides a sense of direction, and gives the organization its unity and purpose. It is the "primordial soup" out of which the successful organization evolves.

A Well Led Organization

A nonprofit with a sense of mission but without leadership is a boat with a set of charts and no pilot. At both the staff and board levels, the excellent nonprofit organization has a strong and committed leadership. The chief staff officer (hereafter referred to as the CSO or CEO) and board leadership work toward common stated goals and provide the example for others. It is evident that the volunteer and staff leadership believe in the cause. Working for the organization is thus more than a job, more than an honorary post; it's a sizable dedication of one's waking hours.

A Professionally Managed Organization

In all but the youngest and smallest nonprofits, carrying out the mission defines the roles of staff and volunteers, and both groups need to be well managed. According to John Garrison, former president of the National Easter Seal Society, "Some nonprofit people used to think that if you're doing good, somehow God will provide. But almost everyone now realizes that commitment isn't enough anymore. You also have to have professionalism, or you're going to go out of business."[6]

Precisely because they do not have a bottom line orientation, nonprofits have to develop the discipline of sound management. This will be even more true as the next century approaches.

Volunteers and Staff Who Understand and Appreciate Each Other's Roles

"The relationship between the CSO and the board is one of mutual trust and respect."[7] There is an understanding, revisited as necessary, of the differing roles of volunteer and staff. Each has an awareness of the strengths that the other brings to the organization. Communication between staff and volunteers is open and frequent.

A Fiscally Sound Organization

Fund raising is an integral part of the successful organization, carried out by both staff and volunteers. The organization enjoys a positive reputation and is able to attract major gifts. Donors can be assured that their donations are both accurately recorded and prudently managed.

HOW THE BOOK IS ORGANIZED

These five principles . . .

- Mission
- Leadership
- Management
- Professionalism
- Financial Stability . . .

. . . both form the core and permeate the thinking within this book. It is written with the chief staff officer and senior management in mind, whether the positions are described as president, chief executive officer, executive director, administrator, or division or department director. Those who aspire to these positions, or would like to know more about the characteristics of an excellent nonprofit, will be served by its contents as well.

The book assumes that the reader:

- Does not have infinite time; but
- Needs or desires to become reasonably informed about some topics and proficient in others.

On that basis, each chapter begins with an "organizer" in the form of an executive summary. Its purpose is to provide a quick glance into the chapter and a review of its contents. Reading the executive summary should help the reader to decide in what depth he or she wishes to explore the chapter, where there may be some knowledge gaps, and where he or she can skim.

Nonprofit organizations have always been important, but never more so than they will be in the next century. It is not unlikely to speculate that some of the best nonprofits in the next decade will be considered "vanguard," looked to by profit and nonprofit sectors alike for their leadership, organization, and innovation.

Here's to yours becoming one of those nonprofits.

NOTES

1. (No author), "Perception Lags Behind Reality," *Association Management,* 42 (February 1990): 34.

2. Thomas Wolf, *The Nonprofit Organization: An Operating Manual* (New York: Prentice Hall Press, 1984), v.

3. (No author), "What Managers Don't Know," *Communication Briefings*, 8 (no date): 1.

4. Peter F. Drucker, *The New Realities: In Government and Politics, In Economics and Business, In Society and World View* (New York: Harper & Row, 1989), 228–231.

5. "Profiles of Excellence: Studies of the Effectiveness of Nonprofit Organizations," Executive Summary (Washington, DC: Independent Sector, 1989), 3.

6. John Byrne, "Profiting from the Nonprofits," *Business Week*, 3151 (no volume) (March 26, 1990): 67.

7. "Profiles of Excellence," 11.

Chapter 1
Mission: A Sense of Purpose

If you don't know where you want to go, any road will get you there.
—Anonymous

EXECUTIVE SUMMARY

A child being interviewed by Art Linkletter on his popular "Kids Say the Darndest Things" observed that the captain of the ship needs to know two things: where the ship is headed and how to get there. Mission is where, planning is how.

This chapter on mission describes an organization that transformed itself from a nonprofit at risk to a vibrant and growing national entity by first asking: "What is our business?" The chapter points out how the mission statement is used and why it is important that it be written down. Visioning is described in the context of planning, along with some tools to conduct visioning activities. Some noteworthy examples of mission statements are presented. The chapter concludes with a look at some trends that will affect the missions of many nonprofits and a thought about "making a difference."

What makes a nonprofit outstanding? What singles out some nonprofit organizations above the rest? Why is it that some organizations always seem to be doing the right thing, while others seem to founder, moving from project to project, with no apparent sense of direction? The primary characteristic of the outstanding nonprofit is a clearly articulated, jointly held, commonly valued sense of mission.

A CASE IN POINT

Frances Hesselbein took over the national executive directorship of Girl Scouts of America at a time when that organization was foundering. In an increasingly multicultural world, Girl Scouts was largely white and middle class. It held little appeal for many of the teenage girls whom it wanted to attract and membership was, understandably, a problem; so, too, was volunteer leadership.

Hesselbein began asking questions that went to the very heart of the organization: "What is our business? Who is the customer? And what does the customer value?"[1]

Hesselbeing created a *mission* for the Girl Scouts of America. They would be neither a women's rights organization nor a religious organization, nor a source of cheap labor for door-to-door sales. Girl Scouts of America would be in the business of helping girls and young women achieve their potential.

Out of this mission, this clarified focus, grew new programs and new initiatives—a new strategic plan. And out of the plan: a reinvigorated, thriving organization.

Strategic planning, which is described in Chapter 2, begins with the creation of a mission statement. Because it is so central to the success of the nonprofit organization, developing the mission is concerned in this chapter in depth

STATING YOUR MISSION = KNOWING YOUR MISSION

It is not uncommon for groups working on planning to balk at the time being allowed for the creation and articulation of a mission statement:

"We all know what the purpose of this organization is. Why on earth are we wasting so much time on this matter, when we could be getting on with the real work of planning?"

"I just can't see why it's necessary to state the mission in one or two sentences. There are dozens of important things that we do. How can we possibly write a mission statement that includes all of them?"

"Let's go ahead with the rest of the planning process and come back to this mission statement. Maybe it'll be clearer once we know just what it is we want to do."

Avoid the temptation. If the organization accomplishes nothing else in its planning process, it is important to have consensus on your mission. Why?

- The mission statement is the organization's essence.

  When someone asks, "What do you do?" it is essential that everyone—staff, board, other volunteers—has the same answer. Imagine trying to convince a funder to support you when you can't agree about your purpose.

As a corollary: you should be able to state that mission in one sentence. Two, at most. If you can't, perhaps the organization hasn't crystallized its mission. Perhaps it is trying to go in too many directions.

- Clarifying mission clarifies purpose.

As your organization digs into analyzing its mission, what you'll find is that different "players" have different ideas, usually reflecting their own biases and favorite programs, understandably. Writing the mission statement forces the issue.

- The mission statement should "set the charge."

It should be stated in terms that command attention. A mission statement worth its salt says: "Hey, this is who we are! We're the first/the biggest/the only . . . . And what's more, we're *going* to be. . . ." Said another way: the mission should evoke pride on the part of your volunteers and staff and get others to think: That's an outfit that I want to know more about.

DOES YOUR ORGANIZATION REALLY NEED A MISSION?

The classic case of failing to understand one's purpose (which every teacher of planning drags out if given enough time) is that of the American railroad, which failed to grasp that it was in the business not merely of hauling freight, but of "transportation." The suggestion is made that if the owners of the railroad lines had thought of themselves in a larger context, the railroads might be thriving today, as they are in Europe and Japan.

Here is another, perhaps more poignant example. Consider the American school system. From its inception, it was generally an effective institution, in part because it complemented other institutions—notably the family and the church and the family doctor—which were well established. Each had its unique place in society providing services which together make for a whole and healthy person. There were common bonds among the three, and a common sense of values pervaded. As society became more complex, more diverse, and more mobile, it created a situation in which the educational system, almost by default, took on additional responsibilities. As a consequence it today faces enormous challenge, brought on in large part by changes that it did not anticipate, and has been forced to address after the fact:

- The traditional family (two parents, one at home; at least two children; a detached house) now characterizes only about half of the American homes.

- There has been a decline in the numbers of persons practicing traditional religion.
- The family physician is now a health care system, to which many have limited access.

Stated simplistically, if the challenges to teaching in 1950 were talking in study hall, chewing gum, too little money, and how to deal with varying degrees of ability, today they are teenage pregnancy, drugs in the school, heightened violence—and too little money (some things don't change).

Had the educational system been considering their mission and monitoring these trends, they may have been able to construct a broadened mission for the schools as a focal point in the community. Imagine a school facility open to children and adults: a point of entry to the various educational and health care systems; a source of respite care for single parents; a daycare facility for the elderly; a job placement center. In short, conceive of a school that plays a central role in the life of the community—that indeed makes it a community.

There are arguments that can be made counter to this line of reasoning, to be sure; but the point is: no one anticipated major social changes; they did not ask, "What role should—or could—the school play?" The result is that they are playing catch-up, saddled with a mission that is flawed.

This kind of reasoning needs to be applied to the nonprofit organization. Management needs to keep abreast of changing demographic and other trends (as will be covered in a subsequent chapter), and periodically reassess their mission in light of a rapidly changing society.

CREATING A VISION

Does any of these sound like your organization?[2]

The organization hardly lacks for good ideas. Department and division staff are often coming up with plans for a new project which they would like to implement. Some of the most loyal and active board members have developed their own "pet" projects, working solo or with selected staff.

৬ ৬ ৬

As CEO, you're having trouble getting people "charged up about" the organization and its possibilities. Perhaps it's just that many of your staff and volunteers have been with the organization for a number of years, and are a bit jaded; perhaps it's because the organization's relatively good success has made people complacent. Whatever the cause, the result is a notable lack of vibrancy. Even when new ideas surface, they don't sustain interest for very long.

ꕷ ꕷ ꕷ

You feel a little greedy complaining about the organization. It actually runs quite well. Staff and volunteers are committed to the organization's well being. There is general agreement about where the organization should be headed. What bothers you is that you are convinced that the organization has not begun to realize its potential.

In each of these instances, what is lacking is a sense of organizational *vision*.

Visioning is a proven method which can be used to create a picture of where you (singly or collectively) want the organization to be some years hence—the vision of how the organization might appear. It is a journey into the essence of the organization, engaging visioning participants in creating word pictures.

The mission statement is a crystallized answer to the question, "What business are we in?"; the vision is an imaginative depiction of what the organization wants to be. It speaks in bold language. For example:

- We are nationally recognized as one of the finest business schools in the country, able to attract the top graduate students.

- The XYZ Institute is a major factor in the elimination of Alzheimer's disease worldwide.

- We have gained a national and international reputation for excellence in the performing arts. Our annual Bach festival sells out six months in advance.

Once you have the mental picture, or pictures, the mission becomes a crystallization of that far off goal, and perhaps how to reach it.

As an opening activity, if the nature of the planning group (and the skill of the moderator) seem to lend themselves, you can perform visioning exercises that help to loosen up the group and lighten the task ahead. For example:

- Ask the group's members to close their eyes, and picture what the organization might look like in five or ten years.

  Ask them to imagine they are walking into the building and down a main corridor. What do they see along the way?

- Ask one or two persons from the group to volunteer to demonstrate how someone from the organization might talk or walk in the idealized organization. (Cue: Are they happy? Do they appear proud? Confident? Impressive?)

There are several ways in which to go about conducting a visioning exercise. Whichever approach one takes, it is important to keep in mind that for the vision to drive the organization it must be shared—which means that those most closely linked to the organization feel a sense of ownership of the vision.

One approach is to convene a group of key stakeholders (a planning retreat might be the ideal setting). Ask each, individually, to describe in writing for someone unfamiliar with the organization, how it might look in five years' time. How large is it? What types of clients is it serving? How is it perceived by the community, by donors, by consumers of its services? Where is it located? What kind of staffing does it have? (For the sake of time and ease of discussion, keep the descriptions to under one page.)

Allow up to a half hour for the group members to write their personal visions. Then, depending on the nature of the group, you may want to ask members of the group to read what they have written; or, if there is benefit to anonymity, you may want to collect the samples and read some of them aloud yourself. Capture key elements of each person's vision visibly (on a chalkboard, overhead projection, flipchart, etc.).

A variation on this approach is to work in small groups, with each group charged with coming up with a vision. This approach forces dialogue and some give-and-take. As above, capture the key points of each small group's vision when the larger group reconvenes.

A third approach is to serialize the process. Each member of the group writes out the answer to one question; for example: "How is our organization perceived by the local community in the year 2000?" Then have each member of the group pass his or her paper to the left. Ask the members to then write down a response to another question on the sheet which they have received. Continue the process until your list of prompting questions has been covered. The advantage of this serialized visioning is that it leads to composite visions. Often what will occur is that a member of the group will read the response of the person from whom he or she has received the paper and will consciously or subconsciously consider that response when answering the next question.

Whichever means are used to have the group picture the organization of the future, remind the members of these ground rules:

1. **State the vision in positive terms.**

   Say what the organization is, rather than what it is not. (Negative statements set the wrong tone, allowing members of the group to concentrate on what's wrong with the organization and not on what it might accomplish.)

2. **Write in the present tense (as if what is envisioned is already a reality).**

3. **Live dangerously.**

   At this stage, don't let the group's thinking be confined. The message is : Assume that money is no object, that if we can imagine it, we can make it ours.

4. **Be concrete and specific.**

   Don't say: "Our organization is a model of success"; describe how it is successful, and why it is a model.

Once the essence of the individual visions have been displayed, it is time to coalesce them into a common picture of what the organization might become. If the group is functioning harmoniously, the moderator may want to engage it in a discussion toward this end (*caution*: getting a committee to agree on language can quickly degenerate into quibbling over semantics and word choice). A better alternative may be to take a break during which one member of the group who is not strongly identified with any particular point of view undertakes a composite vision.

What to Do with the Visioning Statement

The visioning statement is an excellent precursor to formal strategic planning. It might become crystallized and compressed from a statement of several hundred (or even several thousand) words to a mission statement of a few dozen. Parts of it might be culled into planning goals.

In addition to its use in the strategic planning process, the vision can be a tool to engender enthusiasm among staff, volunteer leadership, financial supporters, and potential supporters.

THE MISSION STATEMENT: SOME NOTEWORTHY EXAMPLES

It might be helpful as the organization crafts (or revises) its own mission statement to consider a few better examples. Note that each captures the essence of that organization, that it has a certain excitement to it—sometimes even a sense of urgency, and that it would serve well as a rallying point for staff, volunteers, and others whose belief in the organization is critical to its success.

• The mission of the Nature Conservancy is to preserve plants, animals, and natural communities that represent the diversity of life on Earth by protecting the lands and water they need to survive.

- To protect and improve the quality of life for present and future generations. —The Cousteau Society
- Our mission is to be the preeminent provider of quality health care services to infants, children, and youth in our region. Children's Hospital will strive to enhance the health and well-being of all children through responsible programs of excellence in research, education, and advocacy. —Children's Hospital, National Medical Center
- Helping people prevent, prepare for, and cope with emergencies. —American Red Cross
- To reduce premature death and disability due to cardiovascular disease and stroke. —American Heart Association
- NAHD is an international association dedicated to the advancement of healthcare institutions and organizations through philanthropy. —National Association of Hospital Development
- The National League of Cities is a membership organization of general purpose local governments dedicated to advancing the public interest, building democracy and community, and improving the quality of life by strengthening the capacity of local governance and advocating the interests of local communities.

TEN TRENDS THAT WILL—AND OUGHT TO—AFFECT YOUR MISSION

Organizations, whether they choose to be or not, are "open systems." To survive, organizations must interact with and adapt to changes in their external environments.[3] To thrive, they need to anticipate and understand forces of change, and then develop new programs, new initiatives, new ways of thinking. The mission statement must be a reflection of the fact that organizations are not closed systems. The business of many nonprofits during the 1980s may be quite unlike the business that will frame their missions in the first decade of the twenty-first century.

Said another way, the organizational mission of the successful nonprofit undergoes periodic refinement in response to major societal trends. The unsuccessful organization either fails to see those trends or to craft a mission that acknowledges them.

As you write or revisit your own organization's mission, here are ten trends worth considering. (Other trends will be addressed throughout the text as they relate to specific topics of nonprofit management. A more in-depth look at trends can be found in Chapter 2 on planning.) Your organization's size, development stage, purpose, and vision may each have an impact on the planning process. As a trend, each of the ten shows some movement, some change. While none is assured (the concept of a "future fact" being oxymoronic), all are likely.

The Society Is Becoming Older

By the year 2000, the median age in the United States will be 36 (by comparison, it was about 28 in 1970).[4] There are several implications:

- An older workforce may be more stable and more dependable; and is likely to be more experienced.
- At the same time, an older workforce is less likely to be flexible, i.e., willing to move to a new location or to become retrained for a new job.
- An older population may bode well in terms of acquired wealth, increasing the prospects for fund raising.

The Society Will Be Dramatically More Diverse

In 1989, persons from minority backgrounds comprised about one-fourth of the population of the United States. In little more than a decade, the population will be one-third minority. For a country of some 250 million persons, this represents a shift of unprecedented magnitude. The organization that relies on the white, male, middle class for its clients, its staff, or its volunteer leadership may be left behind.

The Nature of Voluntarism Is Changing

While there is evidence that the interest in volunteering has increased, the way in which one will volunteer is different than it was a few years ago. The prototypical volunteers of the 1990s will be less willing to commit themselves to open-ended, long-term volunteer assignments. Instead, what they will seek out are volunteer roles that have a fixed end-date and a measurable outcome, and give evidence of making a real contribution to the problems facing society.[5]

It makes sense to involve volunteers in the organization's planning, to stimulate their feelings of ownership and belonging and formulate roles and responsibilities for them that match their individual needs and interests. It may prove necessary to rethink the typical nonprofit governance structure with its reliance on standing boards and committees.

There Will Be Proportionally More Women in the Workforce

Not only will there be an increase in the numbers of women who work outside the home, there will also be a growing presence of women in managerial, professional, and leadership positions. The prescient organization will see the enormous benefits that this brings by its addition to the labor (and volunteer) pool of competent, well-educated, purposeful individuals.

At the same time, the workplace will need to adapt: flexible work hours, options for day care, and changes in health and benefit plans. The enterprising nonprofit will capitalize on new programs designed in response to these changes in the world of work.

The Nation Could Be Facing a Crisis in the Educational System

According to John Naisbett, as many as one-fourth of the high school graduates in the United States cannot read at the eighth grade (functionally literate) level.[6] The situation is no better in mathematics. At the same time, the relative proportion of young people is declining. What this means is that we will have a smaller pool of entry-level employees, and many of those who form that pool will lack the basic skills necessary to perform on the job.

In the nonprofit sector, those on whom organizations rely to enter data, word process proposals and correspondence, maintain the look of the facility, or provide the first line of service as aides and paraprofessionals may be woefully unprepared for these tasks.

Our Society Is Becoming a Service Society

Most industrialized countries worldwide are shifting from an economy based on manufacturing—that is, on the production of goods, to one based on the provision of services. "Instead of the industrial worker, we [will] see the dominance of the professional and technical class in the labor force."[7] Services, from retail sales to government service and from health care to fast foods, are becoming the driving factors in the economies of industrialized (or post-industrialized, as Daniel Bell would have it) countries.

And within that service economy is the growth of the nonprofit sector. Nonprofit organizations will play an ever more important, ever more central role in the economies of the United States, Canada, and other leading countries.

The good news is that it may become easier to attract talented professionals as the image of the nonprofit world, and the value placed on doing something that "makes a difference" increase. The downside is that competition among service providers will be keen. The best managed organization will still be around and active in the twenty-first century.

Delivery of Healthcare Is Undergoing Profound Change

American society is witnessing dramatic changes in where, how, and to whom health care services are provided. Those nonprofit hospitals that failed to couple sound business practice with a caring mission are being replaced by corporations that succeed through economies of scale and rigorous attention to the bottom line.

Although third party reimbursement is still the lifeblood for many health care providers, obtaining that lifeblood will increasingly be linked to cost efficiency and proof of efficacy—that the services provided really make a difference.

The nature of the patient is undergoing redefinition as well. With the advances in medical research, notably the genome project—in which scientists are attempting to discover the genetic blueprints which cause many diseases—whole families of diseases may be eliminated. Health care providers will be seeing persons with severe or multiple disabilities who have survived because of advances in technology.

Mainstream Workforce Values Will Change

Driven in part by the crescive presence of baby boomers, workplace values will reflect a more educated populace. Harvard business professor D. Quinn Mills makes this comparison between those whose values were shaped by World War II and the war in Vietnam (as displayed in Table 1)[8]:

Table 1.
Comparison of Values:
Pre-Baby Boomers and Baby Boomers

Pre-Baby Boomers	*Baby Boomers*
World War II—a war we won.	Vietnam—a war we...tied?
Authority—be a good soldier; follow orders.	Question authority—follow not by title but perceived competence.
Tact—be polite; avoid confrontation.	Candor—speak one's mind.
Group consciousness.	Individualism.

Technology Will Affect Virtually Every Aspect Life

Among technology's true believers lives the opinion that, while technology may not replace social engineering, it is capable of finding shortcut solutions to major social problems: "To solve a social problem one must induce social change—one must persuade many people to behave differently than they have in the past. . . . By contrast, resolution of a technological problem involves many fewer decisions. . . . By contrast, technological engineering is simple."[9]

Among its detractors, the belief is widely held that technology is separating humankind from its roots, that people fail to see the hold that it has over them because they are so enamored by what it can do for them.

Whatever one's stand on the issue of technology, it must be acknowledged that technology will be a force in every individual's personal and professional life. If the nonprofit world of the year 2000 bears only minor resemblance to its progenitors of 1950, the influence of technology will in large measure make it so. The effective nonprofit will need to balance technological advances with the quality of service which only caring professionals can provide.

Change Is the Constant

Change: On every front. In every occupational domain. It has been said that innovations once took a generation to be realized. They can now occur virtually overnight. As nonprofit executives, we need to have the tools to see change coming in order to respond quickly and appropriately.

WHERE NEXT?

This first chapter has focused on mission, considering both how to determine it and how to recognize major issues and trends that may affect it. Visioning has also been considered, and how the visioning process relates to the establishment of an organization's mission.

The next several chapters will look at how to build on the vision and the mission, emphasizing:

- How to develop a strategic plan that gives form and substance to the mission, and
- How to put the plan into operation.

The point of contact between plan and execution is marketing, which is planning as applied to the customer.

Within the context of planning one must consider public relations. Why here? Because in order for a plan to succeed, what others think of an organization must be clear, and then a course of action must be developed to affect that thinking, to create the image that portrays the mission.

PARTING THOUGHTS: MAKING A DIFFERENCE

In *The New Realities,* Peter Drucker argues that there is one thing that all nonprofit (third sector, independent sector) organizations have in common: "their purpose is to change human beings. . . . [They are] human-change institutions."[10] They make a difference in the lives of others. That difference must be understood by all who are engaged in the work of the nonprofit. That is why understanding and articulating the organization's mission is so important.

NOTES

1. John A. Byrne, "Profiting from the Nonprofits," *Business Week,* 3151 (no vol) (March 26, 1990): 70.

2. Michael Doyle, "Quest for Vision," *Association Management,* 42 (September 1990): 30–34.

3. James D. Thompson, *Organizations in Action* (New York: McGraw-Hill, 1967), 4–13.

4. William B. Johnston and Arnold H. Packer, *Workforce 2000: Work and Workers for the 21st Century* (Indianapolis, IN: Hudson Institute, 1987), 80.

5. Virginia Hodgkinson and Murray S. Weitzmann, "Giving and Volunteering in the United States" (Washington, DC: Independent Sector, 1988).

6. John Naisbett, "John Naisbett's TrendLetter" (September 14, 1989): 1.

7. Daniel Bell, *The Coming of the Post-Industrial Society: A Venture in Social Forecasting* (New York: Basic Books, Inc., 1976), 125.

8. D. Quinn Mills, Keynote address, American Society of Association Executives Annual Meeting, Cincinnati, OH, March, 1989.

9. Alvin M. Weinberg, "Can Technology Replace Social Engineering?" In *Technology and the Future,* Albert H. Teich, ed. (New York: St. Martin's Press, 1990), 30–31.

10. Peter F. Drucker, *The New Realities: In Government and Politics/In Economics and Business/In Society and World View* (New York: Harper & Row, Publishers, 1989), 198–199.

Chapter 2
A Guide to Strategic Planning for the Nonprofit

Planner n. One whose job is to think about doing real work.
— *Anonymous*

EXECUTIVE SUMMARY

Let our advance worrying become advance thinking and planning.
Winston Churchill

While individuals cannot control the future, they can exercise consider-able influence over it. They need not inherit and respond; they can initiate and shape. Lest this sound simple-minded, it is not an argument that allows the nonprofit to isolate itself from forces in the environment. To the contrary: it can anticipate those forces and build programs in response to them.

This chapter begins by defining strategic planning in relation to long-range and operational planning and discusses organizations that have used strategic planning to good effect. Also discussed: Why plans fail; key steps in planning; how to set the priorities among goals; planning to plan; how to determine which programs are right for your organization; an in-depth look at trends—and how to assess their impact on the nonprofit, using the normal group technique to establish goals; and converting strategic plans to doable activities. The chapter concludes with a brief introduction to systems thinking—a way of planning by looking at the whole rather than the parts.

STRATEGIC PLANNING DEFINED

What makes planning "strategic"? How does strategic planning differ from long-range or operational planning?

Long-range planning is:

- Long range (obviously)
- General
- Inclusive
- Goal-oriented

By contrast, strategic planning is:

- Shorter range
- Specific
- Focused
- Action-oriented[1]

The two planning modes can complement one another. The long-range plan is built on the organization's vision of where it would like to be several years hence. The vision is reflected in what are often ambitiously written goals.

The strategic plan is more narrowly defined. It focuses on a selected number of goals in order to concentrate the organization's energies and resources for a period of time. It then presents objectives that are to be met within that time frame and strategies to achieve them.

Time Span

Long-range planning might cover a span of ten years; strategic planning typically covers not more than five, and often not more than three. By setting longer range goals, long-range planning allows the organization to keep certain global purposes in mind, reducing the likelihood of continual redirection with changes in board leadership, availability of funding, or fads.

The nonprofit enterprise might create a long-range plan in which there is a goal cast for virtually every key element of its mission statement. For example:

By the year 2005 we will have in place an endowment of $10,000,000.

A lofty goal. Doable? Perhaps. In a properly executed long-range plan, such goals will be reviewed periodically to be sure they are still desirable and possible. The organization may find that it can move up the timetable in its endowment campaign. It may observe that a new (competing) community health center has become active in serving Hispanic children without natural parents, at which time it could be appropriate to reassess the organization's goal relating to that kind of service. This doesn't mean, necessarily, that the goal is abandoned.

After investigation, the planning body may decide to rewrite it (in this, reflecting a desire to work with rather than compete against another agency):

> Working with the Orlando Community Health Center, we will become the premier nonprofit in the greater Orlando area serving Hispanic children who are without natural parents by the year 2000.

Inclusive vs Selective

One of the reasons plans fail to be realized is that they are simply too inclusive. The planning body puts in them virtually everything that is going on within the organizational walls. Why? In part, because it is difficult to find a program that isn't loved by someone. Sometimes a program finds its way into the plan, even when its importance is suspect, so as not to offend a key volunteer, board member, or staff person who has a particular project that she or he thinks is of vital importance.

Long-range plans may be inclusive in order to address the full range of activities and thus may serve as the basis for a monitoring function. They are a kind of institutional audit, a catalog of all important activities within the organization. By leaving nothing out, management has the ability to track activities across the breadth of the organization.

Strategic plans differ in that they deal with specific goals and objectives that the organization wants to achieve over a discrete period of time. Out of 35 major activity areas identified within the organization, five may be identified that are going to receive concentrated attention and perhaps increased resources. For example, the organization may decide as part of its planning process that what it really needs to achieve is an improved public image.

> The community confuses us with at least three other nonprofits. That misperception is hurting our ability to attract potential clients and undermining our fund raising efforts. We need to develop a strategic plan, one element of which is targeted to improving our public image.

Focus

The strategic plan is thus more focused. It says, in effect: "Sure, activities 1–35 are all important for the success of our organization. We've got to have a smoothly running accounting office; we need a strong program in community outreach; we know how important the inpatient research program is. But—for the next two to three years we are going to place particular emphasis on improving and enhancing our public image. We believe that if we do so, it will benefit our community outreach program and provide a larger pool for our research. It will also lead to greater accomplishments in our fund raising, which means more money."

Recognize that committing one's organization to strategic planning has its risks. It is not possible to make every activity a high priority. Some sacred cows will not get the attention that certain members of the board or staff think they deserve. It is important to keep reminding staff and volunteers that the strategic plan is in place for three years (if that's its span). Something else may become the first priority after that time, and, "Yes, outreach is important, and, no, we don't want to abandon it; we just want to concentrate our efforts in public relations."

How do you arrive at the kind of consensus that is necessary to develop a strategic plan? The steps to take follow.

WHO DOES EFFECTIVE STRATEGIC PLANNING?

In the late 1970s and 1980s strategic planning became the thing to do. Planning consultants built homes at the beach on the fees they collected for teaching virtually every major corporation and many nonprofit organizations how to do strategic planning.

In point of fact, strategic planning was—and is—more form than substance. Many organizations have gone through the motions and emerged with some semblance of a strategic plan, only to find that their plan affected very little change. Either the planning was not conducted correctly (often because of failure to involve key decision-makers, gatekeepers, power brokers), or because it was not possible to implement the result.

So, who has done strategic planning effectively? In the for-profit sector, McCormick & Co., for one. McCormick significantly broadened its scope, changed its image, and opened new markets as a result of asking "What is our business?"

In the nonprofit world, the United Way has been notably active in strategic planning, as has the National Association of Home Builders (NAHB). Both developed a strategic planning approach at the national level which they have effectively taught to their counterparts on the state and local levels. Why have McCormick, United Way, and NAHB succeeded where others have failed?

- They were committed to the planning process.

  Those who implemented it believed in it, understood it, were able to explain it.
- There was a sense of urgency.

  McCormick sensed that it needed to expand its business horizon in order to maintain profitability. United Way was challenged by other national nonprofits who wanted access to employee payroll deductions. Home builders suffered variously from skyrocketing housing costs and a questionable image.

Successful planning results, then, when the organization leadership believes it is needed, often because of a perceived threat or need to change. And it succeeds by following a carefully described process. The examples given—McCormick, United Way, NAHB—should not lead the reader to assume that strategic planning is the province solely of the large organization. To the contrary, small nonprofits become major entities by creating their future through planning.

Why Does the Planning Process Fail?

Lack of Commitment

If the board and top staff of the nonprofit are not convinced of the need to plan strategically, and then manage the organization strategically, there remain but three choices for the chief officer:

1. Get rid of those who are not committed to the planning process;
2. Polish up his/her own resume; or,
3. Forget about planning.

Failure to Integrate Planning Into the Way the Organization Does Business

Planning needs to be tied to budget: if you plan to improve your public image but veto funds for a new brochure, you're sending a mixed message. The plan also needs to be reflected, i.e., integrated, in the plans of each department.

Short-Term Mentality

If you are serious about affecting public behavior toward your organization, you must give it time. If you hope to change public attitude, give it even more time. Don't set yourself up for failure by asking too much too soon.

Who doesn't do strategic planning? Sadly, the United States government. Oh, various agencies engage in planning, and of course the Defense Department is big on planning. But that's the equivalent of having each department doing its own planning, without an overall sense of where management and the board want the organization to go. There's no "big picture." As a result, administrations come and go, Congress persists, and many of the largest problems remain unsolved. The same is true for some of the larger corporations in the United States.

Driven by the need to succeed, quarter by quarter, they fail to create and maintain a goal that might only be achievable in five to ten years.

STRATEGIC VS OPERATIONAL PLANNING

Before describing the steps in a typical strategic planning process, it will help to review the distinction between strategic and operational planning.

Strategic planning is focused, of a fixed duration (usually three to five years), with specific, targeted objectives in mind. How these objectives are carried out (i.e., how they are put into operation) is the province of the *operational* plan. Usually one year in length, the operational plan takes the strategic planning process into the world of the day-to-day, depicting:

• Specific activities, with an indication of . . .
• When they will be accomplished, and
• By whom

Table 2 displays where strategic planning leaves off and operational planning begins.

Table 2.
Strategic and Operational Planning

STRATEGIC
Mission Statement
Environmental Scan
Goals
Strengths and Weaknesses
Strategic Directions
Objectives

OPERATIONAL
Action Plans
    Activities
    Due Dates
    Responsibility

KEY STEPS IN STRATEGIC PLANNING

While there are as many versions of what makes for a strategic plan as there are strategic planners with a house on the beach, the variations have certain elements in common.

Mission

As considered earlier, the mission (sometimes mission statement) is the raison d'être of the organization—its purpose, its core. It may include something about the organization's . . .

- Scope (measured geographically or demographically, for example);
- Structure (e.g., is it a public charity, university, pediatric hospital);
- Size (". . . the largest private college in rural Idaho");
- Duration (". . . the oldest daycare provider . . .");
- Services (". . . offers on-the-job training and remedial education to employers and their employees . . ."), or
- Composition (". . . neighborhood action group . . .").

The mission is sometimes stated in the present tense:

Hillsboro Community Center is dedicated to improving the lives of senior citizens in Tuscaloosa County through the provision of better housing and health care.

Or it may be stated in future tense, capturing what the organization sees as its destiny:

Lackawana Area Foundation seeks to become the foremost funder of programs for the disadvantaged in the Lackawana/Old Bridge townships.

Environmental Scan

If anything has been learned about effective planning in the past decade, it is this: planning does not occur in vacuum. It must be done while cognizant of both external and internal factors and recognizing that major societal trends (sometimes called Macro trends) are germane. The fact that American society is aging affects organizations, as do other major trends in demographics, economics, politics, technology, health care. Conversely, being aware of trends is a source of power: major societal shifts can be anticipated and new programs created in response to them. Assuming an organization has been gathering information on trends, how does it infuse that information into the planning process?

One way is the implications wheel (known in futurist circles as the future wheel). Similar to brainmapping, the implications wheel allows graphical depiction of the possible implications of a particular trend or issue. By design, it elicits a wide range of expression concerning an issue or trend, allowing members of the group to record opinions without fear of contradiction. Figure 1 shows how a typical implications or future wheel is constructed.

Figure 1. Implications (Future) Wheel

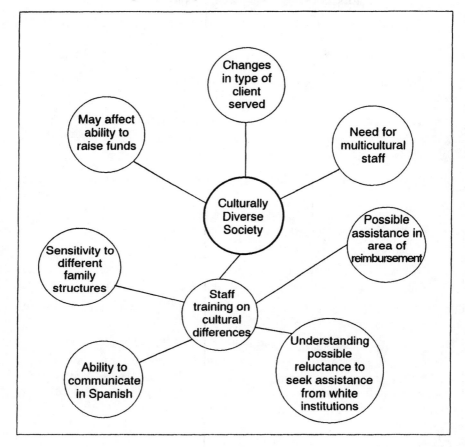

To demonstrate the implications wheel, consider the trend toward a more culturally diverse society. Start by writing that trend in the center circle, and then begin to describe, in the first ring of circles moving outward, some of the major implications that a culturally diverse society may have for the organization. For example:

- Changes in type of client served;
- Need for multicultural staff;
- Staff training on cultural differences;
- Affect on ability to raise funds.

For each of the implications, additional implications can be derived as can possible courses of action. Moving now into the second ring, one might link the following to staff training on cultural differences:

- Sensitivity to different family structures;
- Ability to communicate in Spanish;
- Understanding possible reluctance to seek assistance from white institutions;
- Possible assistance in area of reimbursement.

How might you use the implications (future) wheel with your institution's planning committee?

1. Give a wheel to each member of the committee.

   Ask the members to work independently for a few minutes, listing implications, and then implications of implications.

2. Have each member of the committee pass his or her wheel to the person on the right.

   Ask the committee members to add to the wheel now in front of each of them. They may ask their colleague on their left for clarification ("What did you mean by this?").

3. Go around the room, asking each member to mention one implication and what it means for your organization.

   Capture these visually (on a chalkboard, flip chart, overhead, large screen computer display).

As you proceed in this fashion through the trends, it will become clear that the group perceives certain trends are going to have special affects on your organization. Some will lend themselves to exciting new programmatic opportunities. Do they fit your mission? If so, you may want to capture them as possible goals.

Goals

A goal, in the words of author and management consultant Ken Blanchard, "is a dream with a deadline."[2] Goal statements are sometimes included within the mission as further definition, indicating how and perhaps when the organization will achieve its mission. Within the strategic planning process, goals help to clarify intent. Every department and every committee may have a goal. One needs to remember that it will be hard to find a program in your organization that isn't special to somebody. If every favorite program were a priority in the strategic plan, what would result is a laundry list, not a strategic planning document. The challenge is to find a way of acknowledging that each program is important, while allowing only a small percentage of them to make it into the strategic plan.

Having gone through a review of major trends, and their potential impact on the institution, the planning group is now in a position to come up with possible goals. The strategic planning process determines which goals to include by forcing the planning group to set priorities. Of the numerous ways to begin, one, the Nominal Group Technique (NGT), will be described in the following section.

The Nominal Group Technique[3]

While this is a group activity—involving perhaps as many as 20 persons—it is controlled, i.e., nominal in terms of how the discussion flows, as compared to a less controlled technique such as brainstorming. The reason for the control is to encourage full group participation and discourage dominance by any one faction. There is a tendency in group discussions for some individuals (and not necessarily those with the most worth hearing) to dominate the interaction. The Nominal Group Technique works to avoid this problem by insisting that everyone be heard from in turn. Here are the basic steps:

Generate Ideas

Ask each member of the group to write down three or four goals that he or she believes to be most important. Assure the group that every idea is valued: "Don't limit your thinking; let your imagination run. Don't be bound by what you think is affordable or doable at this stage."

Allow some time for thought in this first stage. Good ideas need time to percolate.

Record Ideas

After the group has had the opportunity to jot down what it thinks may be the most important goals for the organization, ask each person in turn to list his or her ideas, one at a time. Support the ideas—at this stage, each has value. And support "hitchhiking" (building on another's idea).

Discuss Each Idea

The next step in NGT is to allow for consideration of each idea presented, but in serial order. Here, too, the purpose is to focus discussion and avoid having the meeting agenda revised on the spot by a dominating personality. The author of each goal may wish to comment on her or his nomination or be asked to explain just what it would entail. By moving item to item, the NGT coordinator manages the discussion.

Conduct Initial Vote

The NGT process may yield several ideas of merit. Discussion will help to winnow out those that seem unrealistic, and only one or a few desirable goals may surface in the process. That is where voting comes in.

As is the case throughout NGT, the voting process allows for independence of thought free of influence by the more verbal (or apparently powerful) members of the group. Each member of the group selects up to five items he or she believes to be most important, voting for his or her first, second, third, fourth, and fifth choices. Results are then listed in rank order.

Discuss Results of Initial Voting

If there is still wide variance among participants as a result of the initial voting, with several items receiving relatively high ranking but no clear concurrence, it is useful to re-enter the discussion. The coordinator (in our case, the committee chair) may wish to ask for comment on voting patterns: "I see that this item received three number one votes, but two number five votes. That's quite a discrepancy. Would anyone who voted on this item care to share with the group how he or she came to that evaluation?"

Often what will result is a better understanding of the item in question and its relative merits, making it easier to take the final step.

Take Final Vote

As with other group process techniques (Delphi survey, for example), the discussion-voting-discussion-voting process in NGT leads toward consensus as items become grouped with other items, as the rationale behind choices becomes clearer, and as the number of items considered is narrowed. The final vote often serves as a ratifier, bringing closure to the discussion, allowing participants to feel that they have acted in a democratic fashion in choosing goals for the organization.

It is essential to effective strategic planning that there be no more than about five or six major goals. Much beyond that, and the organization is operating inclusively, not strategically. Sometimes the chair of the planning committee needs to remind the group that strategic planning implies that the institution is going to focus on a few goals. Employing a process such as the Nominal Group Technique makes the job easier for both chair and committee.

PLANNING TO PLAN

Involving the Key Players

Plans are made—and killed—by people, by the degree to which they are committed both to the planning process and its outcomes. While the actual development of the plan can be assigned to a planning committee (perhaps a subset of the board or a board/staff task force), the work of that committee must not occur in isolation. In laying out the planning process, it is important to ask:

1. **Who on the board should be involved directly in the planning process?**

   Who has had experience in planning, perhaps in a company or within another nonprofit, and considers himself or herself a forward thinker?

2. **Who on the board may not have the interest or the time to commit to a planning committee?**

   Nonetheless, these participants need to be brought in from time to time, asked for advice, and given a chance to review committee documents in draft.

3. **Who among the staff should be actively involved?**

   It may not necessarily just be the person who thinks in terms of planning. It may be the one or two staff members who have the unofficial power to make or break an idea. They can virtually assure its survival with a modest endorsement or scuttle it with a few words of ridicule.

4. **Who among constituent groups needs to be kept informed during the planning process?**

- Key local government officials with whom the organization interacts?
- Major donors?
- Potential major donors?
- The head of the volunteer auxiliary?
- Consumers of the organization's services, or their families?

Picture the players involved in the planning process as concentric circles. In the innermost circle may be the actual planning committee; in the next ring, perhaps key board members and senior staff; in the third ring, other board members, department heads. The number and composition of the circles will vary by circumstance. The important element is to be sure that every key player is involved at certain stages and that thought has been given in advance as to when and how that involvement should occur.

The Planning Process[4]

The planning process should be laid out in advance, with consideration given to variables that can affect its success:

1. What is the organization's experience with planning?

Is there a history of successfully developing strategic plans? Unsuccessful plans? Or is this the first attempt?

Would it be wise to engage an outside facilitator who not only knows the planning process but brings objectivity to it?

2. Is the leadership committed to strategic planning?

It makes little sense to charge ahead if the president of the board of trustees believes planning to be a waste of time. There needs to be at least a critical mass of support, if not general consensus.

If no consensus exists, what steps need to be built in to ensure feelings of ownership about the plan and the planning?

3. Over what time period will the plan be developed?

Is there urgency? Can at least a first iteration of the plan be written at a weekend retreat? How much time will the key stakeholders be willing to spend, and how best can that time be used?

4. Where might problems arise?

What can be done ahead of time to mitigate the problem? Can you identify "idea champions" who will support the planning process among their colleagues?

DECIDING WHICH PROGRAMS ARE RIGHT FOR YOUR ORGANIZATION

Four questions ought to be asked when planning programs (or goods and services) for the nonprofit organization:

1. Does it fit the mission of the organization?

2. Is it in concert with the current focus of the organization as delineated in the strategic plan?

If not: the program should be shelved or given a low priority, or perhaps the plan itself needs revisiting.

3. Is there a market?

   Chapter 3 discusses this variable in some depth.

4. Does the organization have the resources to carry out the program?

   Is there sufficient funding in the current budget, and if not, can other sources of funds be tapped? Does the organization have the staff resources to carry out the program?

   What are the long-term implications? By launching the program, what is the organization committing itself to?

It may be useful to develop a New Program Rating Scale, with 1–5 points awarded to each of the four questions. Programs that attain a determined score are given further consideration; those below are deemed not ready for prime time.

UNDERSTANDING—AND USING—INFORMATION ON TRENDS

It is virtually axiomatic that nonprofits succeed to the degree that they understand their environment and react to it appropriately. In the terminology of organizational theory, organizations are "open systems," subject to the environments in which they exist. To develop a usable plan, it is incumbent on the organization's planners to scan the environment, identify trends, and interpret their potential impact on the institution.

In addition to the future wheel described earlier, there are two tools that futurists employ to help management decide whether major trends will have an impact on a particular organization.

The 9-Box

The 9-Box is a tool used to assess a group's perception as to the relative probability of an issue or trend and its potential impact. As its name implies, the 9-Box contains nine cells or boxes, distributed in the overall box as three layers of three boxes each (Figure 2).

The east to west axis describes "impact," and the north to south axis "probability of occurrence." Suppose your organization were considering the potential impact of the trend toward a more racially and ethnically diverse population. The 9-Box allows the planning group to evaluate the degree of probability that this trend will continue and the impact that it may have.

Each person in the group is provided with a marking pen and asked to indicate with an "x" on a flip chart, on which the 9-Box has been drawn, where he or she thinks the trend falls. For example, if a member of the group thinks the trend towards diversity is very probably going to continue and is likely to have a high impact on the organization, he or she might put an "x" in box number "1."

Once each member of the group has marked his or her choice, it is useful to ask those who ranked the trend differently than most (sometimes referred to as the "outliers") if they are willing to share their thinking with the group. Doing so often reveals some insight that is useful. Using the 9-Box, the planning group can come to consensus on which trends seem to warrant most attention.

Figure 2.
The 9-Box

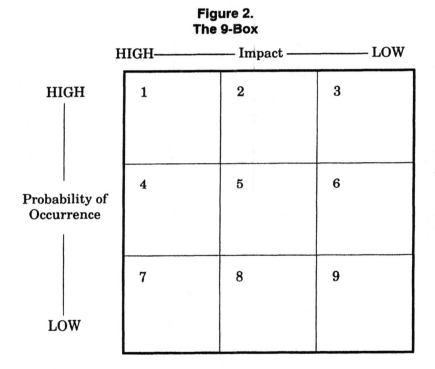

Trend Line

The trend line provides a graphic representation of the planning group's opinion on the impact of a trend *over time*. As indicated in Figure 3, the completed trend line depicts the group's collective opinion on whether the trend being considered is likely to increase, decrease, or remain about the same.

Figure 3. Trend Line

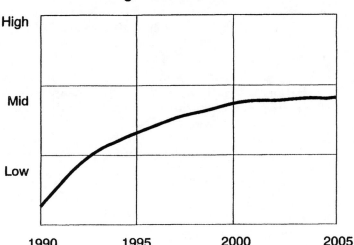

The east-west axis on the trend line depicts movement over time (in this instance couched in five-year increments). The north-south axis is used to portray relative impact on the organization.

Imagine again that the planning group is considering the trend toward diversity among the population. Each member of the group is asked to draw a line denoting how he or she thinks the trend will change over time. For example, some might think that the trend already has high potential impact and will continue; their trend line will start in the "high" box and move across.

It is helpful to provide each member of the group with a different colored marking pen in order to distinguish among the lines drawn. As with the 9-Box, what often happens is that there will be a clustering, with several members of the group drawing similar trend lines. Here, too, there is benefit to hearing from the outliers.

MAKING THE PLAN "DOABLE"

Poll a randomly selected number of organizations that have engaged in strategic planning and ask: "To what extent is the plan affecting the direction of your organization." The response may be disheartening: strategic plans do not, with regularity, become the driving force for the organization as was intended. Inertia, incumbency, politics, and a lack of implementation strategy all contribute inversely to the plan's effectiveness. Recognizing their import is the first step toward assuring that the plan does not become a collector of dust.

Translating Multiyear Plans to Measurable Activities

The strategic plan tends to be written in fairly broad, although hopefully immeasurable, objectives. For it to be implementable, it must be translated into time-specific objectives, which are assigned to particular units or staff within the nonprofit.

To illustrate, consider the example of a facility whose mission is to provide remedial and educational services that enhance the development of skills among children with learning disabilities. The facility believes it has the potential for national recognition as a comprehensive provider of research, direct service to clients, and training. In pursuit of its mission, it has established goals for itself relating to:

- Becoming nationally recognized for the quality of its service, research and training;
- Developing assessment and therapy procedures;
- Reaching maximum enrollment;
- Designing high-quality research;
- Remaining viable fiscally while enjoying growth.

In order to realize these goals, the facility's CEO meets with the department heads, all of whom contributed to the plan's development. She or he asks each department to come up with a set of objectives that will address the goals pertinent to them. In addition, certain administrative objectives which will improve the facility's functioning are laid out.

Department heads then meet with their staffs to prepare department-wide objectives. For example, the overall strategic goal of designing high-quality research and the goal of maintaining financial viability have been operationalized by one unit into this general objective:

By July, 199-, the Research Division will be sufficiently productive in contributing to basic and applied knowledge in the education of children with learning disabilities that its record can be a major source of financial support.

That general objective, which may not be fully realized for several years, is captured in the facility's institutional objectives for the year. The research department, in turn, has crafted the following time-specific objectives:

- By August 199-, produce sufficient funds to underwrite research costs for the fiscal year from sources other than regular contributors of unrestricted gifts.
- By October 199-, working with the Development Office, identify sources and develop a schedule for contributions and grants which will assure support for the next three fiscal years.

- By November 199-, establish a colloquium on research needs which will involve other research centers in the United States and Canada.
- By December 199-, submit three manuscripts reporting data derived from studies on the efficacy of the interdisciplinary teaching model.

Each unit within the facility completes a comparable set of objectives. These then are attended to during the year in three ways:

1. The office of the CEO sends out a memo to department heads each quarter, reminding them of objectives which have completion dates in the following quarter.

2. The objectives are reflected within the individual performance management plans for each staff person. Performance plans are reviewed between supervisor and staff being supervised at least quarterly.

3. The facility-wide objectives are reviewed monthly during meetings of the staff executive team, which comprises the department heads and the CEO.[5]

SYSTEMS THINKING

Virtually anyone who has ever worked with or studied organizations has dealt with unintended consequences: Thinking one is correcting "A," only to throw "B" out of whack. What seemed like a solution yesterday has become a problem today. For example, developing a strain of poison to kill roaches, only to create a new species of roach which can withstand that poison. Then the stakes are raised: a more lethal solution, which leads to a more virulent problem, and so it goes, until not only has a roach when created which can withstand virtually anything, but the air has been polluted with hydrocarbons in the process.

Systems thinking would suggest that one is dealing with parts and not with the whole. The symptom has been isolated but the environment in which the symptom existed has been missed.

Systems thinking (general systems theory) is a means of understanding the cause and effect relationships within organisms (of which an organization is a complex example). It takes as an assumption that a network of interrelationships underpins the organism; studying the network reveals a pattern of behavior.[6] Said another way, the parts do not function independently but form a whole, with the various parts interacting with one another.

Systems theory, which grew out of observations of how organisms function, recognizes that in order to survive systems must have the ability to cope with change and live through it. The more complex the organism, the more energy is expended in gathering and interpreting information and in maintenance of the organism.

Applied to organizational planning, systems thinking argues in favor of taking a long-term perspective in order to consider possible side effects, possible unintended consequences. "Systems thinkers ... realize from the beginning that all stable systems have, by definition, ways of resisting change. Instead of stubbornly fighting against the system, they study it.[7]

Additionally, systems theory acknowledges that organizations are affected by their environment. To understand how the organization functions, one must look at it in the context of the larger environment in which it operates and understand the forces that influence it, threaten it, provide it with stability.

What does this mean in terms of what management must consider when planning for the organization?

1. **Consider solutions that take into account the larger whole.**

   One of the tenets of systems theory is that for every decision there is an intended and an unintended consequence.[8] If a change is made in the way the accounting office functions, e.g., changing the way expenditures are coded, what impact will that have on the development office and its need to track fund raising costs? How will it affect the reports provided to the board?

2. **Play out the various possible scenarios.**

   What is the range of ways that a proposed solution might affect the organization? What are the long-term implications of the action proposed? Will a short-term solution only create a problem later on? If so, is the new problem going to be worse than one now being addressed?

3. **Acknowledge that change, especially if it is to have long-term positive results, may be a long time in coming.**

   There are times when unilateral decisions have to be made: there is no point in debating on whether to leave a burning building. But where such decisions can be avoided, it is probably wise that they are.

   If changes are to take place, you will be well served to acknowledge that the organism by its very nature is averse to change; that change must be incremental; that those most affected need to be an active part of the change and not part of the underground resistance movement.

PARTING THOUGHTS

Planning is based on a bold premise: that management can exercise control over the future of the organization and can invent the future that it desires, and not merely respond to what happens. If it were not so, organizations would be indistinguishable from fire departments.

Organizations are created around goals; plans show how to achieve those goals.

NOTES

1. John M. Bryson, *Strategic Planning for Public and Nonprofit Organizations* (San Francisco: Jossey-Bass Publishers, 1988), 6–7.

2. Kenneth Blanchard, speaking at the First Future Leaders Conference sponsored by the American Society of Association Executives (ASAE), June 1988.

3. Andre L. Delbecq, Andrew H. Van de Ven, and David H. Gustafson, *Group Techniques for Program Planning* (Glenview, IL: Scott, Foresman and Co., 1975), 7-10.

4. Some of the thinking regarding the planning process comes from Bryan W. Berry, *Strategic Planning Workbook for Nonprofit Organizations* (St. Paul, MN: Amherst H. Wilder Foundation, 1986), 16–17.

5. Appreciation is expressed to Frank R. Kleffner for providing the model for operationalizing planning objectives.

6. Kathryn Johnson, "Rethinking Association Management: A Systems Approach to Solutions." Presentation at the American Society of Association Executives (ASAE) annual meeting, August 15, 1989.

7. Draper L. Kauffman, *Systems 1: An Introduction to Systems Thinking* (Minneapolis: Future Systems, Inc., 1980), 19.

8. Johnson, ASAE annual meeting.

Chapter 3
Marketing

"To market, to market, to buy a fat pig."

—Children's poem

EXECUTIVE SUMMARY

Marketing is becoming a core function within the nonprofit organization. This chapter provides an introduction to many of its tenets: What is marketing, and how does it apply to the nonprofit? The four "P's" of marketing; marketing trends; how to determine if your organization is market-driven, and how to make it so; how to begin a marketing program, and where it should be placed within the organization; elements of market research, knowing your constituencies and how to segment the market universe; ten reasons why marketing fails; and, finally, applying marketing principles to both fund raising and public relations.

BUYING FAT PIGS

The principle of marketing has been in existence for a rather long time. Farmers and others brought produce (and fat pigs) to be purchased by those who needed, or wanted, a certain item which they did not or could not produce themselves. The marketplace was the common ground on which an exchange occurred.

It is not surprising, in this age of information, that the term marketing now connotes a whole body of thought. To their credit, scholars of marketing have brought a sophistication to the approach of buying and selling. Yesterday's farmer brought a fat pig to market on the assumption that someone would buy it. Today, he or she could hire a marketing firm to determine not only whether someone might buy that pig, but also:

• Is pig "out"? Should the farmer be producing something else?

- What benefits should be extolled about the pig? *"Grain fed. Listened to Vivaldi. Raised in a pollutant-free pen."*
- What should be avoided or played down? *"Contains lots and lots of fat. . . . Spent most of its days wallowing in mud."*
- What price can be charged?
- Are there times of year when pork is most likely to be purchased?
- Does the buying public need to be educated before it will purchase a rather homely, fat animal?
- How should pork be positioned vis-a-vis chicken? *"Anything you can do with a chicken you can do with a pig."*

MARKETING AND THE NONPROFIT ORGANIZATION

The term marketing is no longer foreign to managers in the nonprofit world. But, on the assumption that the term may mean different things to different people, consider some principles.

Marketing Defined

Marketing is a process by which exchange is effected—voluntary exchange. As a process, it is systematic. It employs well crafted programs as opposed to random actions to achieve results. And the desired result? Exchange. Product or service for cash. Contribution to a cause. Commitment of time as a volunteer. In each instance, a voluntary exchange occurs.

The Four P's

People are not primarily interested in my seeds, they're interested in their lawns.   *—David Burpee*

For virtually as long as it has been considered a science, marketing has considered four controllable elements as essential. Applied to the example of the pig farmer, they are:

- Product (having something to sell—preferably, something for which there is consumer interest);
- Price;
- Promotion (letting the buyer know of the pig's availability);
- Place (the common ground on which a sale—an exchange—might occur between farmer and hungry consumer).

The Four P's in the Not-for-P

Within the nonprofit sector, here's how the Four P's apply:

Product

Call it higher education or health care, member benefits or publications, what the organization has to offer is a product that must be of interest to others if it is to survive, much less thrive. Knowing what the constituents of the organization want and need is at the core of any effective marketing plan.

Price

If your organization is offering continuing education, selling pamphlets on how to quit smoking, or providing a service for which there is stiff competition in the community, the concept of pricing is hardly foreign. Where many nonprofits fall down is in failing to fully consider their real costs, both direct and indirect; the result is that they price their services too low.

Fair price is also driven by perceptions. The same four-bedroom house that fetches a seven-figure sales price in Palm Beach may go begging at a quarter of that cost in a less affluent region. This is true as well for services in the nonprofit sector: if what an organization does is perceived as of particular value, the organization will be able to charge for it accordingly.

Promotion

Good products can rot on the shelves if no one knows of their value. So, too, for the goods and services that an organization provides. Promotion becomes increasingly important in a world bombarded by noise.

Place

"Place," for the nonprofit organization, is both location and visibility. Place may mean opening up a satellite campus or facility; it may also mean increasing the public's awareness that the organization exists.

In the classic for-profit marketing paradigm, marketing is a direct two-way exchange. You sell; I buy. The marketing function simultaneously encompasses both resource allocation (providing goods and services) and resource attraction (obtaining revenue).[1] The classic nonprofit marketing paradigm often involves a third player—a contributor, third party reimbursement source—who provides the revenue to the organization for a service it has or is going to render to a client.

Classics don't change, but paradigms do. Many for-profit companies, such as health care conglomerates, routinely access the third player for revenue, while many nonprofits offer products and services which are purchased directly by the consumer through fees.

MARKETING: A LOOK AT SOME TRENDS

Marketing pioneers knew some extraordinary successes precisely because they were pioneers, because they asked questions and analyzed the marketplace with greater sophistication than ever previously. As a consequence, they were able to develop products and position those products in a way that made them desirable if not downright essential in the mind of the consumer.

Times change. Here are some trends worth considering as you set about marketing your organization.

1. **Product differentiation is becoming more difficult.**

   There was a time when offering outpatient weight-loss clinics might have made a unique institution. Now if a hospital doesn't offer a whole range of outpatient services, it is probably also a hospital in some financial difficulty.

2. **There is growing competition from the for-profit sector.**

   Virtually every corner of education and health care has become fair game for for-profit entrepreneurs, some of whom provide services of high quality and at reasonable price. More than one nonprofit has found it economically attractive to contract out for services even of a professional nature. What is more, within health care, larger companies are swallowing up the smaller.

3. **Price is not always a determinant.**

   As certain segments of the population acquire or inherit wealth (including those who in the '80s were called the "Yuppies," for example), they tend to ask questions and demand more. But they are also willing to pay for services they believe to be desirable. Consider, for example, the thriving business enjoyed by some hospitals that have created special menus, and even whole wings, for the well-heeled patient.

   At the same time, trend watchers note that those with disposable income are not always ready to spend it indiscriminately. The upper middle class suburbanite who spends $50 at the French bistro on Friday evening can be seen checking out cereal coupons in the local supermarket the next morning.

4. **Customers are ever more interested in quality of service.**

   Increased competition means increased options. As purchasers of products and services, individuals are less willing to accept passively what is offered and more inclined to go a little out of their way for that supplier who offers better service.

   A case in point: Stories about the service offered by Nordstrom's department stores have fast become legend—how they train even part-time and temporary help to provide quality attention to customers; how they invest in the customer, rather than in the product (avoiding the systems adopted by some competitors in which clothing is virtually locked up); and how they have been known to accept return on items that don't even come from their store!

   Service is not merely a competitive edge. It is becoming *the* competitive edge. And that is no less true in the nonprofit sector. "Customers" of nonprofits—those who avail themselves of these organizations' services, join the associations, buy the products—can afford to be choosy.

   Ask yourself:

   - Does staff of your organization share the attitude that those to whom they provide service come FIRST?
   - Is it easy to get through your switchboard?
   - Would you take your son or daughter to your facility?
   - Would you use the services provided yourself, or would you shop around if you had the need and the money to do so?
   - Do you ask your clients how they feel about the services the organization has provided? And then act on their suggestions?

5. **Time is a commodity.**

   Two jobs. The house. The lawn. Take the kids to soccer practice. To ballet lessons. Make lunches. Get the car fixed.

   There is more to do and less time to do it. On average, people are working longer hours on the job and then filling in what remains with quality time. They work in order to have the money to pay for services that they could have done if only there were enough time.

   Nonprofit executives must be sensitive to the fact that, for their marketplace, time is a valued commodity. The organizations that they manage will need to adjust the hours during which they are open, including nights and weekends; provide services close to and perhaps even in the workplace; and in the near future perhaps be capable of offering some services via telephone line and computer.

6. Society is becoming a cultural mosaic.

In most of the largest American cities, "minorities" are becoming the "majority" (giving new meaning to those terms). The image of the melting pot is giving way to that of a mosaic—a whole, but comprised of many distinct parts. If your organization is providing service based on a white, male society, it is dangerously behind the curve.

IS YOUR ORGANIZATION MARKET-DRIVEN?

Becoming market-driven means thinking first not of your organization but of the person to whom you are or wish to be providing some product or service.

Pop Quiz

Here is a little test to see if your organization is in fact market-driven. Put a check next to any of the following statements that represent the way you and your staff think and act:

1. We look at other organizations in order to copy programs or services that worked for them.

2. We rely heavily on our board; the board members tend to know best what programs to provide.

3. Our education program (health care program, whatever) is more than satisfactory to most of our clients.

4. We make a point of communicating regularly with our clients and with potential clients.

5. Each department in our organization has the autonomy to operate pretty much on its own.

6. As an organization, we believe: "If it ain't broke, don't fix it."

7. Our job is to identify needs and develop programs to meet those needs.

8. We have a pretty secure market share.

9. People today rely too much on "hard data." Most of the really good ideas come from instinct.

10. We're actively looking for new programs that we can offer to those whom we serve.[2]

How many of the ten apply to your institution? Only three clearly represent the thinking of a market-driven organization: numbers 4, 7, and 10. If you checked several items other than those three—and equally important, if you didn't select those three—you may want to think twice about calling yourself market-driven.

Becoming Market-Driven

The first step in becoming market-driven is commitment. From the top, chief staff executive, board chair, board members, senior staff, there must be commitment to a marketing environment. What does that mean?

- Being willing to listen to what your organization's customers—students, clients, patients, families, agencies, funders—have to say about the organization;
- Asking those customers what they want and need, what programs they value, what programs don't exist that should;
- Providing appropriate staff to a marketing effort;
- Creating an atmosphere in which the marketplace drives the decision-making;
- Rewarding creativity and risk-taking.

LAUNCHING A MARKETING PROGRAM

While there is no formula for launching a marketing program, there are some steps that ought to be considered.

Initiate Market Planning

Marketing is planning. When an organization develops a strategic plan, it looks at the environment, both internal and external, to assess strengths and weaknesses, opportunities and threats. It then frames a mission statement, develops goals and objectives and a series of activities to meet those objectives.

Developing a marketing plan is much the same. Indeed, the internal and external scan conducted for the strategic plan (cf. Chapter 2) will yield valuable information for the market plan.

Conduct a Situation Analysis of New Products or Services

Before your organization creates a new program or product based on the recommendation of staff or volunteer leadership, ask:

- Is there any other similar product or service currently being offered? If so, with what success?
- Has the organization developed a product or program, the results of which would provide useful information in terms of the income that was generated?
- Does the proposed program or service meet a clearly stated need? By what measure has that need been determined?
- Can the proposed new product or service be adequately "positioned"?

  Will the buying public for the product or program perceive that your institution is appropriate to offer it? Can anything enhance the organization's image relative to the proposed product or program?
- What is required in terms of pricing in order to recoup all costs, direct and indirect, of researching, developing, producing, promoting, and distributing the new service or product?

  Will that result in a price that is acceptable to the buyer?
- Can any of the costs be offset, for example, by securing grant funds, getting donations of materials, having the product underwritten by a third party?

Ask. And Then Listen

Establish a mechanism by which your organization can hear the needs, wants, interests, desires of its constituent groups. Some suggestions:

- Create a consumer advisory that meets periodically throughout the year.
- Conduct occasional focus groups (see later in this chapter on how to set one up)—targeted to specific topics, such as a new program that the organization is thinking of starting up.
- Survey the organization's donors, volunteers, clients, and members on at least an annual basis.

Evaluate

Be rigorous in asking hard questions: "Do we need to keep this service? What are the true costs of running that program? Will the market bear a price increase? Would we increase sales if we lowered the price?"

Establish an Entrepreneurial Climate

Encourage risk-taking. Reward it. There are companies that actually provide incentives—bonuses, certificates—to employees who "screw up" trying something new. Why? Because in the long run risk-taking pays off.

Harvard business professor Rosabeth Moss Kantor believes that there are three new sets of skills required of organizations wishing to create environments that stimulate entrepreneurship:

Power Skills

Power skills are the ability to convince others to buy into the idea, to invest in it a new initiative.

An Ability to Manage Teams

To be innovative, the organization needs to encourage participatory decision-making, building teams in which there are no bad ideas. Managing teams is a skill that differs considerably from traditional hierarchical (boss/staff) structures.[3]

An Understanding of Change

Understanding change means both appreciating the nature of organizational change and recognizing that it may happen in incremental steps.

Be sure that your organization has at least one member of the board who will champion an entrepreneurial spirit.

And, as management, welcome change. Use it as a stepping stone and not as something to resist.[4]

Encourage lots of ideas. Create a suggestion box, if your institution doesn't already have one, and publicly acknowledge those who contribute to it.

Cut Your Losses

One of the things the not-for-profit world is not very good at is looking at programs or services as cost centers and making decisions based on financial viability. Nonprofit organizations are hesitant to ask if people like the programs and services that are offered or if some of them remain because the services have become "sacred cows."

That is not to say that no program should survive unless it turns a profit. Nonprofits are, after all, in business for educational, charitable, or scientific purposes—that is, for the common good. And there may be very legitimate reasons for keeping a program alive on which the organization is taking a bath. But be sure of those reasons.

SHOULD YOU CREATE A MARKETING OFFICE?

In a word: yes. And no.

Yes: The marketing effort should have a focus, and creating a marketing unit may help frame that focus. Some nonprofit organizations are hiring staff with marketing backgrounds, and a handful of MBA programs address marketing for nonprofits. You might also look within your existing staff for someone whose potential as a marketing specialist can be cultivated.

Consider as well going to a company that enjoys a positive relationship with your organization and request a loaned executive, someone who, at the company's expense, will come in and help you set up a marketing function.

And No: Don't create the impression that because you have established a marketing office that no one else needs to think in marketing terms. ("Oh, that's a marketing issue. Don't worry about that. Marketing will handle that aspect. We're program people, not marketing experts.") All senior staff should be trained in and familiar with the terminology of marketing and required to ask some hard marketing questions of themselves—i.e., who wants, who needs what we have to offer?

CONDUCTING MARKET RESEARCH IN THE NONPROFIT ORGANIZATION

Assume that you have made the commitment to make your organization market-driven. You understand that neither a *product orientation* (if we have a good product, it'll sell) nor a *selling orientation* (if we promote it hard enough, people will buy it) are the way to go. Rather, you need a *research orientation,* which begins with an identification of needs. How do you go about compiling that research information?

Conduct Exploratory Research

Your organization may elect to conduct exploratory research through the methods that follow, the purpose of which is to identify the marketing needs that your organization may want to address. Consider:

- Who are our constituents? (There will be several.)
- What are the characteristics of those constituent groups? What are their interests? What do they *need*? What do they *want*?

- Is the nature of the organization's constituency likely to change in the next three to five years?
- How is the organization perceived by its constituents? Is that perception likely to change? For the better?
- Who would the organization like to have as part of its constituency? And what are their needs and interests?
- Who comprises the organization's competition?
- What are the ways in which the institution can reach its markets? [5]

Ask Internally

The first stage of market research begins within your institution. Pose the questions indicated above to your board and other volunteer leadership, to your staff—at all levels, to yourself. Compare the returns. Do you have consensus on who your constituency *is*, or is there a discrepancy among the opinions of staff and volunteers? Is there agreement on whom you would like to reach? Have you identified any promising new markets for your programs?

Ask Externally

There are several methods from which to select in order to learn about your institution's constituent groups. The decision on which to choose will be dictated by the organization's size and the extent of its external constituencies.

Interviews

If your nonprofit already conducts some type of intake interview, be it in the nature of a client questionnaire or an interview with a prospective student, you have a framework in which to learn more about your constituents, about how they perceive your organization and why they chose it. By adding a few questions to that instrument, the organization can establish a systematic information-gathering process.

Do the same with existing clients and with clients who have "graduated" from your organization.

Be sure that the person being interviewed knows why you are asking marketing-related questions ("We want to learn from you both how we're doing and what we might do differently.") Make it clear whether responses will be attributed or aggregated and reported anonymously. And be certain that the person conducting the interview understands why he or she is asking these questions and has good people skills. There is no point in turning a client off by conducting the interview poorly.

Interviewing can occur face-to-face or by telephone. Construct a set of questions, but build in enough flexibility to the respondent to say what is on his or her mind.

Mail Surveys

In addition to telephone interviews (which are themselves a form of survey), some organizations routinely conduct mail surveys of their constituencies. Properly structured, the mail survey yields quantifiable information which can be categorized along a number of variables (e.g., age, race or ethnicity, gender, geographic location).

Focus Groups

The benefit of focus groups is that the group interaction produces "data and insights that would be less accessible without the interaction found in a group."[6] Typically comprised of six to ten or twelve participants, focus groups provide an opportunity to probe in some depth the feelings, opinions, and perceptions of your institution's constituents.

In forming a focus group for marketing purposes, you may want to attempt to bring together individuals with some homogeneity, reflecting the market segment that you seek to penetrate. For example, you may want to convene a group of recent retirees to see if the idea of launching a senior fitness program will have appeal; or you may want to bring together a dozen former students for the purpose of learning what they think were the strongest and weakest parts of your educational program.

Normally, focus groups have a moderator who briefly explains the purpose of the session, sets out any ground rules (e.g., "All opinions are valued; don't be afraid of saying what's on your mind." "None of this will be attributable to any one person.") The moderator may be quite directive or may choose to give the group wide latitude in terms of both topics and length of discussion of an item. Either way, to be sure that you get the answers you need, construct a set of questions to guide the discussion.

It may be useful to start the session by having participants briefly introduce themselves and respond to an opening question in order to break the ice and set the tone of the meeting. Stress the fact that everyone's comments are welcomed.[7]

It is also typical to audiotape the session (be sure to inform the group that you will be doing so), in that it is difficult to serve as moderator and reporter. You may even want to transcribe the entire discussion in order to analyze the data in some depth.[8]

Undertake Developmental Research

Assume that you have gathered some information on your constituent groups. You've asked for and received feedback on what they would like to see in terms of new programs and products. And you have a staff/board task force working on designing a new product line. As the products are being conceptualized, you may want to return to some segment of your constituency to be sure that what you are developing will fly. If it's a new service, you may want to try it out on a pilot group. Sometimes before a new restaurant officially opens its doors to the public it will invite people in for a free meal in order to test the quality of the menu and the quality of the service. You can do the same.

If it's a new product such as a publication, you may want to show a mock-up of it to a test market sample and ask some hard questions: "Does the 'look' of the publication appeal to you?" "Do you like the layout?" "Are these the kind of articles that would interest you?" "Would you subscribe to such a publication?" "Would you be willing to pay $24 a year for it?"

Conduct Formative Research

Even the best of ideas need to be revisited from time to time. As part of your ongoing market research, plan to periodically reevaluate products and services that you offer. Sometimes, sales figures will supply all the information you need. At other times, it may be necessary to dig deeper, using the research methods described earlier.

WHO ARE YOUR CONSTITUENTS?

There is a tendency sometimes to underestimate the potential constituent pool. How many different constituent bodies would you say a university might have? Three? Five? Here's the list that marketing expert Philip Kotler came up with:

- Local community
- General public
- Mass media
- Prospective students
- High school counselors
- Current students
- Alumni
- Parents of students

- Faculty
- Administration and staff
- Trustees
- Competitors
- Suppliers
- Business community
- Government agencies
- Foundations[9]

The list, while extensive, is by no means exhaustive. Kotler might have included: professional societies, regulatory agencies, accrediting bodies, institutions with whom the university engages in cooperative projects, local and state politicians, etc. The point is: think wide. You may find an audience for your institution's products and services that you had overlooked.

SEGMENTING YOUR MARKET

Whether it be for the purpose of selling a new pamphlet, attracting registrants to a new course, or interesting major contributors, segmenting allows the nonprofit to make the most efficient use of its resources. Segmenting may be accomplished across three dimensions:

1. Geographic (Are there zip codes that yield the best return for direct mail fund raising?)

2. Demographic (Is the new pamphlet on stuttering going to be of appeal to new parents?)

3. Psychographic (What kinds of likes and dislikes characterize the typical enrollee in the stress reduction clinic?)

Geographic data are, of course, relatively easy to obtain. For a mailing announcing the offering of a new weight-loss center, mailing to an entire zip code may be warranted, in that being overweight is, sadly, not confined to any segment of the population. For a course on child rearing, by contrast, the marketing staff may want to target only those sections in the community which have a high concentration of young families.

Demographic data are usually collected according to cohorts, i.e., groups of people with some common characteristics—age range, gender, race, or ethnicity.

Psychographic data reveal opinions, attitudes, feelings, beliefs. Compiling and analyzing pyschographic data allow the organization to better understand how a particular constituency group (e.g., direct mail contributors) feel about the organization and the cause that it represents.

TEN REASONS WHY MARKETING FAILS

Marketing is a science, albeit an imperfect one. It requires care and commitment to succeed. Here are some reasons why the marketing effort may fail:

1. The market is either inaccurately or incompletely analyzed.

2. There is a failure to recognize that the market is "thin."

3. The timing is poor.

   The organization gets into the market either too early (before sufficient numbers of people are interested) or too late (when the market is already saturated).

4. There is insufficient consideration given to actual sales.

   Product development can be seductive. Staff may be desirous of retaining a product because it is well written, looks attractive, won an award—even though the sales are flat.

5. The organization's commitment to marketing is half-hearted.

   It does not invest enough money in the marketing function; or the marketing function is isolated, not integrated into the culture of the organization.

6. The marketing research did not accurately read the consumer's wants and needs.

7. Promotion is inadequate.

   Virtually nobody knows about the product or service.

8. The competition was underestimated

9. The cost of developing and producing the product cannot be fully recouped through sales.

10. The distribution is poor.

    (Example: offering a bilingual program in childcare which low-income Hispanic parents cannot attend because there is no transportation.) Commitment to a marketing orientation need not be a function of budget size. The small nonprofit can exhibit a marketing orientation if the staff and volunteers continually think in terms of the publics whom they serve.[10]

WRITING A BUSINESS PLAN

In virtually every major corporation and in many sophisticated nonprofit organizations, the decision to develop a new product or service is made on the basis of a business plan. The business plan lays out the argument for the new program or product: why it is needed, who will buy it, what strengths of the organization it builds on, what variables may affect the success of the product or service, how it will be accomplished, how much it will cost. In your nonprofit organization, you may want to consider using business plans for three purposes:

1. To assure yourself that your marketing staff has given careful consideration to the idea being proposed

2. To convince your board, budget committee, or other decision-making body of the wisdom of your proposal.

3. To persuade a potential contributor that the idea merits his or her contribution as an investment.

Writing a business plan is akin to strategic planning. As a precursor to actually writing the business plan, the author (read "marketing team") may begin as do many planning processes—determining (or affirming, if you have a strategic plan in place) the business in which your organization is engaged. The process continues with an identification of key players and of the forces that may affect the organization as it launches this new venture.

The actual business plan may contain the following elements:

*   Cover Sheet or Title Page
*   Executive Summary
*   Table of Contents
*   Definition of the Organization's Business (mission, purposes, audiences, uniqueness)
*   Environmental Scan (relevant trends, strengths and weaknesses, competition, threats and opportunities)
*   Description of the Need (and what benefit can be offered)
*   Description of the Product or Service
*   Definition of the Market (description of the target audience and the potential which it offers; this section may provide specifics in terms of anticipated sales)
*   Marketing Plan (specific strategies, timeframes, personnel to be assigned)
*   Financial Data (anticipated costs, pricing information, income projections over time)
*   Appended Material (charts, related documents, letters of support, detailed time schedules).[11]

APPLYING MARKETING PRINCIPLES TO FUND RAISING

Effective fund raising is the result of effective marketing. The day is long gone when nonprofit organizations can rely on the "Help, the roof is leaking" approach to raising money. Prospective donors want to invest their resources where they will do the most good, in an organization that is well run, well planned, financially solid. In the 1990s, nonprofit organizations that continue to think of themselves as charities will be fortunate to survive.

To survive—and thrive—nonprofit organizations will need to apply proven marketing techniques to their fund raising.

The Four P's of Fund Raising

The 4 P's of marketing were discussed earlier in this chapter: product, price, promotion, and place. These may now be applied to effective fund raising.

Product

One of the reasons fund raisers fail is that they have nothing to sell. How often have you heard a colleague in a nonprofit organization (perhaps your own) say something like: "We need to hire someone who'll do some fund raising for us. . . . Someone who knows where the bodies are buried." How many organizations have you seen that have gone through one fund raiser after another without ever establishing a successful fund raising program?

Why? In part, because the organization failed to think of fund raising as an integral part of the whole. It's the "fix it" mentality: if we hire a fund raiser we'll be all right. Fund raising, as marketing, begins with a product to sell. Which means that for fund raising to succeed, the organization should have a plan in place, know where it's going, know what it does well, have some ambitious but achievable goals. Then the fund raising can occur in earnest because those charged with raising the money can identify who might be interested in the goals and programs proposed (the products) and how to get to them.

Price

Some years ago an organization for the mentally retarded hired a fund raiser who asked in the interview what the expectations would be of him—how much the board expected he would be able to help the organization raise, and over what period of time. The board could not provide an answer. Board members knew they needed money, but they had not thought about how much they needed, for what, or what was realistic. They had no idea of what the market would bear.

In order to effectively raise funds (especially large funds) it is imperative to have some understanding of the market potential, from two perspectives:

A. What is the amount of money that might be raised from the universe of donors and donor prospects, *in toto*?

    If the organization has had a limited fund raising history, it may be difficult to make any reasonable estimates. The safest bet is to assume relatively modest incremental growth.

B. What size gifts might be realized?

The donor who is willing to contribute $100,000 to her or his alma mater may be prepared to contribute only $1,000 to a local charity that holds some interest.

Chapter 5, on fund raising, describes one method of determining fund raising potential, the feasibility study.

Promotion

Fund raising materials that work—that sell—paint a picture of an organization that has its act together, that is, in effect, a good venture in which to invest. Promotional materials may take the form of direct mail letters, case statements, brochures, proposals; but in each, the central message that emerges is: This is an organization that understands the real needs and is doing something about them.

Place

In fund raising, "place" means several things:

- The physical entity; when prospective donors come for a visit, are they impressed—and hopefully moved—by what they see.
- Being at the right place at the right time.

  Fund raising is built on contacts, on "who knows whom"; being visible in certain settings enhances the image of the organization, making it a more attractive place in which to invest.
- A place not yet built.

  Some of the most successful fund raising occurs with capital campaigns, especially when the organization can paint an exciting picture of what the new facility will look like and be able to offer.

Segmenting

As with other marketing efforts, fund raising relies on an understanding of who wants and who needs the products and services that the institution can provide. Assume, for example, that you want to undertake a new center for infants and toddlers, offering infant stimulation activities, parent counseling, and health care. What companies in your area or nationally, what private foundations, what individuals, what government agencies are likely to have an interest in early educational intervention or childcare or healthy babies? Are there companies that target their products particularly to young parents?

In order to begin raising money, it is necessary to cull out of the organization's universe of constituents those who will need or have an interest in this new service and have the ability to support it financially. Segmenting the constituent universe allows the fund raising staff and volunteers to make best use of their time and resources, targeting those who have the highest probability of wanting the product or program being offered.[12] (For information on the *tools of fund raising*, and the advantages and disadvantages of each, see Chapter 5.)

MARKETING AND PUBLIC RELATIONS

Chapter 4 addresses public relations in some depth, but the following will place it in the context of marketing.

When some organizations think of public relations (or public information) they think of press releases. Create a new service and write a press release on it: "For Immediate Release . . . ." Send it off to the local newspaper and the radio and television stations in the hope that somebody will pick it up. That's neither effective public relations nor effective marketing.

To be effective, the public relations program needs to be built on an understanding of the organization's goals and needs and how these match up with the goals and needs of the public with whom the organization seeks to communicate. The application of marketing strategy to public relations is realized through the implementation of the following seven steps:

1. **Identify the overall goals of the organization.**

   The goals of the public relations program, first and foremost, need to be consonant with the overall purpose and goals of the organization, as presented in the mission statement, strategic plan, and other key documents stating the organization's raison d'être.

2. **Determine the goals for the public relations program.**

   The public relations effort can be doomed by vague goals which mean different things to different people. Board and staff should articulate a set of goals (preferably, no more than five) toward which the organization will work in the next several years. Obviously, these goals need to both reflect and be an outgrowth of the larger organizational goals.

3. **Identify the relevant "publics."**

   If there is no public relations goal having to do with improving the image of the organization among the general public, there is little reason to target that audience for public information. The public relations publics should parallel those of other organizational efforts; for example, the organization may decide to target the corporate sector in order to lay the groundwork for a major corporate fund raising campaign.

4. **Assess the images and attitudes of the organization which are held by the relevant publics.**

   It is important to gather baseline data on the targeted publics: How do they view the organization? Is their image accurate? Is it positive? What changes in their perceptions should frame the public relations effort?

5. **Establish a public relations plan.**

   Make the plan replete with measurable objectives, strategies, activities. How will the goals be addressed, by whom, using what resources, and over what time period?

6. **Implement the plan.**

7. **Conduct both formative (i.e., ongoing) and summative evaluations of the effort.**[13]

PARTING THOUGHTS

> The aim of marketing is to make selling superfluous. The aim is to know and understand the customer so well that the product or service fits him and sells itself.   —*Peter Drucker*

Knowing the market, knowing what the customer wants: these are ideas that many American companies are espousing with renewed vigor. Competition both at home and abroad has made it necessary to do so. This will be no less true among nonprofits. We now know two principles about marketing: One, it is a body of knowledge and skills that is extensive; and two, that notwithstanding, it is a concept that needs to permeate the nonprofit of the 1990s.

NOTES

1. Benson P. Shapiro, "Marketing for Nonprofit Organizations." In *Marketing in Nonprofit Organizations*, Patrick J. Montane, ed. (New York: AMACOM, 1978), 17.

2. Alan R. Shark, "How to Become a Market-Driven Association." Presented at the November 15, 1989 Management Forum of the Greater Washington Society of Association Executives.

3. Rosabeth Moss Kanter, *The Change Masters: Innovations for Productivity in the American Corporation* (New York: Simon and Schuster, 1983), 35–36.

4. Robert R. Tucker, "Unleashing the Innovator in You!" American Society of Association Executives Annual Convention, August 13, 1989.

5. Robert M. Smith, "Knowledge Is Power: Research Can Help Your Marketing Program Succeed," *Case Currents*, 8 (May/June 1982): 8.

6. David L. Morgan. *Focus Groups as Qualitative Research.* (Newbury Park, CA: Sage Publications, 1989), 12.

7. Morgan, 12.

8. Smith, 11.

9. Philip Kotler, *Marketing for Nonprofit Organizations* (Englewood Cliffs, NJ: Prentice-Hall, Inc., 1975), 18.

10. Christopher A. Smith and Goodwill Industries of America, Inc. *Marketing Rehabilitation Facility Products and Services* (Menomonie, WI: Materials Development Center, Stout Vocational Rehabilitation Institute, 1987), 109–115. This text provided some of the thinking regarding why marketing efforts fail.

11. Jonathon Peck. "Business Plan Writing." A presentation at the American Society of Association Executives Annual Convention, August 14, 1989.

12. Kathleen S. Kelly, "Pass the Alka-Seltzer: How Market Research Eases the Pain of 'Gut-Feeling' Solicitation," *CASE Currents*, 8 (May/June 1982): 32.

13. The application of marketing principles to a public relations effort draws on Philip Kotler and Alan R. Andreasen, *Strategic Marketing for Nonprofit Organizations*, 3rd ed. (Englewood Cliffs, NJ: Prentice-Hall, Inc., 1987), 577.

Chapter 4
Public Relations: Marketing the Organization's Story

EXECUTIVE SUMMARY

Organizational theory reminds us that organizations depend on the environment for their survival: interaction is the key; isolation is fatal. Among the measures of a nonprofit's health are the amount of communication that it has with its various publics, what those publics think about the organization as a result of that interaction, and what the nonprofit learns about its constituencies and itself as a result of that dialogue.

This chapter on public relations attempts to show what public relations is today and how those who practice it well create public relations strategies. The chapter considers how to decide on—and then work towards—a desired image for the nonprofit. Also discussed: Is desktop publishing for your institution?; looking at the organization as others might see it; how to hire and manage an efficacious public relations staff (including a sample job description); getting media coverage; and a look at some trends in public relations for the 1990s.

PUBLIC RELATIONS . . . IS MORE THAN PRESS RELEASES

Chapter 3, on marketing, discussed the fact that some nonprofit organizations have a limited understanding of what public relations is all about: "Let's get a little PR on this . . . ." "What we need is a press conference" (to which nobody from the media shows up, all too often).

Communications with one's publics has evolved into a sophisticated and vital function in the nonprofit organization of the '90s. Colleges and universities are now offering courses on public information on both the undergraduate and graduate levels, and those who wish to pursue it as a career can become certified. Public information (or public relations) has its own body of knowledge that the executive director and management of a nonprofit institution would do well to recognize.

WHAT TO CALL IT

The terms "public relations," "public information," and "communications" represent something of an evolution. The organizations that created this function some years ago referred to it as "public relations," which, unfortunately, soon became "PR," which came to possess a rather unpleasant, even sleazy aura. PR staff manipulated information, painting unrealistic pictures of their organization, being less than candid with the press who called.

Perhaps because it carried such untrustworthy connotations, many changed the name of this unit to "public information," implying that the organization was not engaged in the practice of smoke and mirrors, but rather was interested in providing the public with information about itself. The problem with the term is that it suggests a one-way flow. As discussed in Chapter 3 on marketing, in order to be effective, staff of organizations need to listen as well as talk, and preferably in that sequence. They need to learn what it is the organization's publics want, what they think of them, what needs they have.

We need to communicate with the public. Hence, the current fashion, which is to refer to this function as "communications." While this is admittedly a more accurate representation of what the function ought to be, it does lend itself to some confusion. Many universities, for example, have a communications department that offers courses in radio and TV. Many nonprofit service organizations have staff who assist in alleviating communication disorders and lay claim to the term "communication science."

The main point, it would appear, is to have a function that is two-way. Name it for what it most does. The public will come to understand the name if the function works.

CREATING A PUBLIC RELATIONS STRATEGY

Public relations is in effect a marketing activity that is rooted in planning. Much of the process that characterizes good strategic planning applies to the establishment of your public information program. Planning is a process of assessing the future and making provision for it.[1] Public relations is a process of determining the image that the organization would like to project in the future and how to create that image.

The Public Information Audit

In addition to considering major trends that are likely to have an impact on the organization, the public information audit asks: Who are our publics and what do they know and think of us? Imagine, for example, that yours is a local Easter Seals affiliate. You offer some educational programming for young children, occupational and physical therapy, dentistry for children with orthopedic handicaps, and counseling to parents of children with disabilities. In order to accomplish a thorough audit of your publics, the public information staff may want to contact:

- Graduates of your program—disabled young adults who were served by Easter Seals when they were younger;
- Parents, other family members, other caregivers;
- Relevant segments of the medical community—pediatricians, family practitioners, neonatal nurses, pediatric dentists, the local medical school;
- Directors of head start programs;
- Preschool teachers and building principals;
- County health agents;
- Your board;
- A representative sample of your staff;
- Funders;
- The media

You will want to find out not only what each of these groups knows about your Easter Seals program, but whether their information is accurate, whether they have a positive mental image of what you do, if they would refer a family to you (or send their own child there). You will also want to observe any discrepancies, e.g., differences on how you are perceived among various publics. And you will want to know what needs these publics have which your program might address.

Chapter 3 details ways to go about collecting this information in marketing—interviews, surveys, focus groups. What your organization may want to consider is having the data collected by someone who will come across as objective and disinterested. If there are sufficient funds, consider a public relations firm. If that option is not available, perhaps one of the classes in your local college—public relations, journalism, health science—would be interested in conducting the audit as a class project.

DECIDING WHAT IMAGE THE ORGANIZATION SHOULD PROJECT

The decision on the image you want to project ought to be driven by two factors:

1. What the nonprofit's "publics" now know and think of it.
2. The mission and goals that frame the organization's strategic plan.

The plan, in turn, is hopefully based on some understanding of trends. If, for example, the mean age in your community is rising faster than the national average, that should be reflected in the programs you will be offering. What do the trends say about the relative financial health of the area, about the increase in the proportion of minorities, about the numbers of single parents? Is the image which you portray likely to change as the demographics change?

As you decide on what you want to accomplish, keep in mind the following inverted hierarchy:

- Awareness
- Information
- Knowledge
- Attitude
- Behavior

Achieving some level of awareness may be relatively straightforward, e.g., setting a goal of name recognition among 30 percent of the community residents. Getting those residents to truly understand what you do, think well of it, and become involved voluntarily, are progressively more challenging tasks. Don't doom your public relations effort to failure by asking for attitude change when all you need is general awareness.

The hierarchy needs to be applied separately to each constituent group you want to reach. It may be unimportant that the general public know anything about your program as long as the pediatric community knows of you and will make referrals. It may not be important that social workers know what the Easter Seals organization does, but it may be absolutely vital that prospective donors do.

CREATING THE IMAGE

One of the complaints that some people have had about public relations is that it is too "soft" as compared, for example, with fund raising, where it is pretty clear if you are or are not succeeding. That concern can be somewhat laid to rest. It is entirely possible to establish and implement a public relations strategy, and then, at some point, measure if, in fact, you have made a difference.

Once you have completed the goal-setting stage of your public relations plan, and have decided what you want to accomplish with which publics, you can proceed to the development of specific objectives and the activities that allow you to meet those objectives. Be sure to decide upon:

- Measurable objectives;
- Who's responsible;
- Over what period of time;
- At what cost; and
- How results will be evaluated.

Who Writes the Public Relations Plan

If you don't have a public relations committee or subcommittee of your board, this may be the time to create one. That group, which includes your senior public information staff person, should have the responsibility for crafting and presenting the plan to the full board and getting its commitment. There needs to be the same level of commitment among staff. Everyone on staff plays a public relations function, every day. It is important that your staff has input to the planning process and buys in to the goals and objectives.

DEVELOPING A "LOOK" IN PRINT[2]

One of the ways in which to position an organization is bring some consistency and upgrading to the look of its printed materials in what is referred to as "image management." This does not create printed pieces that all look alike, but manages the appearance of the various print media, so that they all send a similar message to those receiving them.

Information Gathering

The process of developing an image begins by asking some basic questions about the organization which relate to its mission, vision, and strategic plan:

- Who are we? What do we do well?
- What do others think of us? What strengths do we portray?

- What image do we portray? What image do we want to portray?
- What is our long-range vision?

It is important in this information gathering stage to ask enough questions of enough people so that some clustering of opinions begins to emerge. Informal focus groups, one-to-one interviews, and surveys all may be used to assess the image that the organization currently portrays.

The results are captured in a report which is then shared with the organization's leadership. For example, the report might reveal that the organization's mission seems well understood among its more immediate constituencies but that the general public lacks awareness of its activities and raison d'être. Among those who know the organization but are not involved with it, words and phrases such as "does good work," "caring," "meeting some needs of society" recur.

It is not uncommon to learn that there is confusion about what the organization actually does.

On the basis of the information gathering and discussions which ensue, a position statement is written, which is an attempt to capture verbally what the organization wants to say about itself; as such, it forms the basis for the organization's communications program.

The position statement is used by graphic artists to design some exploratory symbols. These may be displayed on mock-ups of the organization's letterhead so that volunteers and staff can see how the various options might work.

Finally, a design symbol is selected. The symbol, together with a "logotype" (representing the typeface and design for the name of the organization), become the organization's signature. That signature should then be carried throughout the organization's publications, often with an indication of the color or colors that work best with it. There may also be guidelines developed on the kinds of paper stock to be used and suggestions on typeface for printed heads and printed copy.

IS DESKTOP PUBLISHING FOR YOUR ORGANIZATION?

Not everything that relates to your public relations outreach is a product of your public relations staff. A notable exception may be the printed material produced by virtually every other department in the organization. In the past, you may have required that everything that went to a printer had to go through your public relations people; now, that dictum is being negated (if not at times consciously circumvented) by the infusion of desktop publishing.

From another vantage point, the question, "Is desktop publishing for you?" is probably a moot point. With the ever increasing capability of desktop computers, whether your organization has an MS-DOS (IBM and clones) or Apple system in-house, it is probably using a desktop publishing system. And if you're not, be assured that it is virtually inevitable that your organization will be doing so in the future. There-fore, the more practical question is, "How can the organization do desktop publishing in a way that will be efficient and of high quality?"

How to Use Desktop Publishing in a Way That Is Efficient and of High Quality

1. Provide sufficient equipment.

Yes, one can create a reproducible piece of copy on any word processing equipment. But if you are developing something for distribution to one or more of your organization's constituencies, do you want to send something out that looks vaguely like a ransom note? Or do you want something that reflects positively on the image you are trying to portray?

"But the cost." Unquestionably, a Macintosh Plus, an IBM PS/2, or similar equipment is not inexpensive. Neither is skilled personnel. It's worth investing in both. Perhaps your institution can get a donation of equipment in return for giving a credit line in publica-tions you create.

2. Maintain quality control.

Have your public relations or graphics staff prepare guidelines, including:

- Standard margins;
- Sample typefaces;
- Information on design—e.g., the use of white space.

It may be appropriate to require that any piece produced on desktop publishing be reviewed with your graphics staff in order to decide how the project will be laid out.

3. Provide ongoing training.

Training is expensive; less expensive, however, than mistakes and poor quality made public. Be sure those using the desktop equip-ment understand its capabilities and limitations.

4. Set aside a "yoyo" room.

One of the dangers in getting into desktop publishing is that everyone on staff will want to be creating flyers, brochures, and reports. The public relations and graphics staff can find themselves inundated by requests for help if you are not careful. Some organizations have addressed the problem by creating a yoyo room, which stands for "you're on your own." It's a centralized facility in which desktop equipment is provided. The graphics staff maintains quality control, but the actual creation of materials is up to the staff themselves.

In summation: make the best use of desktop publishing by setting and maintaining standards, while giving staff a chance to be creative in the materials that they produce.

ABOUT YOUR APPEARANCE

Well, not your appearance exactly. But consider, if you will, how your organization might appear to a visitor. What kind of impression might you make on a prospective client, student, board member, or major contributor? Put yourself in the place of an important visitor (and what visitor isn't?).

1. When a visitor calls to arrange a visit, what kind of response would she or he receive?

Will the telephone be answered within the first five rings? Will the voice on the other end of the line sound friendly, welcoming, knowledgeable, nonintimidating; or does she or he come across as the first of several barriers to good service?

Is there an adequate reception area, complete with reading material for both adults and children? When the caller is put through to a department, will someone answer promptly? If the individual being sought by the caller is out of the office, what might the caller hear?

- "Oh, he's not in yet; I don't know when he'll be in."
- "She's probably taking a long lunch hour."
- "Who's calling again? I didn't catch the name the first time."
- "What's the nature of your call?"

2. Does the outside of your building look neat?

Does it need a coat of paint? Are the shrubs well trimmed? Is there any litter on the lawn, sidewalk, or street in front of the building?

3. **How's the appearance of the offices that might be seen by a visitor?**

   Are boxes piled up all over? Does it look as if the people working there enjoy what they're doing? Is attractive artwork hung (perhaps by the children or adults served by your institution)? Are there pictures on display that capture what you are all about?

4. **Do you and your staff refer to the people whom you serve by name?**

   Do the staff speak of "individuals" or "clients"? Of "Mrs. Banyon in Room 103" or "the gall bladder in 103"?

5. **If you were a visitor:**

   - Would you feel welcome or intimidated?
   - Would you be able to find your way around the building? Is it well marked, with signage designed with visitors in mind?
   - Would staff offer to help if you appeared lost?

6. **If you were a parent or family member of an individual receiving service:**

   Would you feel you were an integral and welcome part of the team, or would you feel as if you were intruding on others' valuable time?

   Try it sometime. Call your office. Walk through the halls. Send in a letter asking for general information. Have someone make a call and ask how to make a donation. Try filling out the standard application forms.

   Be prepared to be alarmed. Even in the best run organizations, it is easy to become complacent. Indeed, in the organizations with the best reputations, it is hard not to.

HOW TO HIRE AND MANAGE AN EFFECTIVE PUBLIC RELATIONS STAFF

Not that long ago it was both easy and difficult to hire public relations staff: easy, because anyone who had a modicum of writing ability might apply for a position in public relations; and difficult, because anyone with a modicum of writing ability might apply for a position in public relations. The field has become more refined. It is now a career of choice. One can pursue it with academic and experiential rigor. For the executive director of an organization, that is clearly good news.

In part perhaps because it did not have its own arcane body of knowledge, as contrasted with medicine, or law, or even engineering and accounting, public relations was the kind of job that anyone could apply for—and everyone on the board thought he or she knew how to do it better than the staff.

At times, they did. Another observation which one could make about public relations was that it was less than a profession, populated by individuals with little or no training. Virtually no one working in the field of public relations got there by design.

The third challenge that public relations has had to overcome as a profession was that, as a term, it was a catch-all for . . .

- Hollywood publicists, who would stage any stunt if it got a few lines of copy for their client;
- The person in the fund raising office who sent out press releases ignored by most of the press;
- The huckster selling cars, or new homes, or political candidates.

The most negative aspect of the person working in public relations could be captured in this rather cynical motto:

The big thing in this business is honesty. Once you learn how to fake that, the rest is easy.

The Public Relations Professional: What to Look For

Fortunately, the public relations professional today is schooled in his or her craft, skilled as a communicator, considered a trusted source of information by the media, and bound by a rigorous code of ethics. How do you find such an individual?

What to Look for on the Resume

Decide up front what the organization wants:

- Someone with background and knowledge related to your organization, who has acquired public relations experience; or
- Someone who has chosen public relations as a career.

With either choice, your will want to see evidence of sound communication skills, both oral and written. The candidate should evidence experience communicating with a public, and preferably several publics; have a record as a writer (and not only as an editor—you'll need both skills); and demonstrate a career path consistent with someone who wants a long-term job in public relations. Beware the jack-of-all-trades resumist. While public relations does require many generalist's skills, what your organization does not need is someone who sees this job as a stopgap.

If you are seeking someone with solid public relations credentials, look for college course work, preferably at the graduate level. Better still: Is the candidate a member of the Public Relations Society of America (PRSA), the membership society for public relations practitioners? And even better, has he or she become a certified public relations executive (denoted by "APR," for accreditation in public relations)?

Where you look for the public relations staff person will depend in part on the nature of your organization—whether it's local or national, a college or hospital, with a staff of 10 or 110. Professional and trade journals can be good sources, as can *The Chronicle of Higher Education*. You might look to head hunting agencies, as long as you are prepared to pay the fee. When the resumes starting coming in, here are some things to look for:

1. Sound communication skills.

   Is there a record of experience in writing—extensive writing, writing under deadline, as contrasted with writing for academic journals?

   Does the resume give indication of public speaking?

   Is it well written? Are they any typos or mistakes in grammar in either the resume or cover letter?

2. Credentials.

   Does the candidate's resume reflect any coursework in public relations, either preservice (before starting a career) or inservice? Has the candidate participated in any special workshops relating to some aspect of public relations?

3. Commitment.

   What evidence is there that the candidate sees public relations as a career, and not just as a job? Would yours be the first organization in which he or she was in a job with a title relating to public relations? If the candidate is a member of PRSA, has she or he been active—attending local meetings and annual national meetings, serving on committees?

4. Career Path.

   Does the resume suggest that this candidate is moving up a career ladder? For example, do the job titles go from "public relations associate" to "director of public relations?" Are you going to be getting someone who sees this as a positive career move, or someone who's just looking for a way to pay the mortgage?

   Do you want an "up and comer" or a seasoned veteran?

Do you want someone who'll do a great job for two years, but then want to move up; or are you looking for an individual who will make a long-term commitment?

What to Look for in the Interview

The review process has narrowed the search to five acceptable candidates. A couple look really good on paper. Interviews are scheduled.

Here are some traits worth looking for in a skilled public relations professional:

1. "Speed and quickness."

If you've ever listened to a football broadcast, you're probably familiar with the distinction between *speed* (the ability to get downfield) and *quickness* (the ability to change direction rapidly). Both attributes apply to public relations:

- Speed = the ability to write well, quickly; and
- Quickness = the ability to shift from one crisis to another and back again.

Public relations often requires the ability to produce acceptable, understandable copy in short order. Many people can write a comprehensible page of copy if given unlimited time. You won't have that luxury. Nor will the public relations person be able to focus on one task to the exclusion of others. Someone who gets rattled by a day full of interruptions may not be the person for you.

2. Organization.

Public relations staff may at times need to respond to crises, but ideally they shouldn't be the cause of it. Your organization should seek someone who can manage myriad tasks without letting small or large ones fall through the cracks.

3. Vision.

If strategic planning helps to create the big picture, public relations helps to articulate it—creating word pictures to excite the imagination. Ask the candidates: "From what you know of this organization, what do you think it might become in five years?"

4. Ask yourself: How would I respond?

If you were a television reporter, how would you respond to the person applying for this position? Admittedly, this calls for subjective judgement—but public relations deals with appearance as much as with fact.

Every organization has a culture. The person who fits in well in an environmental advocacy organization might be singularly out of place in a nonprofit cancer hospital. Your public relations staff will be the identity that many media think of when they think of your organization. Is the image presented by this candidate what your organization wants to project?

Public Relations: Sample Job Description

Figure 4 displays a sample job description for a director of public relations.

Figure 4.
Job Description
Director of Public Relations

The Wellmeaning Institute, a residential program for children and adults with eating disorders. The Institute is a nonprofit organization, located in the heart of North Carolina, and easily accessible to most major cities. The Institute serves about 300 persons annually and is in its tenth year.

Wellmeaning is seeking a senior level public relations professional to direct its public relations program. The successful candidate will be responsible for all of the activities related to public information, media relations, graphics and printing, and in-house communications. The public relations program also works closely with Wellmeaning's fund raising department.

The director will supervise a staff of five professionals and three support staff. He or she will work closely with the Institute's board of overseers, especially its public information committee. The director will also be responsible for preparing annual goals for the department and for reporting on its progress in meeting those goals.

Qualifications: Masters degree in a field relating to public relations, communications, journalism, or writing. Clear evidence of excellent writing skills. Sound organizational and interpersonal capabilities. Knowledge of major issues facing nonprofit organizations. Understanding of eating disorders desired but not required. Interested candidates should submit . . . .

MANAGING THE PUBLIC RELATIONS PROGRAM

One of the historical difficulties in managing a public relations program is how does one evaluate it? How can someone supervising the public relations program know when it is successful?

- By the number of press releases the staff puts out in a month's time?
- By the frequency, during a year, that the organization is mentioned on local TV or in the most prominent newspaper?

- When it receives a favorable evaluation by the members of the board's public relations committee?

A related question: over what period of time should the relative success of the public relations program be evaluated? Is a year too short to see any change? Is two years too long to invest in a losing cause?

Setting Realistic Goals

One of the reasons why public relations programs fail—and the staff along with them—is that organizations tend to set unrealistic expectations.

- "We need to get on the 6:00 o'clock news. Let's get somebody who can do that."
- "Did you see the big article on the Romer Clinic in yesterday's *Dispatch*? When will we have the expertise that'll get us that kind of coverage?"
- "How about seeing if we can get Bob Hope to emcee our annual dance. He does a lot of charity work. Every newspaper in the county would want to be there."

While the staff may not ever be fully successful in discouraging members of the board who are convinced that if they just try, they can get a Bob Hope for the charity event, realistic objectives can be established on which to evaluate the public relations program.

The process starts with a marketing assessment. Whom does the organization desire to influence? With what message? Forget about getting a big story in the weekend section of the local paper—unless the readers are the audience you really want to reach. More likely, you're going to want to capture the attention of the business community. What do businesspeople read in your community? Is there a program that your organization is conducting that might be of interest? Something having to do with . . .

- Stress reduction;
- Hiring older workers;
- A training program that works with undereducated entry-level employees;
- Research on motivation;
- Information on the global marketplace;
- Job sharing.

As with any market, the public relations program needs to ask: What does the business community want and need to know about? Who are potential buyers and what are their characteristics? How does one find, train, and retain good employees? How should staff be motivated at all levels? How can the latest technology be used effectively? What are the new product ideas?

Review your institution's programs. Chances are good that you are addressing one or more of these topics. You have information and skills that are of interest to the business community. The questions are only: What match can be made between business interest and organizational programming? And, what's the best way to get the organization's message across?

Setting realistic goals also means tying the public relations program to the accepted goals and objectives of the overall organization. Public relations is a service component. Its goals should echo those of the institution. It's easy to accept that the public relations objectives should tie into the objectives of the fund raising program. Public relations helps to create the image that makes the organization attractive to potential donors.

But the same logic should hold for other organizational objectives. The public relations objectives should interstice with the objectives of other units:

- Recruitment of new students or clients;
- Success of the outreach project;
- Getting more financial support from the state;
- Getting the attention of donors from the more affluent areas of the community.

Public Relations in the Small Nonprofit

While the principles of effective public relations apply across the spectrum of nonprofit organizations, the mechanics of getting the job done will vary according to organizational size and budget. In many nonprofit organizations, there simply are not the resources to staff a full public relations department or to undertake sophisticated market surveys.

Some strategies which the management of the small nonprofit might want to consider follow:

1. Expand the public relations staff through the use of volunteers.

Constitute a public relations committee or task force (a committee typically being ongoing, a task force short term). There may be volunteers already known to the organization who can help in preparing copy, contacting the print or electronic media, serving as tour guides. It is important that all parties understand up front that when volunteers engage in such activities, their work must meet the same kind of standards of review as if they were paid staff. Timelines must be adhered to, and the volunteer should be prepared to have his or her work edited by someone else.

2. **Start an intern program.**

Local colleges are often excellent sources of bright, energetic young people for whom an internship is a win-win proposition. They gain invaluable experience for their resumes, and the nonprofit has a cadre of individuals who can supplement the efforts of staff.

3. **Ask a university public relations class—or the local chapter of the Public Relations Society of America (PRSA)—to use your organization for a special project.**

It may be possible, with some advance planning, to work out an ongoing relationship with a local higher education facility, which has a program in public relations, whereby the class takes on the nonprofit as its semester project. Increasingly, organizations such as PRSA are looking for ways to become more involved in the local community.

4. **Ask for an in-kind contribution from a local company.**

One nonprofit had its entire public relations program, including the design of print materials, created by the public relations staff of a local employer. Another possibility: obtain the loan of a public relations staff (referred to as the "loaned executive" program).

5. **Seek funding specifically for the public relations program.**

An argument can be made to a funder known to the organization that a grant to augment the public relations effort will pay dividends in improving and expanding the nonprofit's image, thereby increasing the chances of attracting additional constituencies, including funders.

GETTING INTO PRINT AND ON THE AIR

Visibility in the general media—newspapers, radio, television—can be helpful to the organization for three reasons:

1. **Media exposure can expand the pool of persons interested in receiving goods or services.**

There is no way that the typical nonprofit can afford to purchase advertising that reaches the number of people reached by a newspaper story or mention on television or the radio.

2. **Media visibility can be a source of contributions—both financial and in-kind.**

While it is not likely that the organization will receive unsolicited contributions as a result of a newspaper feature article, it is probable that the organization's chances to raise funds increase proportionally to its name recognition. Being well known also increases the probability of attracting volunteers.

3. **Media coverage is perceived as implied endorsement.**

Assuming that it is favorable, receiving media coverage suggests that the media source believes the organization to be worthy. It is one thing for the organization to tout its good works; it is quite something else again for an apparently objective third party to do so.

Working with the Editor

Both print and electronic media rely on editors to determine what news will appear. Understanding that editor's needs and interests—that is, applying marketing principles to public relations—will improve the chances of being covered. Editors are literally bombarded with news releases and requests for media coverage, much of it patently self-serving. In addition, the editor is tracking major national and local stories and deciding how best to present them in the space allotted. Operating on a tight timeframe, he or she must decide what stories are most newsworthy, that is, which ones "offer the most information with the most urgency to the most people."[3]

The organization that is desirous of obtaining media coverage, then, needs to think in the editor's terms: What about the organization is newsworthy? Are there any breakthroughs that might be of interest to the general public? Has anything been learned that might be applicable to a wide audience?

Consider this fictionalized example. Appleway Nursery is a daycare center. Most of its children are from two-income families. One of the teachers comments at a staff meeting that it appears a growing number of the children see their grandparents only a few times during the year, and she has started inviting senior citizens to visit the center periodically to read to the children and play with them. Early indications are that the program is a great success: the kids love it, the older persons feel needed and valued, and the parents notice what a calming influence the senior volunteers have on their children.

By linking it with current trends in society—the changing nature of family life, the increase in two-income families, the aging of the populace—Appleway Nursery could have a story of interest to an editor.

A Look at Some News Outlets

Getting on the 6 o'clock news is only one of several alternatives (and frankly, among the more remote). Consideration should be given to the range of options available.

Radio Talk Shows

Talk shows are a growing phenomenon. The Appleway story might well be of interest to a talk show whose audience includes older persons. Appleway might want to recommend a team of persons who could be interviewed: the teacher, one of the "grandparents," and a working parent (the parent interviewed by phone from his or her office, to further make the point).

Magazines

Many newspapers prepare and run their own Sunday supplement magazines. Most major cities have magazines bearing the name of the city. In addition, there is a magazine for virtually every segment of the population. The Appleway story could appeal to all three outlets—the Sunday supplement, replete with photographs; the city-named magazine, many of which are aimed at upwardly mobile families; and a magazine designed for retired persons.

The Organization as Expert

Molding a newsworthy story is one way of garnering publicity. Another is to present the organization, or persons working for it, as sources of expertise. Both electronic and print media seek organizations and individuals whom they can turn to for further information, clarification, analysis. Within your organization, there may be staff or volunteers whose expertise could be made known to the media in areas such as:

- Science
- Technology
- Health care
- Modern art
- Substance abuse
- Child care
- The economy
- Management
- Changing racial and ethnic demographics

The Special Event

Chapter 5 addresses the advantages and disadvantages of using special events for fund raising. Special events can also be used for the publicity that they attract—especially if that publicity is positive and favors the kind of image that the organization wishes to portray.

For example: a nonprofit hospital in the Washington, DC area decided to hold an event in honor of all living persons who had been born at the hospital. The public relations staff was able to secure the Mall on which the Smithsonian Institutions are located. The idea had such appeal that newspapers, radio stations, and television all ran stories about the event, encouraging area residents who had been born there to get in touch with the hospital.

When the event was held, still more publicity was generated. The participants spanned several generations and were themselves the source of a number of human interest stories.

As a special event aimed at publicity, the reunion had a lot going for it. It was a "feel good" activity that everyone—members of the media included—could identify with.

What to Do When the Media Call

Some interaction with the press and electronic media comes uninvited; the possibility of such interaction should be anticipated and planned for. Staff should know who the organization's spokesperson is (to whom all calls from the media should be directed). It is not a bad idea to simulate an actual emergency in which the nonprofit might find itself in order to see how prepared the organization is—one element of that preparedness being able to respond to the media effectively.

This is not to suggest that the staff should be skilled in cover-up. To the contrary, if anything has been learned from observing organizations handling disasters it is that those who act quickly and with candor, accepting blame and laying out a corrective course of action, ultimately come out ahead. Consider how well Johnson & Johnson handled the scare some years ago when it was found that some person or persons had tampered with bottles of Tylenol. Rather than attempt to minimize and cover up, the company took the lead—removing its products, coming up with a solution, and keeping everyone informed. The outcome: the public's confidence in and respect for the company is high, and the profits reflect that.

PUBLIC RELATIONS IN THE 1990s: AN OVERVIEW OF SOME TRENDS[4]

Planning for your organization's public relations program will be enhanced by first considering the changing nature of public relations.

1. **The 1990s Will See a Demand for Greater Accountability**

   Some nonprofits have had bad press, especially in terms of their fund raising practices. That leads to additional public scrutiny, which in turn heightens the demand for the public relations staff to be able to present a portrait of the nonprofit which is at once forthright and reassuring. If your nonprofit can withstand close scrutiny, it may be navigating through heavily mined waters.

2. **Those at the Vanguard of Public Relations Are Employing Sophisticated Techniques**

   They are familiar with multimedia, and can work alongside both printer and filmmaker, graphic artist and image consultant. They are conversant in the use of databases, computerized graphics, desktop design, and publishing. They understand how television stations operate and are developing interactive media programs using combinations of computer, compact and optical disk, video-tape, and print.

3. **Public Relations Is Communication, Not Manipulation**

   One of the reasons why some public relations practitioners had questionable reputations a generation ago was that they saw their jobs as manipulation—manipulating events, manipulating the press, massaging the facts. Public relations practitioners are coming to realize that they share a common interest with those in the print and electronic media: the desire for a good story. Helping the media reporter to find and develop that good story results in a win-win situation.

4. **Communications Is Becoming More Targeted**

   Sending out the same information, in the same format, to every audience known to the organization, is akin to what is known as shotgunning of proposals in fund raising: taking the same proposal, and sending it to dozens if not hundreds of funding agencies, every one of which recognizes the proposal for what it is.

   Public relations practitioners on the vaguard in the 1990s are educated in tools of marketing. They conduct focus groups and analyze what their various publics know about the organization; they study those publics' wants and interests and develop strategies that match organizational goals to consumer needs.

5. The Competition for Visibility Is Ever More Fierce

With the proliferation of nonprofits, with federal and state funding cutbacks, and with occasional uncertain economic conditions, nonprofits are increasingly looking to the media to help solidify their position in the mind of the potential client or contributor. The successful public relations director will need a cogent story to tell and skill in telling it. He or she will need to be imaginative, and the nonprofit executive will need to remind staff that everyone is in the business of telling the organization's story.

6. Implicit in Several of the Other Trends Is That Public Relations Is Increasingly Concerned with and about Ethics.

Nothing will bring down the nonprofit faster than a story in the press about how it fudged facts in order to present an unjustly positive front to the world. The savvy nonprofit CEO will pick up on the trend towards ethics and help his or her organization play a visible role in promoting ethical behavior.

PARTING THOUGHTS

Public relations professionals get the message out about the organization; they should not be looked to for the purpose of molding the image. That compromises not only their integrity, but also the integrity of the organization. In an age of scrutiny, asking the public relations staff to paint an undeservedly rosy picture of the organization is asking to hasten its demise.

Given a mission that is exciting and programs that hold promise, the skilled public relations practitioner can bring positive attention to the organization, which in turn increases the likelihood of investment in it, and hence its success.

NOTES

1. Philip G. Kuehl, "Strategic Long-Range Planning: Concepts and Techniques." American Society of Association Executives annual convention, August 9, 1980.

2. Some of the thinking in the section on creating a "look" is thanks to Will Linthicum, personal communication, July, 1990.

3. Martin Bradley Winston, *Getting Publicity* (New York: John Wiley & Sons, Inc., 1982), 19.

4. Some of the trends in public relations were drawn from Thomas A. Harrison, "Six PR Trends That Will Shape Your Future," *Nonprofit World*, 9 (March/April 1991): 21–23.

Chapter 5
Successful Fund
Raising

EXECUTIVE SUMMARY

Fund raising has become its own profession with its own body of knowledge and skills. Nonprofit management needs to know something of that profession in order to direct it effectively. This chapter addresses: Probable trends in fund raising in the next decade; evaluation of fund raising methodology—direct mail, corporate and foundation solicitation, special events, major gifts, government grants; applying the specifics of marketing to fund raising; four steps to successful grantseeking; how to hire capable fund raising staff, including a job description; knowing when the organization is ready to fund raise, and how to know it; and, finally, what motivates the donor?

FUND RAISING: ART, SCIENCE, OR SCAM?

Picture this scenario. You're the head of a nonprofit organization— human service, education, whatever. The organization is in generally good health; has a capable staff, a reasonably steady client pool, a balanced budget (barely). While you're not exactly a household word, in certain circles your organization enjoys a positive reputation—no scandals that have reached the media; accepted by the community that knows you as a worthy enterprise. Your board, while not entirely of the caliber you might wish, is for the most part dedicated and desirous of doing what's best for the organization.

If asked to rank your nonprofit organization on a scale of one to ten, with one being near bankrupt programmatically and fiscally, and ten being a nonprofit superstar, would you give it a . . . six? seven? five?

The point of this scenario building is twofold:

1. Most people think that they work for an organization that is pretty good—not great, perhaps; but a lot better than most (or why would they be working there?).

2. And yet, they see ample room for improvement. Staff salaries still don't compete with the for-profit world. Reserve funds are not sufficient to carry the organization if disaster were to strike. There are programs that the organization dearly would love to launch, if only the funds were available.

Typically, when an organization goes through the kind of assessment just described, the chief staff person and the board may decide: "Let's do some fund raising." This usually translates to: "Let's hire someone who will come in and raise big bucks." A search is conducted, a candidate selected, work begins. After a time, the enthusiasm diminishes, the fund raiser doesn't work out and is replaced, and the cycle continues.

Fund raising: art, science, or scam? In truth, it's all three. Art, because it requires talented individuals who have a feel for how to raise money. And art because fund raising means painting an attractive picture for potential donors. Science, because much of fund raising is now systematic, logical, and to a degree predictable. And science because the whole field of fund raising is becoming codified, with its own body of knowledge and code of ethics. And scam because there are still too many people who call themselves fund raisers who don't raise funds, and con artists calling themselves fund raisers who line their own pockets.

There is some very good news in all of this. More is known about what makes for successful fund raising today than at any time in history. Much has been learned that can be applied to your organization.

The purpose of this book is not to teach the reader how to become a fund raiser, but instead to provide him or her with the information necessary to make sound decisions on a fund raising program.

FUND RAISING TRENDS: WHAT TO EXPECT IN THE '90s

One mark of the successful nonprofit CEO in the '90s will be the ability to monitor trends in order to plan accordingly. That is nowhere more true than in raising funds for the organization. Below are listed six trends worthy of a closer look.

The Nature of the Donor Is Changing

Baby boomers, an aging population, a culturally diverse society, women in the workforce—all of these will have an impact on fund raising.

Baby Boomers

Because of its size, the baby boom generation has a great influence on American thinking and behavior. Baby boomers act differently from the generations preceding them. They are less motivated to "give something back" to [societal institutions], more inclined to ask questions about how their contributions will be used, and less inclined to contribute because someone in authority . . . asked them to.[1]

As donor "cohorts," baby boomers want to be sure that the organization to which they are contributing is managed well and that their dollars will be used appropriately. They will be most inclined to give larger sums to causes in which they believe, and which relate to their own personal interests, rather than giving small amounts to every charity that asks.

By the year 2000, the oldest baby boomer will be in his or her mid fifties—typically, the peak earning years. They will thus be a group that should be of particular interest to nonprofit fund raisers.

The Older Person as Giver

The median age of persons in the United States will be 36 years as we enter the twenty-first century—compared with about 28 years in 1970.[2] A sizable proportion of the population will be retired (or at least of retirement age). The superannuated (sometimes called the "old old") will be a burgeoning part of the population. Assuming the economy is sound, the persons over the age of 65 should represent a rich source of financial support for worthy nonprofits. They will also be a source of volunteers; this involvement on a personal level often translates into financial support as well.

Cultural Diversity

Peter K. Francese, president of American Demographics, points out that whether your organization's cause is health care, education, or some other aspect of human service, it will be essential to "think in multilingual as well as multicultural terms."[3] What might work for a predominately all white, Lutheran community in Minnesota may have no bearing on the polyglot that is Miami (or virtually any major city in the northern hemisphere).

Women in the Workforce

Father as breadwinner is an image that went out with Ozzie and Harriet. Of necessity and choice, in its place are families in which both adults work. For those who have children, issues of daycare, education, safety, and drugs will all likely have appeal. For those without children, the patterns of contributions may reflect leisure interests—the arts, for example, as well as social and environmental concerns.

Women with earning power will be making their own decisions about the causes that they will support. It is becoming commonplace for each spouse within the two-income family to have his or her own charitable interests.

The Level of Sophistication in Fund Raising Continues to Rise

Fund raising will always be an art, but is also a science. Successful fund raisers are becoming market-driven, asking "Who wants, who needs" the services that the nonprofit organization provides—or might provide. They are analyzing and segmenting the marketplace in order to target best prospects and maintain a favorable cost/benefit ratio.

The use of sophisticated fund raising techniques is flourishing, spurred by technology, which allows for computer generated "original" letters and proposals, analysis of data, and desktop preparation of elegant solicitation materials.

One university uses state-of-the-art technology in its telemarketing. Students hired to call prospective donors among alumni can retrieve computerized information on these prospects, have the calls automatically dialed, and then "branch" into some 60 different topical areas, allowing them to tailor their conversation to the interests of the alum being called.[4]

The Scrutiny of Fund Raising Is Likely to Expand

In 1988, the National Charities Information Bureau (NCIB) published its "Standards in Philanthropy," which specified for the first time an allowable percentage in terms of the funds raised that should be used for programs (NCIB calls for no less than 60 percent going to programs).

State legislatures, concerned with the abuse of a small number of fund raisers, have been reviewing their codes and, in a number of states, revising or writing new legislation requiring registration of persons soliciting funds and periodic reports.

Both the IRS and Congress continue to examine nonprofits for reasons similar to those of the state legislatures. It can be expected that the trend from both of these bodies will be towards more scrutiny.

Increased Competition for Funds Appears Inevitable

Substantial growth in the economy may be unlikely in the next decade. This may be especially true in light of the massive federal debt. The United States went from being the largest creditor nation to the largest debtor nation in the years 1980 to 1986.[5] Unless and until that debt is brought under control, federal support of nonprofit institutions will do well to remain at level funding in real dollars.

The need for funds, however, is likely to advance due to drug abuse, "crack babies," AIDs, rising health care costs, spiraling costs of education, and the aging of the population. As evidence, consider that there were some 100,000 new nonprofit organizations created in the 15-year period between 1975 and 1990,[6] each of which is dependent on fund raising to survive.

Overall, There Should Be a Continued Growth in Philanthropy

Here again, assuming a relatively healthy economy, the level of philanthropic support should continue to rise. Many corporate CEOs appear personally committed to philanthropy, as noted in a report from the Council on Foundations, which observed that the "CEO remains dedicated to the fundamental principles of corporate giving. . . . In this framework, increases in both cash and non-cash contributions and expansion of matching gifts programs are expected."[7]

Individual giving in the 1980s outpaced growth in the Gross National Product. If history is any indicator, the level of support from individuals should continue to grow, especially as the population ages.

Some Things Don't Change

It is easy to become caught up by the trends and forget some basic truths which seem to withstand change:

- People give to people, not to places or things.

  Although the giver may be demographically different, the way in which gifts, particularly larger gifts, are made is unlikely to vary.

- Fund raising is at base the art of people who believe in what they are doing asking others to share that belief.

PRO'S AND CON'S OF VARIOUS FUND RAISING METHODS

There are numerous ways in which money can be raised for a nonprofit cause. Here are some of the most typical, with a description of how they work and what's good and not so good about each.

There was a popular song some years ago entitled "You Gotta Have Friends." That is nowhere more true than in the nonprofit organization. Virtually any of the numerous definitions of "friend" listed in *Webster's New Collegiate Dictionary* obtains:

- "One attached to another by affection or esteem";
- "Acquaintance";
- "One that is not hostile";
- "One that favors or promotes something."

Friends of nonprofits run the gamut of those who are acquainted with the organization sufficiently to provide some financial support and little more, to those who are linked to it emotionally and actively promote it. It is the number one job of those charged with raising funds for the organization to identify, cultivate, solicit, keep informed, and express appreciation to those who are or might become friends. Keep in mind as you review the various fund raising methods that friends are the paying customers of the nonprofit organization; their active involvement needs to be nurtured by board and staff alike.

Direct Mail

Direct mail means, simply, mailing a solicitation directly to the person from whom you are seeking funds. In direct mail, the letter, brochure, or other mailed piece does the asking for you. Whom do you ask for money by means of direct mail?

Those whom you know:

Dear Mrs. Moneyflow,
It's been a good year here at Shadyside Camp. We had 120 campers from broken homes, all of whom had a chance to hike and swim and sleep out under the stars, thanks to your generosity.
As a supporter of Shadyside for the past five years, you know that we charge no tuition. Our kids come from environments where it wouldn't be possible to come up with the money that it costs for two weeks of camp. Friends like you make it possible. We count on you, as do "your" campers. Can you see your way clear to renewing your support with a generous donation of $50 at this time?

To be successful, the letter writer should reflect the perceived interests of the donor. Presumably, Mrs. Moneyflow cares about the camp and its campers. She will want to hear how things went, who the kids were, what they liked best. Pictures, notes, and quotes from the children themselves all serve to bring her closer to the organization.

And those whom you don't know:

Dear Friend,
For 120 kids, the difference between another hot summer in the city and a summer of fun is Shadyside Camp. . . .

Whether writing to someone known to the organization or to a mailing address, the principles of marketing apply. For a direct mail mass mailing to succeed, it is necessary to segment the universe of names. For example:

- Is it a church-affiliated camp?
- Will it appeal to persons who have a liberal bent?
- Are families with relatively modest incomes more likely to support the camp than the more wealthy, who perhaps cannot identify with the experience?
- Will the camp's message appeal more to some ethnic groups?

One of the most effective ways to segment the mass direct mail appeal is by testing mailing lists. These can be rented from list brokers in units of 1,000 names. Your fund raising staff might test, for example, 5,000 names drawn at random from a list of known contributors to Save the Children. Usually, the measure of success in such a test mailing is to break even or to "pull" one contributor for every 100 names. What one is attempting in mass direct mail is not so much making money as it is, in effect, buying the names of people who will become contributors to the organization.

Direct Mail—Pro

1. **Direct mail is the most scientific of all fund raising.**

    Drawing on proven marketing tools, direct mail solicitation allows the organization to identify potential markets, determine which approaches work best, at which times of the year. Will a short letter work better than a long one? Will including a brochure help? Does the color of the envelope make a difference in the return ratio? Test it.

2. **It can be tested in relatively small quantities.**

    Because direct mail can be sampled in small batches, it allows the nonprofit to control costs, putting its resources into those approaches that have indicated the most promise.

3. **Fund raising axiom: The greater the potential, the more personal the approach.**

    Table 3 matches donor with approach to use.

Table 3.
Donor and Approach to Use

Category of Donor	Approach to Use
Major Donor	Hold one on one, face to face meeting
Substantial Donor	Invite to organization events
Average Donor	Send annual report with personalized* letter
Smaller Donor	Send personalized letter

(*Personalized = letter includes name and address of donor)

Direct mail is an effective tool for smaller donors. While the definition of smaller will vary from organization to organization, the general rule of thumb is don't spend $8 to get a $10 gift. If you can obtain renewal gifts of $10 with a mailing whose total cost averages $2, so much the better.

Direct Mail—Con

1. **Don't be lulled into complacency by the relatively modest costs of direct mail.**

    The organization saves nothing if it settles for a $25 direct mail donation from a contributor who has the potential to donate $500 if properly nurtured.

2. **The competition is intense.**

    If your organization decides to attempt a direct mail mass appeal, use the sophistication that direct mail has to offer in order to minimize your risk exposure and maximize the potential dollar return.

Foundations

Foundations are in the business of giving away money. By definition, private foundations are 501 (c)(3) organizations with a corpus of money which is invested, yielding interest monies that can be expended on nonprofit ventures.

Foundations—Pro

1. **Foundation solicitation can be very cost effective.**

    Whereas direct mail mass solicitations do well to break even, the foundation proposal which costs $500 to prepare (counting staff time) might yield a grant of $25,000.

2. **Information about private foundations is extensive and accessible.**

   The Foundation Center, with cooperating collections around the country, is a vast source of information on foundations—their purposes, their giving history, their board members, their assets. Information on foundation giving can be accessed via computer, via telephone, and via the printed page. Foundations are a segmentable market.

3. **Many foundations are willing to underwrite new and sometimes risky ventures.**

Foundations—Con

1. **Foundations usually have very specific programs in which they are interested and do not want to offer general financial support.**

2. **While they have become more open, foundations are still to some extent a closed society.**

   At their worst, they do not issue annual reports, will not entertain telephone inquiries, and give only to pet projects. It is helpful to have a contact on the inside.

Corporations

Ten years ago, foundations provided considerably more funding than did companies. Today, the two are on a par in large measure because of the increase in corporate giving. More companies are contributing to nonprofit causes, and some companies are contributing larger portions of their profits—up to 5 percent in the most philanthropic.

Corporations—Pro

1. **It is fairly easy to seek corporate contributions.**

   No long proposals. No indepth research on ethnographic characteristics of the donor, as with direct mail. Sometimes a simple letter will suffice. Look for companies in your community that have a reason to give to your organization—you serve their employees, or family members of employees; you offer a positive public image.

2. **Companies can be a source of in-kind contributions:**

   • Gifts of equipment (computers, building supplies, textbooks, prizes for special events)

- Donations of time, in the form of loaned executives, who bring expertise in management, accounting, data processing

Corporations—Con

1. **Companies are in business to make a profit.**

   While many have a social conscience, they are nonetheless driven by the bottom line. They must consider what's in it for them when looking at your request.

   This has led to the growth of cause-related marketing, in which a company contributes a portion of its sales profits to a nonprofit organization as a means of both making a donation to the nonprofit and making a profit for itself. For example, imagine your organization is contacted by La Femme, which owns a stable of boutiques selling women's designer dresses, with an offer. You host a fashion show. For every dress sold, you get a percentage. The risk, of course, is crossing the line—losing sight of your organization's mission in order to obtain substantial funding.

2. **Corporate giving may be quite modest.**

   Many companies continue to use corporate giving as a means of improving or maintaining their image within the community. As such, they spread their budget across a wide number of applicant organizations, none of which receives a very sizable amount as a consequence.

Special Events

Special events is the term given to everything from bake sales to first night Broadway premiers. The common elements of a special event are usually that . . .

- They occur in real time—they're live.
- Their success is dependent on large numbers of people purchasing something—flea market items, raffle tickets, bids in a silent auction.

Special Events—Pro

1. **Special events can attract attention to your organization.**

   Choose the event carefully for the image that it portrays. If your organization offers speech therapy, for example, it would not be prudent to host a benefit performance of *A Fish Called Wanda*, in which one of the principal characters is ridiculed because he stutters. The organization may be better off hosting a communications awards banquet, recognizing those in the community who are outstanding communicators.

2. Special events can provide entry to persons whom the organization wants to get to know.

Hold a sports event at your own facility and you may attract some of your neighbors and sports enthusiasts. Hold a celebrity tennis match and you may be able to get to know some of the community's socially prominent.

Consider the event as more than a onetime activity. Ask yourself and those working on the event: What can we do to interest participants in us and not just in the event? How can we add to our donor prospect pool through this event?

Special Events—Con

1. Special events do not offer a positive ratio of energy expended to dollars raised.

Compare the amount of effort that goes into netting $10,000 from a special event with the effort in researching and writing a foundation proposal.

2. When special events fail, they fail in public.

Try facing your board when you decide to hold a benefit opening night performance of the local symphony, under the stars, and it rains. Pours. Gowns drenched. Performance cancelled. All of it captured on the 11:00 o'clock news.

Major Gifts

Of every $100 contributed in the United States in a given year, only about $10 comes from companies and foundations. The vast majority comes from individual donors, especially those capable of making sizable contributions.

Major donors are at the top of the donor pyramid. They merit the most thorough, personal, in-depth attention. They demand the organization's best marketing techniques:

- Peruse the organization's contributor list for those with the potential to make large gifts (for example, $5,000 annually).

- Learn all that you can about these prospects

  You may want to ascertain the prospects' club and religious affiliations, their philanthropic interests, their giving history, the boards on which they sit. Much of this information is publicly available—Who's Who, Dun & Bradstreet, the social register etc.

- Ask around.

  Who on your board or other volunteer body knows these individuals well enough to ask for support?

- Determine the best approach.

  Should one member of the board go alone? (Usually: no. Someone on staff should be there as well, providing accurate information and follow-up.) Is there a best time to make the first contact?

- Select an attractive investment opportunity.

  What will hold appeal; what's the best match with the prospect's own needs and wants and interests?

Major Gifts—Pro

1. **The obvious advantage.**

   A great benefit of undertaking a major donor program is that the ROI (return on investment) is among the highest in fund raising, all things being equal (i.e., assuming a good cause, well articulated, by the right person or persons).

2. **Fund raising axiom: the 80/20 rule.**

   The financially healthy organization gets 80 percent of its fund raising dollar from 20 percent of its donors. It is true that you want to have a broad contributor base, so that you are not overly reliant on any one source of support. It is also true that major gifts are a touchstone of your ability to get others to share your vision.

Major Gifts—Con

1. **There are few if any free lunches.**

   Major gifts often come with a bill to be paid. The donor may want some control over how the funds are invested (although legally, once the gift is made, it is out of the donor's hands—or it is not really a gift). He or she may want to have something named for her or him in perpetuity, or a seat on the board, in return.

2. **Major gifts can sometimes be costly.**

    Some nonprofits have learned the hard way to estimate the cost of accepting a major gift before doing so. A number of universities, for example, refuse a donation to build a building unless the donor is willing to provide for the building's ongoing maintenance through an endowment fund.

    Similarly, it may be appealing to accept a major gift to launch a new program without due consideration to how that program will be financed in years to come.

Planned Giving

Planned giving is a technique for raising funds, usually larger funds, by offering the donor one or more of the following benefits:

*   A tax-shelter (for example, making a donation of appreciated property, rather than selling it and paying the capital gains tax);
*   Allowing the donor to make a larger gift than might otherwise be possible (e.g., naming the institution as beneficiary of a life insurance policy);
*   Providing a way to make a donation and still receive annual income (through the creation of a pooled income fund of an annuity trust).

In general, the tax advantages are secondary to the donor's interest in the organization and his or her willingness to support it financially. In other words, don't expect that having a planned giving program in place will attract gifts from wealthy individuals who know little of your institution.

Planned Giving—Pro

1. **Planned giving offers additional opportunities to the organization's donors.**

    While current tax law in the United States is not as favorable to this type of giving as it was, there still can be genuine financial savings for a well-crafted planned gift. Your organization may want to retain a lawyer or trust officer who specializes in this field if you decide to mount a planned giving effort.

2. **Planned giving can boost your endowment fund.**

    The same donor who wants to see his or her annual gift spent on a current project may be willing to take out a life insurance policy in the name of your organization, with the understanding that the proceeds one day will go into an endowment fund bearing his or her name.

Planned Giving—Con

1. **You've got to know what you're doing.**

   Planned giving is perhaps the most complex of fund raising approaches, requiring a knowledge of tax law and facility in accounting.

2. **It requires sensitivity and tact.**

   In many cases, in order for your organization to benefit from planned gifts, the donor must pass away. The effective planned giving officer is able to convince the donor that he or she should act now, without repulsing or scaring the donor by raising the specter of his or her imminent demise.

Government Funding

Government grants are a specialty. It is unlikely that you will be able to hire someone who is proficient in private sector fund raising—alumni relations, direct mail, planned giving—who also knows the intricacies of government funding. Nonetheless, it is an area that you should investigate at all levels—local, state, and national.

As with foundation grants, information on government funding is in general rather accessible. Government agents are public servants (although they sometimes need to be reminded of that fact). And, as with foundation grants, usually the funding will be for a specific project of interest to the funding agency. Government funding is either in the form of a grant (in which the agency invites organizations to submit proposals reflecting their own ideas on how the need specified by the agency, e.g., personnel training, might be addressed); or a contract (in which the agency describes, in a Request for Proposal (RFP), what it wants done and attempts to select the bidder whom it believes can do the job best, most inexpensively, or some combination of the two).

Government Funding—Pro

1. **Government contracts can sometimes provide a steady, dependable source of income.**

   For example, the city in which your organization is located may decide to contract out for certain health services. If your institution is the winning bidder, you may garner a contract that not only pays for staff, but also allows you to charge your negotiated overhead rate. For some institutions, the overhead is in excess of 75 percent. Thus, on a contract in which the direct costs amount to $100,000, the winning organization may end up receiving $175,000.

2. **Government grant proposals are typically read by expert reviewers, which means that a sound proposal has a reasonable chance.**

To put it another way, who you know is sometimes less important in government grants than in other sources of support.

Government Funding—Con

1. **Paperwork.**

The Paperwork Reduction Act notwithstanding, government proposals are on average longer and more detailed than other proposals that your staff will write. One consequence, expect to commit resources to the proposal development if you are hopeful of obtaining a government grant.

The paperwork continues (at times increases) once your organization receives funding. In addition to program reports, you will need to submit periodic financial statements in order to receive payment.

2. **Payment typically comes after the fact.**

Whereas you may receive a foundation grant, in its entirety, up front, you will typically have to lay out your own funds in order to get a government project underway.

MARKETING AND FUND RAISING

Throughout the description of various funding methods, an attempt has been made to address the importance of marketing. Effective fund raising is effective marketing. Unless your organization is well-endowed financially, it will not be possible to pursue every fund raising method described. You will want to examine the range of options and select among them, beginning with those that offer the best ROI (return on investment) for the funds allocated.

Within the fund raising methods, marketing principles apply. Shotgunning proposals—sending the same proposal out to several foundations or agencies in the hope of hitting on one—is a waste of time. Better to research the pool of agencies or foundations first, and select your best prospects (those that seem to reflect your own needs and interests). Then craft a proposal that makes it clear to the reader that you understand the need and know how to address it.

FUND RAISING WITHIN THE SMALL NONPROFIT

Not every nonprofit is in a position to undertake a full range of fund raising activities, and the smaller nonprofit will have to decide which ones offer the best potential for the smallest dollar investment. The fund raising program can be enhanced by employing some of the strategies suggested in the Chapter 4 on public relations:

- Use volunteer "staff
- Institute an internship program
- Obtain in-kind support from a local company (software, loaned staff, graphics design and printing, for example)
- Seek grant support specifically to expand the fund raising potential.

THE BUSINESS OF GRANTSEEKING: FOUR KEY STEPS

As with any strategic marketing, developing a plan for grantseeking follows certain definable stages: (1) analysis of factors (the situational analysis); (2) setting of goals; (3) establishing and implementing a course of action; and (4) evaluating the results.

1. Analyze Influencing Factors

Use the SWOT analysis:

- Strengths:

  What do you do in terms of fund raising? Where have you had your greatest successes? Given your staff and volunteers, what types of fund raising might you be most likely to undertake with some assurance of success?

- Weaknesses:

  Running special events may require a sizable volunteer cadre, and most certainly requires someone with superb organizational skills. If your organization lacks either or both of these, perhaps you should look to another fund raising vehicle (or be prepared to make some changes or additions to your human resources).

- Opportunities:

  Do any of the changing demographics present fund raising opportunities for your nonprofit? For example, it is likely that a substantial portion of the population will be wealthy, retired, and in good health. If that's true of your community, what can your organization do to tap that resource for contributions and for assistance in fund raising from others?

- Threats:

  Is your organization prepared economically to weather a financial downturn? (If not, can you turn this to your fund raising advantage, appealing to certain donors to assure that the organization is on a sound financial footing?) Do you have the resources to commit to direct mail or to start up a planned giving program?

2. Set Goals

Fund raising goals need to reflect the stated strategic planning goals of your organization. (In fact, fund raising goals ought to be a part of the strategic plan.) Setting the actual fund raising goals, i.e., how much you can raise and over what period of time, should involve all of the key players in your fund raising milieu (development committee, other key board members, fund raising staff), and may involve outside counsel, particularly if you opt for a feasibility study (a description of which follows shortly).

Paradoxically, you need to go in two directions when setting fund raising goals: (1) Be ambitious. "Faint heart ne'er won fair lady." If your organization doesn't set ambitious goals, it and you will never know what might be achieved. (2) Be realistic. Management consultant Tom Peters argues that it is best to establish expectations that you are confident of meeting—and then exceed them.[8] Peters' recommendation has the ring of truth. Have you ever read of a college or religious institution that had to admit it was behind in achieving its fund raising goal? Doesn't give you a lot of confidence in that organization, does it?

3. Establish a Plan of Action

Here's where your organization needs to get very specific. Fund raising is daunting work. It requires board members and staff to pick up the phone, make an appointment, and ask someone else to part with some of their money. There is a great temptation to find every excuse why it's not quite the right time to actually ask for the gift.

The Indian poet Kagore once said: "I have spent my days stringing and unstringing my instrument, while the song I came to sing remains unsung." If they are not monitored, those charged with fund raising will spend their time practicing and tuning their instruments in order to avoid having to fund raise. The way to get past that understandable procrastination is to establish concrete action plans, including deadlines and persons responsible. Keep the plans visible; make them a regular part of meetings with the development office staff, and encourage the chair of the development committee to do the same with his or her colleagues.

4. Evaluate

Even if your staff and board are having success in fund raising (and in some ways, especially then), make evaluation a regular part of the fund raising plan of action. It's not enough to know whether you have or have not reached your fund raising goal; you need to know why. What are you doing right? What clearly is not working? What corrections need to be made midcourse?

HIRING CAPABLE FUND RAISING STAFF

One of the reasons why fund raising sometimes gets a bad rap is that there are too many people out there who call themselves fund raisers but aren't. So how do you weed through the resumes to find capable individuals, and what should you be looking for?

Know What You Want

Before you begin soliciting resumes, much less ploughing through them, do three things:

1. Come up with a list of characteristics for the ideal fund raiser for your institution.

    If you could hire someone with all the right qualities, what would those be? (See the next section for some ideas.)

2. Write a job description (a sample description for a Director of Development comes later in this chapter).

3. In cooperation with the development committee of the board, describe your expectations of the fund raising staff person.

    How will you (collectively) measure whether he or she has succeeded?

Commit each of these—characteristics, expectations, measures—to paper. Distribute them to your board and other volunteer leadership, senior staff, colleagues. Doing so will both begin to get the word out and establish expectations for what this person will (and will not) be asked to accomplish. If a member of the board disagrees with what kind of person to hire or what the development officer should achieve, better to know and deal with it now. One of the unfortunately consistent reasons why fund raising staff have such short tenures within organizations is that their expectations of the job and the board's (or CEO's) do not coincide.

Characteristics of the Ideal Fund Raiser

Characteristics can be formal as well as informal. Formal characteristics might include:

- Educational background:

  A bachelor's degree at minimum, master's preferred. Master's (and in some instances a doctorate) in a relevant area (either relevant to your organization's purpose or to fund raising) is so much the better.

- Continuing education:

  Ask for evidence that the candidate is keeping up and expanding his or her knowledge base—learning the latest in fund raising trends and mechanics, mastering new technologies, maintaining currency with societal issues that may affect your organization and its ability to raise funds.

- Memberships:

  Does the resume list membership in the National Society of Fund Raising Executives (NSFRE), the National Association for Hospital Development (NAHD), the Council for Advancement and Support of Education (CASE), or some other association of fundraisers? Is there any indication that the candidate has held office in such an association? If so, it might suggest that he or she has received recognition from fund raising peers.

- Certification:

  Members of NSFRE can obtain certification as fund raising executives (CFRE), meaning that they have demonstrated their knowledge of fund raising practice.

As to some informal characteristics, Jerold Pannas, in *Born to Raise,* lists 63 qualities of top-notch fund raisers. He culled the list after interviewing 50 persons whom others deemed as among the best. Here is some of what the 50 thought to be essential qualities:

- Inveterate reader;
- Goal-oriented and goal-driven;
- A stickler for details;
- Not afraid to ask for the gift;

- Possessing a high level of commitment to the purpose of the organization for which they work;
- A good listener;
- A hard worker;
- Not afraid to hire the best staff;
- Capable both of seeing the vision of what the; organization can become—and communicating that vision to others.[9]

Sample Job Description

The particulars of your fund raiser's job description will of necessity vary according to organizational goals, size, board composition, and fund raising history. But there are some commonalities. What follows is a sample job description for a Director of Development in a midsize, hospital-affiliated organization that serves persons with disabilities.

Figure 5.
Sample Job Description for
Director of Development

The LaBlanche Center for the Developmentally Disabled is seeking qualified candidates for the position of Director of Development. The position is full time and will be filled as soon as an acceptable candidate has been selected.

Background. The Center has been providing services to persons with developmental disabilities and their families for 15 years. These services include: job training and placement; occupational and physical therapy; group housing; sheltered employment in horticulture; and advocacy. The Center is affiliated with the Alma Petersen Community Hospital and provides a setting for interns in the graduate programs of several colleges and universities in the Walmouth area.

Job Summary. The Director of Development reports to the Executive Director and is responsible for the successful planning and implementation of the Center's fund raising programs. These include an annual fund drive, special events, and a new planned giving program; the Center is considering a major capital campaign which also will be the responsibility of the Director of Development.

The Director supervises the staff of the Development Office, including a Director of Public Affairs, a Records Assistant, and a part-time Secretary. It is anticipated that the Director will work closely with the Center's Board of Trustees, and in particular with its Development and Planning committees.

Figure 5. (continued)

Specific responsibilities of the Director of Development include the following:

1. Work with the Board and relevant committees to establish short- and long-range funding goals, and a plan of action to meet those goals.

2. Facilitate and coordinate the work of the Board and other volunteer leadership involved in fund raising.

3. Oversee the public relations of the Center.

4. Prepare or direct the preparation of print and multimedia materials for use in raising funds.

5. Identify potential sources of funding.

6. Maintain accurate records of all donations received.

7. Prepare periodic reports on the progress of the fund raising efforts and make recommendations for changes or additions as deemed appropriate.

8. Represent the organization with its several publics.

Qualifications. The successful candidate will possess at least the following:

*   Bachelor's degree (master's or doctorate preferred), with coursework in either a field relating to disability or fund raising.
*   Seven years of experience in clearly related fund raising activities, with a demonstrated record of accomplishment.
*   Proficiency in oral and written communication skills.
*   Evidence of leadership (within an association, community agency, or other body).
*   Excellent organizational skills.
*   Evaluative skills (i.e., the ability to assess progress in achieving stated goals and to determine the reasons why).
*   Finely developed interpersonal skills.
*   Managerial capability.
*   Commitment to helping others.

Interested persons should submit a resume and letter which taken together give a clear picture of experience and capabilities. Candidates should be prepared to provide the names of at least three persons who can comment confidentially about candidate qualifications.

Making the Selection

If fund raising is important to your organization (and it's hard to imagine that it is not), the CEO needs to be an active participant in the selection process. Resumes can be screened by other staff in whom the CEO has confidence, using the job description, expectations, and characteristics as a means of ranking resumes and eliminating those that obviously don't fit.

The resumes that survive this first cut should then be read carefully by a candidate review team in order to identify three to five candidates meriting personal interview.

Development staff must relate to the board and other volunteer leadership in order to do their job, but they report to the executive director or some other senior staff. For that reason alone, it is not advisable to have a member of the board or another volunteer sit on the candidate review team. Instead, it may be appropriate to schedule a meeting of the board (or some portion of it) to introduce the selected candidate. That provides a chance for the candidate to get some sense of what working with the board might be like as well. If he or she doesn't see the importance of such a meeting—be concerned.

Conducting the Interviews

It's been said that the job interview is like a first date. That's misleading. All the first date may lead to is a second date. The interview can lead to an offer of marriage to the organization. The interview needs to be structured to allow for an intelligent, informed decision to be made by both parties, candidate and organization. The interview is nowhere more important than when hiring fund raising staff. Why? Because fund raising is not like medicine, where you can examine extensive educational credentials; nor is it like accounting, where you can rely on the independent judgement of others. Fund raising is anything but exact. When it comes down to it, you have to select a candidate to become your Director of Development because it feels right.

Questions that can be asked to elicit information to help make the selection include:

- "I see on your resume that the Whyanot Institute for which you worked raised $1.5 million annually. What role did you personally play in that?"
- "Tell us what you would do to motivate a board member who has superb contacts but shows no interest in fund raising?"

- "You've had a chance to look through some materials on our Center. What do you see as the major strengths on which you would capitalize?"
- "What would your role be in raising funds as compared to the role that needs to be played by senior staff or volunteer leadership?"
- "Suppose we offered the position to you. What concerns would you need to have addressed before deciding that this would be a good career move for you?"

What Salary Do You Offer?

It is important to recognize that experienced, qualified, competent fund raisers do not come cheap. (In fact, if the salary requirement of a candidate seems low to you, consider that a potential warning sign.) You will have to weigh your own salary structure, including the salary paid to persons at a comparable level in the organization, against the likelihood that a truly skilled fund raiser will be expensive.

Organizations at times attempt to address this potential inequity (and perhaps also hedge their bets) by asking if the fund raising candidate will work on a percentage of funds raised—the theory being that the fund raiser will be more motivated to succeed if there is a direct correlation to his or her salary. In addition to the fact that this smacks of questionable ethics, it is also not sound practice. What you want of a fund raiser is belief in the organization's cause and the desire to work hard for it; you want someone with good judgement, who will build a sound fund raising program rather than looking for quick hits.

KNOWING WHEN YOUR ORGANIZATION IS READY TO RAISE MONEY

The readiness is all.
— *Shakespeare*

In fund raising, as in any enterprise, "there is a tide in the affairs of men [and women] which, taken at the flood, leads on to fortune" (*Julius Caesar*, IV, iii, 217). How does one know when the conditions are right to set afloat a major fund raising effort? One way is to conduct a fund raising audit.

The Fund Raising Audit

The audit is a series of confidential, one-to-one interviews with board members, other essential volunteers, key staff within and without the development office, and is preferably conducted by a disinterested party, such as a researcher or fund raising consultant.[10] The interviews may be supplemented by audit displays: summaries of fund raising accomplishments, evaluations of the organization conducted in other contexts (e.g., higher education or hospital accreditation), and/or the organization's strategic plan. Both the review of documents and the interviews should be guided by the following questions, the answers to which will form the basis of an audit report:

- Have the goals of the fund raising effort been clearly stated, and are they generally understood?
- Has a budget been allocated for the fund raising effort envisioned, and is it serviceable?
- Are the board members and other key volunteers pledged to the organization and willing to work in its behalf?

  Specifically, is it evident that they will take leadership roles in raising funds?
- Will the staffing be adequate to the tasks proposed? Do they possess the requisite skills?
- Is the development office properly positioned within the organization?

  Will it get the support it needs from professional and administrative staff? How is the development office viewed? And do other staff members perceive that fund raising is related to their jobs?
- Does the chief staff person share a high level of commitment to the fund raising goals?

  Is it likely that he or she will be willing to devote solid blocks of time to the effort?[11]

The Feasibility Study

The fund raising audit is directed internally: Is the organization ready to mount a fund raising campaign? Its counterpart is the feasibility study, which is for the most part directed externally: What is our potential to raise funds?

The feasibility study is thus a market analysis. Through a series of interviews, it seeks to discern the answer to three questions:

1. Who are the organization's best prospects for fund raising?

2. Are the mission, goals, and programs of the organization well-known among its targeted constituencies, and, if so, how do these groups value the organization?

3. If the organization launches a fund raising campaign, what level of success is probable?

The feasibility study is best conducted by an outside firm with experience in this aspect of fund raising counsel. History has shown that using a third party for the feasibility study not only assures objectivity, it also increases the richness of the information obtained. The organization's own key leadership may be more inclined to talk candidly to someone who has no direct involvement with the organization.

The feasibility study might involve 50 to 100 persons, interviewed face-to-face or by telephone (typically not by mail survey, in that it does not allow for additional probing by the interviewer). Those interviewed might include:

- Members of the Board of Trustees
- Other key volunteer leadership
- Current major donors
- Perceived prospects for major individual gifts
- Foundation and corporate giving officers
- Community leaders

There are several potential outcomes of the study. First, it will provide information on the organization's potential to raise sizable contributions, according to the three research questions noted earlier.

Second, it may reveal some weak spots. For example, the firm conducting the study may learn that there is a substantial donor pool, but that there is no one on the board or development committee with the capability or the interest to head up a major development campaign.

Third, the organization will learn which of its goals and programs have the most appeal, and to what types of donors. For example, it may find out that its scholarship program would have considerable appeal to the corporate sector if a company could have its name associated with scholarships awarded.

Fourth, the organization will have the groundwork for a fund raising strategy, which can be refined and expanded into a full-blown development plan.

Selecting the Firm to Conduct the Feasibility Study

There will be no shortage of fund raising firms interested in conducting the feasibility study—in part because it often leads to additional work with the organization, especially if the decision to mount a fund raising campaign is affirmative. In order to make a careful selection, some organizations use a Request for Proposal (RFP) which lays out the scope of work desired and asks potential firms to submit a proposal. The RFP should ask for detailed information on:

- The steps which will be taken;
- The timeframe in which the study will be completed;
- The number of persons who will be interviewed, and an indication of the interview instrument;
- Qualifications of the firm and the person(s) who would be assigned to the study;
- Products which will be delivered as a result of the study;
- Costs.

THE ROLE OF THE CEO IN FUND RAISING

The CEO is the linchpin of the nonprofit organization's fund raising efforts. His or her commitment to fund raising, evidenced in enthusiasm, support, and active involvement, can make or break the organization's fund raising. Enthusiasm needs to be reflected on both the staff and volunteer levels. If it is evident that the CEO finds fund raising distasteful, the board and staff can hardly be blamed for a lack of enthusiasm themselves.

Support is required in several instances: arguing for fund raising as a priority in goal setting; requiring that it be addressed in the goals and objectives of all departments, and not merely the development office; and providing sufficient financial and human resources to meet the fund raising targets.

Active involvement means what it says. The CEO needs to do more than lend his or her name to the fund raising effort; he or she needs to model the desired behavior: make phone calls, visit prospects, ask for support. At the same time, it is important to acknowledge that, even in the smallest nonprofit organization, the CEO should not typically be the principal fund raiser, although he or she may be the only person on staff who is directly charged with that responsibility. The success of the fund raising effort is, in organizations small or large, directly proportional to the role played by volunteer leadership.

WHAT MOTIVATES PEOPLE TO GIVE?

Why do people willingly part with some portion of their disposable income? This is a question that has been asked at one time or another by everyone attempting to raise money. In marketing terminology, what needs or wants or interests are filled by making a contribution?

The answer needs to be split into small and large gift categories. Small is defined less by dollar amount than by how it feels to the individual (a $100 contribution by millionaire H. Ross Perot is small; by someone on a fixed income, it may be substantial). People tend to make small donations with a minimum of consideration. Someone comes to the door, asking for a contribution to a cause for which they hold some positive feeling, and they make a donation without giving it much thought. What are the motivators for such a small gift? A sense of community, perhaps; an avoidance of the feeling of guilt if they said "No"; and a general feeling of altruism. Making such a contribution is not unlike impulse buying; individuals do it "because it's there" and not because of either long held commitment or thought.

This kind of impulse gift may also be made out of a sense of avoidance (Here, now leave me alone), or relief (Thank God I don't have that disease).

That the organization that relies on guilt, avoidance, or impulse for its fund raising is not likely to thrive in the decade ahead. Increasingly, as the competition for funding escalates, when contributing to an organization, a donor will want more in return. The contributor will be motivated to make a larger gift (either incrementally or onetime) by factors such as these:

Personally deciding that the cause is important. For example, deciding to do something to improve the environment. When someone receives a solicitation from The Wilderness Society, he or she gives it consideration in large measure because of a conscious decision that the environment is an important issue. The Wilderness Society becomes a beneficiary of that decision.

Believing that the organization is well managed. A public television station for several years conducted a year-end campaign asking current contributors to make a special gift to help balance the station's budget. In doing so, they were inadvertently sending the message that they did not manage their resources very well.

Believing there is some status involved. Colleges and universities do some of their most successful fund raising from those classes which are having important reunions (10th, 25th, etc.). Special events often succeed when they offer the participant a chance to "rub elbows" with someone of prominence—a sports figure, television star, politician, person of social status. (Poll virtually any group, and there will be someone who knows a person of prominence—friend, relative, fellow alum.)

Feeling a sense of obligation. A sense of obligation is one of those motivators that may still work among older members of the community, but is unlikely to prompt giving from the younger. Among the baby boomers, for example, respect must be earned; as a giving cohort, they are unwilling to recognize a sense of obligation as sufficient rationale for any sizable gift.

Giving as an expression of gratitude. If guilt is the dark side of the moon, gratitude is its light side. Hospitals and other health care settings know that the grateful patient is a prime prospect, as is his or her family. A similar gratitude may be the driving force behind capacious gifts to an alma mater.

Giving because it is good business. While this may be more commonly a motivator for corporate giving, it should be looked at as a crescive motivating factor for individuals who are engaged either full- or part-time in entrepreneurial or consulting ventures.

Giving to be part of something larger than self.[12] It is to the more mature motivators—gratitude, being part of something larger than self, and the perception that it is good business—that organizations should direct their fund raising. These are the motivators that can lead to long-standing, win-win relationships.

PARTING THOUGHTS

In the section within this chapter on trends, it was mentioned that there has been a proliferation of new nonprofits in the past 15 years. If the odds ratio for business ventures applies, at least one in four of those new nonprofits is no longer in existence. A key reason is the inability to raise sufficient funds. All organizations have three basic functions: input, process, output. Fund raising supplies key input; it should not be its own end, but it should be viewed with the same kind of respect and attention given to other programs that further the organizational mission.

NOTES

1. James P. Gelatt, "The Bigger Picture," *Executive Update*, no volume (December 1990): 41.

2. William B. Johnston and Arnold H. Packer, *Workforce 2000: Work and Workers for the 21st Century* (Indianapolis, IN: The Hudson Institute, 1987), 79–80.

3. (No author) "The Fragmentation of Consumer Markets," *Fund Raising Management*, 19 (November 1988): 69–70.

4. William Olcott, "The Changing Face of Philanthropy," a speech at the Third Annual Philanthropy Day Fund Raising Conference, Portland, OR, November 10, 1988.

5. Rob McCord, speaking at the August 1989 "Colloquium on the Future," American Speech-Language-Hearing Association, Rockville, MA.

6. George Wilkinson, "Nonprofits in the '90s," speaking at the Foundation Center, Washington, DC, June 29, 1989.

7. (No author) "The Climate for Giving: The Outlook and Future CEOs," *Health Funds Development Letter*, no volume (December 1988): 2.

8. From an audiotape excerpted from *The New Masters of Excellence* by Tom Peters, produced by Nightingale-Conant Corporation, 1986.

9. Jerry Panas, *Born to Raise* (Chicago: Pluribus Press, 1989), 180–201.

10. Del Martin, "The Development Audit: Providing the Blueprint for a Better Fundraising Program," *NSFRE Journal,* (Autumn 1990) 28–29, 31, 54.

11. Thomas R. Moore, "Evaluating an Institution's Commitment to a Comprehensive Development Effort," *501(c)(3) Monthly Letter,* 10 (February 1990): 1.

12. Russ Reid, "Why Do People Give?," *Reid Report* (an occasional newsletter without date): 1.

Chapter 6
Fiscal Management

Money is watched with a narrow, suspicious eye. The [person] who handles it is assumed dishonest until [proven] otherwise. Audits are penetrating and meticulous. —*John Kenneth Galbraith*

EXECUTIVE SUMMARY

This chapter on finance presents basic information in order to provide a framework for sound decision-making. Covered is a review of financial terms and functions and an explanation of the difference between cash and accrual accounting. Also addressed: how to keep track of grant funds, understanding debit and credit, the steps in developing a budget, fund accounting, and the independent audit. Building on these basics, the chapter considers what board members should ask about the organization's finances, reporting to donors, being prepared for the worst (including how to determine which programs or products might be dropped), and what to ask when automating the financial functions.

At the risk of oversimplifying, it might be maintained that, when it comes to budgets and fiscal management, there are two types of people:

1. Those who enjoy working with figures and understand the budget process.

2. All others.

Most fall into the latter category. They know that developing budgets and maintaining accurate financial records are necessities but are quite content to leave those functions to the bean counters—if only they would talk English.

The following true-to-life case study exemplifies the situation for many nonprofits and its implications for those who fall into the "all others" category.

Letitia Wilson had been the executive director for the Learning Center since its inception 10 years ago, when it began as a neighborhood program offering afterschool tutoring. Wilson has a masters degree in library science and elementary education, and after her own children were out of high school she decided to provide assistance to children in the immediate vicinity who needed help in reading. She soon came to realize that some of the children whom she tutored had problems in reading that went beyond phonetics; they failed to recognize words and parts of words in the way that was characteristic of most children. Some of them inverted their letters; others seemed incapable of recalling from lesson to lesson how to pronounce a word or what it meant if they could pronounce it. And yet, in most other ways, these children were of normal or above average intelligence.

Wilson's Learning Center came to specialize in children with reading problems long before terms such as "dyslexia" and "learning disabled" were in vogue. She added specialists who had graduated from the local university, secured space in the basement of the Lutheran church, and formally incorporated her little afterschool program by the name it retains today.

Over time, Wilson developed a following; parents whose children had attended the Learning Center gave eager testimony to the success of the program. A volunteer fund raising board was formed and funds were raised, allowing the program to expand significantly.

Today, the Learning Center has an operating budget in excess of $500,000, enjoys a regional reputation—and is about to fold. It is the victim of changes that were unanticipated: the mainstreaming of learning disabled children into the public school; the need for sophisticated computerized equipment for in-class use as well as record keeping; and the unwillingness of faculty to work for noncompetitive wages. An otherwise sympathetic article in the local press has revealed that the Learning Center is $230,000 in arrears and will probably have to close its doors for good at the end of the school year—if it survives that long.

The Learning Center is hardly unique in its failure to understand that running a nonprofit organization means running a business. While it may survive through a last-ditch fund raising effort on the part of its parents organization, its future is in question unless it can start thinking of itself as a bottom-line oriented enterprise.

What This Chapter Will Address

This is not essentially a short course on "Accounting for the Executive Who Knows No Accounting. It will address, and hopefully explain, key concepts in fiscal management, operating under the assumption that staff of nonprofits need not become accountants, but they do need a firm grounding in the aspect of management that addresses finances.

UNDERSTANDING SOME TERMS

Understanding the following terms will be useful in interpreting financial information prepared for the nonprofit organization.

Finance: The economic activity of an organization; the conduct or transaction of money matters. In practice, the terms financial and fiscal are often used interchangeably. Some practitioners make a distinction between financial *statements* and fiscal *accountability*.

Financial Statement: A report of the financial status of an organization. It often consists of three items:

1. Balance sheet (summarizing assets, liabilities, and equity).

   The balance sheet reflects the organization's financial status as of a point in time. Its name comes from the fact that, as with a mathematical equation, the assets of the organization must be balanced by the liabilities and the equity (also known as the "fund balance").

2. Statement of activities (in effect, a profit and loss statement, showing income received, expenses incurred, and the net income; an income statement).

   The statement of activity is sometimes referred to by the catchy title of "statement of support, revenue and expenses, and changes in the fund balance." It is a summary of the organization's financial status over a specified time period (typically, one year).

3. Statement of changes in financial position (also known as statement of sources and uses of funds, or a statement of functional expenses).

Accounting: The means used to measure and report on the financial activity of an organization; the system used to organize and maintain the financial record of an organization. Accounting is considerably more than bookkeeping, which is essentially the record of basic financial information. Accounting, by contrast, is the overall system within which financial information is captured, analyzed, and displayed.[1]

Assets: Items owned by an organization which can be converted into cash; things of value. Some examples: equipment (computers, copiers, etc.); stock; vehicles; office supplies; furniture. Assets can be either current (i.e., short term), meaning the organization expects to convert them to cash; or fixed, such as the building itself and the land on which it sits.

Liabilities: Obligations; debts; promises to pay. Some examples: outstanding loans; mortgage on the organization's building; unpaid taxes. Liabilities can be current, meaning that the organization will pay them within one year or long term (e.g., a mortgage on property).

Equity: Assets minus liabilities; hence, the net worth of the organization. Equity may also be expressed as the "fund balance" or the "general fund." While it comprises the assets of the organization minus the liabilities, in accounting terminology equity is often expressed as a function of assets:

Assets = Liabilities + Equity

Revenues: Financial resources flowing into the organization; income. Some examples: donor contributions; income from sale of products; third party payments; interest on income; grants.

Expenses: Financial resources flowing out of the organization; payments made for goods and services needed so that the organization can operate. Some examples: salaries; consulting fees; payments to telephone company; costs for staff travel; postage.

Net Income: Revenues minus expenses. Table 4 displays a simple income statement reflecting how net income is derived.

Table 4.
Income Statement
Exemplar Nonprofit
For the Year Ending December 31, 1993

Revenues:
Sale of Products	$ 22,000	
Contributions	110,000	
Interest Earned	<u>7,500</u>	
Total Revenues		$139,500

Expenses:
Rent	$ 4,500	
Salaries	48,900	
Utilities	<u>2,000</u>	
Total Expenses		<u>($ 55,400)</u>
Net Income		<u>$ 84,100</u>

CASH VS ACCRUAL ACCOUNTING

To fully understand how income statements work, it is helpful to discern the difference between cash and accrual bases of accounting.

Cash Accounting

As its name implies, it is the method followed by an organization that functions on a cash accounting basis and so records transactions only when cash (including checks) has actually been exchanged. Thus, an accounting record based on cash will not reflect an expense that has been incurred but not paid. Nor would it reflect income (say, from the sale of a publication) until such time as the funds from that sale had actually been received. In a sense, the cash basis is akin to maintaining a checkbook. The checkbook reflects actual cash held in an account and expenses paid from that account. It reflects neither bills to be paid nor income that has been received but not yet deposited.

Accrual Accounting

The accrual method recognizes expenses when they are incurred (as opposed to when they are paid) and income (i.e., revenue) when it has been earned (and not only when it has been received).

Arguably, the accrual method is a more accurate picture of the organization's financial status. It is akin to balancing one's checkbook, in the sense of reflecting deposits made and checks written which have not been recorded by the bank; plus an additional record of income to be received and expenses which must be paid.

In order to reflect those items that fall outside the movement of cash, some additional terms are required which are common to accrual accounting.

Accounts Receivable: An amount of money (cash) owed to the organization. Some examples: a service that has been billed to a third party payor; sale of an item on credit. Because these will be converted to cash at some future date, they are considered an asset to the organization.

Prepaid Expenses: Monies paid in advance of their actual use. Examples: prepayment on the organization's rent; an upfront partial payment to a vendor. (These are also assets.)

Accounts Payable: Costs incurred with the purchase of an item for which the organization will pay at some future date. Example: use of a purchase order (before the organization has incurred a financial obligation).

Deferred Income: Payments received in advance of the organization's providing a product or service (also "unearned revenue"). Example: grant funds received from a private foundation for a project that is not yet underway. Both deferred income and accounts payable are liabilities, because they reflect funds that are obligated and will be expended at some future date.

Projecting Expenses within a Cash or Accrual System

There is a way to monitor and project expenses even if the accounting office follows a cash system. Indeed, the method can be used even with an accrual system. It is particularly helpful with grant funding. The method is shown in Table 5. Note that it lists not only the amount actually expended to date (Column 2), which would be the cash accounting, but also obligations (Column 4) and projected expenditures (Column 5). For example, assume your organization has a grant of $150,000 to conduct an in-service training program. The grant project will incur costs in salary, benefits, travel, equipment rental, printing, postage, telephone, and meeting logistics.

Table 5.
Project Accounting Record (PAR)

	1 Grant Award	2 Expended To Date	3 Balance To Date	4 Estimated Obligations	5 Projected Expenses	6 Estimated Balance
Budget Category						
Salary						
Benefits						
Travel						
Equip.						
Printing						
Postage						
Tele.						
Mtg.						

Using this system, it is possible not only to record the amount actually spent to date on travel (for which a check has been written), but also to indicate outstanding bills for travel expenses and to make estimates for future travel.

Employing the PAR system might have saved The Learning Center (the case study which opened this chapter) considerable headaches.

THE CHART OF ACCOUNTS: KEEPING TRACK

An account is a basic unit by which the financial activity of the organization is tracked.[2] Accounts may be organized numerically in a chart of accounts to reflect assets and liabilities, revenue and expenses, or fund balances. Establishing a chart of accounts makes it easier to track income and expenses accurately.

For example, here is a sample chart of accounts for a nonprofit organization which both raises funds and expends it on training, scholarships, and the support of research in leadership development.

The chart begins with a classification of what is known as "department codes." The Exemplar Fund has four such departments:

10	Development
20	Service Programs
30	Training Programs
40	General Administration

By using ten-digit codes, the Fund is able to further categorize within each department where desirable.

The second part of the chart of accounts then delineates three basic account types (unrestricted, restricted, and designated):

01 to 30	=	Unrestricted
40 to 70	=	Restricted
80 to 99	=	Designated

The Restricted Funds (bearing a general category coded of "40") are further divided into various endowment funds which have been established:

Trustee Fund	=	41
Capital Fund	=	42
Memorial Fund	=	43 etc.

The various designated funds have their own codes as well. For example, funds designated by the donor to conduct a leadership training project for older persons might be coded "82."

The third major area displayed in the chart of accounts reflects activities of the organization. For example:

00 to 09	General Administration
10 to 20	Annual Giving
21 to 30	Trustee Solicitation
31 to 40	Corporate Contribution
41 to 50	Foundation Grant
51 to 60	Leadership Programs
61 to 70	Leadership Research

The fourth part of the chart of accounts is the General Ledger Codes which allow for detailed tracking of assets, liabilities, and fund balances. These are set up according to Assets, Liabilities, Fund Balances, Revenue and Expense. The Exemplar Fund uses a four-digit ledger code. Under Assets are included its investment income ("1100"), land holdings ("1500"), and interests from its restricted funds. Liabilities, in keeping with accounting practice, reflect "accounts payable" and "deferred income."

The revenue codes allow the organization to record contributions with specificity:

Major Individual Gifts, Unrestricted	3000
Major Individual Gifts, Restricted	3001
Annual Fund, President's Club ($100+)	3002
Annual Fund, Patrons ($50–99)	3003
Annual Fund, Friends ($25–49)	3004
Annual Fund, Contributor (up to $25)	3005
Earned Income, Publications	4003
Interest, General Fund	5000
Interest, Endowments	5001
Leadership 2000 Income	6001

Expenses follow traditional categories: salaries and benefits, professional services (consultants), furnishings and equipment, supplies, postage and shipping, travel for both board and staff, expenses according to specific program areas.

When gifts are received, or bills paid, they are coded by staff according to the specific ledger code. This allows the Exemplar Fund to maintain a current record of its financial position and determine shortfalls or over-expenditures that appear to be occurring. For example, a bill for supplies charged to the Leadership 2000 program, for which designated funds have been received, might be coded 20-82-51-7005:

20	=	Service Programs
82	=	Designated Fund
51	=	Leadership 2000 (a specific activity)
7005	=	Supplies

DEBITS AND CREDITS

One of the most confusing elements for nonaccounting staff is the distinction between, and categorization according to, debit or credit. The simplest route is probably not to attempt to apply a logical understanding of the terms debit and credit, but rather to recognize that they visually represent the left and right sides of the double entry financial record.

Simply put, cash going into your organization is a debit (abbreviated DB); cash spent by your organization (flowing out of it) is a credit (abbreviated CR). One other point needs to be kept in mind: accounts need to be balanced. Thus, an action on one side of the equation needs to have a corresponding action on the other side. For example, let's assume that your organization borrows a sum of money. You have received funds (hence, a debit), but incurred a liability. Table 6 shows how that transaction might be reflected.

Table 6.
Debit and Credit on a $10,000 Loan

Cash	Loan
$10,000	$10,000

Thus, your organization shows a debit of $10,000 in its cash, and a corresponding $10,000 in its liabilities.

This "double entry" accounting, as it is known, can be summarized according to the following parallel transactions which might be captured in a balance statement (Table 7).[3]

Table 7.
Summary of Debits and Corresponding Credit Relationships

Debits	Credits
Increase assets	Decrease assets
Decrease liabilities	Increase liabilities
Decrease fund balance	Increase fund balance
Decrease income	Increase income
Increase expense	Decrease expense

DEVELOPING AND USING A BUDGET

Most staff familiar with a budget process think of it as budget preparation—that time of year when the accounting people ask each department to estimate their income and expenses for the next fiscal year. While that is an essential step, there are actually five stages in a sound budget process:[4]

1. Preparation
2. Approval
3. Implementation
4. Monitoring
5. Forecasting

Preparation

Preparation is the planning stage of the budget cycle. While it is common to construct each year's budget by building on the one previous, a cogent argument can be made for following two different approaches:

1. Use zero-based budgeting.

Zero-based budgeting asks the basic question: What does your organization need to function effectively? What goals and objectives do you want to address in the next fiscal year, and what will it cost to achieve those goals and objectives?

One method is to first estimate the revenue that the organization believes it can raise in the coming year, so that senior staff know what the outside limits are. A rather different approach is not to confine the thinking according to preset limits, but rather to come to agreement on programs that should be undertaken and then determine how much will need to be raised in order to do so.

In either case, staff should be required to provide justification for the programs being proposed:

- What goal does the program address? What benefits will it provide?
- Why is it a priority? Why should it be funded ahead of some other program?
- What activities will be undertaken to accomplish the program's objectives? How will these be evaluated?
- What are the negative consequences that might accrue if the program is not undertaken?[5]

2. Link the budget process to the strategic planning process.

If it is to truly drive the organization, the strategic plan should have an impact on the budget process. Objectives of the highest priority in the strategic plan should receive priority in the budget process. The cost of implementing priority objectives needs to be estimated and reflected clearly in the budget—even at the risk of eliminating or reducing other programs in order to do so.

Accompanying the budget itself should be a budget narrative, which describes how the figures were derived and provides explanatory information for any items which might be unclear or appear unusual. In this way, the budget becomes a more user friendly document for staff and volunteers.

Who Should Prepare the Budget?

There are two answers to this question:

- Those most involved and affected
- Those with the expertise

The budget should not be prepared in isolation. As with a strategic plan, the budget preparation should involve those who will be most affected (e.g., the board of trustees and staff) and those who need to feel some ownership (e.g., the development committee responsible for raising funds). Integrating the budget product is a function of integrating the budget process. At the same time, the nuts and bolts of preparing the budget should be left to those who have the knowledge and experience, with input and review by affected parties.

Approval

The approval process will be determined in part by the size and complexity of the organization. However, the same axiom holds true: those affected by it (those who will be charged with making it happen) should have an opportunity to review the budget in draft. Final approval needs to rest with the board of trustees, in which is vested the fiduciary responsibility for the organization.

Implementation

It may be necessary to hold a series of in-house briefings on the budget once it has been approved by the board of trustees so that staff understand what is contained within it, what goals it represents, and how it integrates into their department's own objectives and activities.

Monitoring

The real test of the budget process is the degree to which it influences the operations of the organization—that is, the degree to which it provides a checkpoint for decision-making and review.

Interim Statements

One way in which the budget can have an impact on the organization's functions and operations is to install a system of periodic interim statements. These should follow the format of the basic budget, noting where variances occur between what was projected and what is being realized, either in terms of funds raised or expended. Key staff and the board (or a committee to which this responsibility has been delegated by the board) should study the interim statements with certain questions in mind:

- Were the budget projections realistic? Are there any estimates that ought to be recast?
- Are there areas in which it appears there will be a shortfall?

    If so, what is the reason for the shortfall? Can any midcourse corrections be put into place? Will there be overage in another category which can compensate?

- Are there any expenditures planned which are not in budget?

    If so, how will they be accommodated? Can additional means of support be raised? Are the proposed items necessary? What would be the effect of delaying them?

Reviewing Interim Statements

It is important to remember that the purpose of reviewing interim statements is to be sure that the organization is operating in a fiscally responsible manner. That is an obligation which the board holds and is best met by concentrating on the bigger picture. There is little value in board—or staff—discussions reduced to analysis of the numbers. Those charged with reviewing the interim statements "should be educated to look for significant over or under income or expense categories, and should not waste time on details and insignificant items."[6] That is not to say that board members should feel uneasy about asking questions. Nor should they feel that they need to be financial experts in order to ask questions. To the contrary, there are no stupid questions, but it is entirely possible to let the review of the interim statements degenerate into a discussion of financial minutiae.

Forecasting

The final stage in the budget cycle is where many nonprofits fall down on the job. Review of the interim statements should also be done with an eye to the future:

- Are there any trends that can be discerned?

    For example, do the patterns in which contributions are being received differ from years previous? Are there more small gifts? Is it becoming harder to raise general support funds? Are there trends in the purchase of products which can be used in the planning for future products?

- What are the long-range implications of short-term actions?

Forecasting implies long-range financial planning as well. The financial staff or finance committee should develop a less detailed budget that is projected out over at least two, and as many as five, years. For example, assume that there appears to be room within the budget to purchase a piece of equipment that was not part of the budgeted equipment? Will funds be needed in future years to replace that equipment? Will its purchase lead to any additional costs—service contracts, training, insurance etc.?

Finally, the budget cycle should conclude with an evaluation of the process itself? What changes can be effected in how data are gathered? Is the budget becoming too cumbersome? Are its development and maintenance becoming ends in themselves? Is it a useful tool?

FUND ACCOUNTING

Fund accounting is the system used by nonprofit organizations to account for any program which receives its own funding. By creating and maintaining separate fund accounts, the organization can accurately prepare statements reflecting what has been received and disbursed within each fund.

In theory, the nonprofit would need only one fund if all of the monies which it received were for general operating purposes. That is, of course, not the case. Many donors want to earmark their contributions—scholarship fund, libraries, summer camp program. Grants are typically received in response to a proposal for a specific project. Thus, it is necessary to create a means by which all of the monies received and all expenditures relating to the project can be accurately displayed. The result is separate funds. The intent behind establishing funds is that once they have been created, any monies that go into those funds will be used in accordance with the purposes set forth in the funds' creation.

Funds may also be created by the board as a means of building up monies for a special purpose, such as a building fund or reserve fund.

The most restrictive of funds is an endowment fund. When a donor makes a contribution to the endowment fund, the organization invests that contribution, drawing only on the interest which accrues. The principal is held inviolate.

A caution is in order. Particularly in the early stages of their growth, organizations may be tempted to accept donations that are fairly sizable that carry with them rather confining restrictions from the donor. For example, the donor may wish to contribute $1,500 in memory of a loved one, directing that it be used only for scholarships that reflect the loved one's interests. For our purpose, let's say the fund is restricted to scholarships to children of Middle European ancestry.

The organization may soon find that:

1. It is difficult to locate qualified students meeting this criterion.
2. The fund is so small that the income realized makes for a rather paltry scholarship.
3. There are expenses both direct (e.g., mailings) and indirect (staff time) in managing the fund.

The solution:

1. Establish ways in which donors can honor a friend or loved one without such binding restrictions—e.g., a general scholarship fund.
2. Set a realistic floor for the creation of special funds. Some organizations require a minimum of $25,000; others will create a special fund with nothing less than ten times that amount.
3. Work with the donor to reach a compromise position that recognizes the donor's friend or loved one without unduly tying the hands of the organization.
4. Encourage the donor to agree with terms under which the special fund will be blended into a larger fund after a suitable period of time.

THE INDEPENDENT AUDIT

What makes an audit an "independent audit"? The use of an independent (i.e., not on the organization's staff) certified public account, or CPA. While the independent audit is the product of the individual or firm hired for that purpose, the process of developing the audit can and should be the result of a partnership between the CPA and the organization.

Why have an independent audit?

*   It may be required by state law;
*   Certain funding sources (e.g., federal agencies) may require it;
*   The board of trustees may want the verification from an external evaluator that the organization is sound financially;
*   It provides donors with some assurance that their financial support is going to an organization that is well managed.

Working with the Auditor

Establishing a cooperative working relationship with an independent auditor begins with the selection of the auditing firm, which in turn begins with an understanding of the auditor's role. The firm should not only have a reputation for competence and integrity; it should also have experience with similar nonprofits.

The contact between the auditor and the organization occurs at two points: On a daily basis the auditor will be working with the organization's chief financial officer, but the audited report should be presented to and formally accepted by the board of trustees. The board may want to appoint a body comprising volunteers and staff to interview potential candidates, so that there is accord up front between the board and staff, both on the firm used and on the process which will be pursued.

Staff can greatly facilitate the auditing process by keeping records that are complete, well-documented, and in order;[7] and by assigning someone to work with the auditor who is both informed and cooperative. During the time when the auditor is on site, he or she may be engaged in any or all of the following:

- Reviewing financial statements;
- Making suggestions for changes in the way finances are reported;
- Providing technical assistance to staff regarding generally accepted accounting practices;[8]
- Reviewing time and leave records;
- Analyzing the various funds that have been established;
- Studying investment policies and procedures;
- Reviewing records pertaining to grant funds.

The auditing experience can be a source of information and assistance to the organization which goes well beyond the preparation of an independent audited statement. The auditing staff and the organization's own financial staff may be working literally side by side for a period of several weeks, during which time numerous opportunities will present themselves to learn ways of enhancing the organization's financial procedures. It is incumbent on the organization's CEO to foster a climate of cooperation. If the staff views the annual arrival of the auditor with an "It's that time again already" attitude, the value of the audit may be confined to the printed page.

The board of trustees should also have a chance to communicate directly with the auditing firm. That firm may prepare a "management letter" which in itself may be the most important product of the audit.[9] It can include suggested modifications not only in the bookkeeping and accounting functions, but also in terms of investment policies.

WHAT SHOULD THE BOARD ASK ABOUT THE ORGANIZATION'S FINANCES?

The Association of Governing Boards of Universities and Colleges has compiled a series of questions which boards may wish to pose as they review financial statements and the independent audited statement.

There are three basic areas—Financial Performance, Financial Condition, and Endowment Management—each of which has a number of questions. (They are paraphrased to apply to any nonprofit organization.)

Financial Performance

Financial performance questions seek to determine if the organization is managed well fiscally:

- Is there a history of annual independent financial audits?
- Do the independent auditors' reports contain any qualifying statements?

  The letter accompanying the audit should say something to the effect that "in all material respects" the financial picture as presented by the organization is accurate in conformity with "generally accepted accounting principles."

- If any irregularities or deficiencies were noted in the auditors' report, have these been addressed?
- Does the organization meet its operational expenses with revenues generated within the same fiscal year?

  If deficits occurred, how were they handled?

Performance management questions may also address the sources of revenues and appropriate balance of expenditures:

- Are the sources of revenue varied?
- Is the organization dependent for its operating expenses on income from endowments? Is it using reserve funds to meet its operating expenses?
- Does the organization rely on "soft" sources of funding (such as government grants) for its operations?
- What percentage is spent on overhead?
- Is there sufficient provision for future equipment and maintenance needs?
- How much is being spent to repay outstanding debts?

One way of measuring the organization's relative debt position is to calculate a ratio of current assets (i.e., those which might be converted to cash within one year) to liabilities:[10]

$$\text{Current ratio} \quad = \quad \frac{\text{Current assets}}{\text{Current liabilities}}$$

For example, assume current assets are $345,000, and current liabilities $115,000. The ratio would be 3.0, meaning that the organization has $3 in assets for each $1 of liability. By comparing ratios from year to year, the staff and board can determine trends.

Financial Condition

Questions relating to the organization's financial condition may address both assets and debt.

* Have the organization's assets been increasing?

* Have endowments and other restricted funds been increasing?

* How much short-term and long-term debt obligation does the organization have?

* What effect does the payment of these debts have on the organization's operating budget?

    How much is the organization required to pay out in principal and interest? Is it hampering the ability to launch new programs?

* Would the organization be in a position to pay off its short- and long-term debts (short-term out of liquid funds, and long-term out of assets which it holds)?

* Are the organization's reserve funds increasing in proportion to increase in annual operating expenses?

Endowment Management

The questions on endowment management are concerned both with investment of the endowment funds and the use of income which is generated.

* What is the size of the endowment fund (or funds)?

* Are there "funds functioning as endowment" which have been set aside? (*Note*: "Funds functioning as endowment" are established at times as a middle ground. Because they function as endowments, the organization agrees not to invade the principal and only spend the income. However, because they are not true endowments, the organization may be able to convert them to other purposes should the need arise.)

* By what percentages has the principal within the endowment funds been increasing, if at all?

* What is the rate of return on investment of endowment funds?

- Is the endowment sufficient for the organization's size and growth? (How does it compare with similar institutions?)
- How much of the endowment is needed to balance the operating budget?
- Is consideration being given to reinvestment of endowment income in order to meet future needs?[11]

REPORTING TO DONORS

There are four guidelines to keep in mind in preparing financial reports to donors:

1. Be candid.
2. Be brief.
3. Be first with the information.
4. Be positive.

Candor

There is simply no point in being manipulative with the reporting of financial status. It is unethical, it is probably illegal, and it is certainly bad business. As is noted in Chapter 5 on fund raising, donors are increasingly sophisticated. State and federal agencies are looking with a jaundiced eye at the financial affairs of nonprofits. Obfuscation in financial reporting *might* have short-term benefit, but long term it will surely harm the organization, the area of service in which it is engaged, and nonprofits in general.

If your organization must report a less than positive statement about its revenue shortfall or cost overruns, put the information in context:

- What has been the organization's history? What are its prospects?

    If this is the first time the organization has ended its fiscal year in the red, say so. If the projections for next year appear to make up for the current shortfall, point that out.

- What is the condition of similar organizations?

    Companies offering stock or managing mutual funds learned that having a bad year was more palatable to the investor if comparable firms or mutual funds with similar objectives (e.g., investing in bonds) also fared poorly. The nonprofit world sees shifts as well. There are times when funding for the arts is popular, and other times when health or education are able to attract "center stage" support.

- What is the organization doing about the problem?

What mid-course corrections have been instituted? How long will they take to make a turnaround?

Candid reporting is based on an assumption: The organization is basically sound, but incurs infrequent financial difficulties as might be expected given exigencies of the economy and a fluid sociopolitical climate. The nonprofit that seeks to mask ingrown problems with an inaccurate financial report is doing both itself and the donor a disservice.

Brevity

Most donors do not want, nor do they understand, lengthy financial documents. Make it clear that an audited financial statement is available upon request, but otherwise provide a financial summary, preferably with graphic accompaniment, such as a pie chart highlighting income and programs.

Being First

Another lesson which the corporate sector has learned is that if the quarterly earnings are not going to live up to expectations, it is better to get that word out before the media do so that the organization has some control over what is said. If your organization is experiencing financial difficulties, the board needs to be fully informed and to decide who also needs to know and by what means. If it seems likely the situation can be turned around in a short timeframe, so much the better. If not, the board and CEO may want to schedule personal visits with key stakeholders before the printed financial statements are released.

Being Positive

Here, too, the assumption is that the organization under current leadership has the potential to achieve its goals and even excel. Asking donors to contribute to a cause that the CEO doubts can meet its objectives is unethical at best.

On the other hand, even a dip in the organization's financial growth can be cast in positive terms. For example:

- The shortfall may represent a onetime expenditure;
- Although there was a problem, it has been addressed;
- The organization has learned a lesson that will allow it to move forward.

BEING PREPARED FOR THE WORST[12]

In good times and bad, the prudent nonprofit will have contingency plans in place, lessening vulnerability to shifts in the economy and changes in funding patterns. The board of trustees, or the committee to which budgeting and finance have been delegated, should develop these contingency plans which respond to certain basic questions about the organization's financial health and viability.

Cash Flow

Does the organization have sufficient cash flow to provide a buffer should the receipt of funds diminish? Can the organization withstand delays in payments from grants, contracts, third party reimbursement? It may be wise as times become less certain to increase the cushion within the cash flow to anticipate delays or shortfalls.

Cash Reserves

In addition to the operating funds, does the organization have ready cash reserves of sufficient magnitude to weather a drop in client revenues, reduction in fund raising income, burgeoning expenses due to inflation? Could the reserves offset a sudden drop in the sale of products?

Program Income

The board or finance committee may want to analyze existing and planned services or programs for their income potential. The Boston Consulting Group developed a framework that can be used to analyze products according to the share of the market which they hold and their growth potential. The framework can be used to describe four types of products or services:[13]

1. Star: A "star" is a product or service which holds a sizable share of a growing market with potential for additional growth. Stars provide revenue that can be reinvested, as well as visibility for the organization.

2. Cash Cow: A "cash cow" product or service also has a significant portion of the market, but the growth has leveled off. Because of its stability, the cow can be milked to provide income for new products or services.

3. New Venture: The term "new venture" is applied to new product or service opportunities that show real potential. Investment in them could result in dramatic growth.

4. Dog:[14] The name is self-explanatory. "Dogs" are those products or services that do not perform well. The organization needs to ask if the visibility that they provide is worth the investment in time and financial resources.

The four-fold description developed by the Boston Consulting Group is essentially a marketing device; the board or budget committee would do well to draw on the organization's marketing staff as it reviews products and services according to these designations and to consult with the staff most directly involved.

Cost Containment

Virtually every organization has some fat; some programs are overstaffed and, for other programs, the time has come and gone. It is a painful but necessary task to review all of the organization's programs from time to time to be sure they are relevant and the staffing for them lean.

Fund Raising

What were the successes in the fund raising arena in the past few years? Are there segments of the fund raising market that show particular potential? Would it make sense to inaugurate a new fund raising program—say, in an area of planned giving—in order to respond to the potential for major gifts? Are there elements of the fund raising program that should be abandoned because of their poor cost/return ratios?

Volunteer Potential

Is the board contributing up to its capability? Are other volunteer leaders contributing their fair share? Are there aspects of the overall organization that could be performed as well by volunteers, rather than by hiring staff or consultants?

Staffing

Each department should have a contingency plan of its own. Should it become necessary to cut back on staff, what procedure would be used to determine who goes and who stays?

What is the rate of normal attrition? Should the contingency plan include delaying the replacement of staff who have left?

Other Options

What would the chances be of joining services with other organizations, or of actually merging with another organization? Are there revenue streams which have never been fully explored, such as the spinoff of a for-profit enterprise?

AUTOMATING THE FISCAL FUNCTIONS

This section is not an attempt to describe the various software packages that might be used to automate the fiscal functions of a nonprofit, but rather to suggest some guidelines.

Know Your Requirements

The surest way to create problems for the organization is to select a software accounting package and then try to force fit it into the organization. It is equally risky to have the accounting software selected only by those in accounting, however capable they might be. The requirements should reflect the entire financial operations of the organization, and the software selected should at least be compatible with those requirements if it cannot accommodate them all.

Thus, while it is essential to consider all of the uses to which the software will be put in the business department, it is also incumbent on those making the selection to consider other units as well. For example:

- Does the research division have grant funds which could be better tracked on computer?
- Will the software selected for accounting purposes be useful for fund raising as well? Can it create and track funds? Can it keep multiyear records of donors? Can it be used as a tickler to remind the development office staff of pledges due?
- How will the business department software relate to the purchasing and receiving functions? Is it possible, and desirable, to be able to follow an order from time of placement to the time when the invoice is paid?
- Will it be possible to provide regular reports to department heads, board, and chief staff person, comparing this year with the same time last year?

Anticipate Growth

Needless to say, buying a hardware system with accompanying software is a major step. Buying only according to current needs may prove costly in the very near future. At the same time, purchasing a system that the organization will not grow into for five years is probably not prudent either, given the rapid improvements in technology. That may saddle the organization with outmoded equipment while they attempt to recoup the initial layout.

Find an Acceptable Tradeoff between Hardware and Software

Some of the best software available will not run on the system that most suits your needs. Conversely, selecting to accommodate software requirements may box the organization into a system that precludes use of additional software later on. It is worth remembering that there is no perfect hardware/software system and that the organization exists in a political climate. The choice of what to purchase (or build) in terms of fiscal automation should be considered on rational grounds, but with a keen awareness of group decision-making and group process.

SPECIAL STRATEGIES FOR THE SMALL NONPROFIT

The importance of sound fiscal management will not vary by size of organization, but the means of managing the nonprofit's financial resources probably will. More than one nonprofit CEO has wrestled with how to keep accurate records and provide timely financial information with a modest staff. Here are some possible strategies:

1. **Make the best use of available ("off the shelf") software.**

   At the low end, accounting software can be purchased for as little as $50–$75. While the software is essentially a computerized checkbook register, it does reduce the manual recording of data and allow for simple printouts.

   For somewhat more, the nonprofit may want to consider standard spreadsheet applications such as Lotus 123 or Excell. These can also be used for budget preparation (including grant proposal budgets) and do not require extensive computer experience to master.

2. **Seek in-kind contributions of customized software.**

   There are at least three options here: (1) See if a local college or university class will create a software package as a class project; (2) Identify a local company that might allow you to use its customized software as an in-kind contribution; (3) Pursue the loan of staff from a company with a large data processing staff.

3. **Look for solutions which meet several needs.**

   It may be possible to identify a software application that can be used not only by the financial staff but also for development office records keeping, tracking of patient or client records, or analysis of research data.

4. Use the KISS (Keep It Simple, Stupid) approach.

Donors do not typically require exhaustive programmatic budgets or extensive accounting of expenditures. Be sure that the information, input, and analysis are needed before you embark on a complicated program.

5. Educate nonaccounting staff.

Considerable time on the part of the accounting staff can be saved if other staff within the nonprofit know how to apply ledger codes to bills requiring their signatures. Convene a brainstorming session to determine what financial information is really needed (as opposed to desired) and how financial information can be collected more efficiently.

PARTING THOUGHTS

The foundation of wealth is the first decision well made.
—*J. P. Morgan*

Managing the financial health of the organization is a question of making good decisions. This chapter has sought to provide the fundaments of finance. The nonprofit CEO needs to understand these basics in order to conduct his or her own cross impact analyses, weighing financial data against human capability in order to assess the organization's well-being and potential. Financial decisions need to be made with an understanding of finance, but also with a view of the whole. Therein lies the role of nonprofit management.

More than one nonprofit CEO has been replaced because he or she did not monitor the financial affairs of the organization. The other extreme, however, can be equally terminal—that is, immersing oneself in the minutiae of budgeting and financial statements to the exclusion of the larger picture.

Know enough about the financial workings of the organization to ask hard questions and stimulate effective decision-making and enough to be able to assure its viability. Those who support it with their time and resources expect no less.

NOTES

1. Glenn A. Welsch, Robert N. Anthony, and Daniel G. Short, *Fundamentals of Financial Accounting* (Homewood, IL: Irwin, Inc., 1984), 67.

2. Andrew S. Lang, *Association Finances for the Non-Financial Manager* (Washington, DC: American Society of Association Executives, 1989), 35. Appreciation is also expressed to Armondo Quinones for his review of the material on developing a Chart of Accounts.

3. Lang, 43.

4. The five stages of the budget process are based somewhat on those contained in A. Michael Gellman, "The Budget Cycle," *The Budgeting Process* (Washington, DC: American Society of Association Executives, 1990), 3–5.

5. Some of ideas regarding zero-based budgeting were drawn from Linda J. Shinn and M. Sue Sturgeon, "Budgeting from Ground Zero," *Association Management*, 42 (September 1990): 45–48.

6. John Paul Dalsimer, "Understanding Nonprofit Financial Statements: A Primer for Board Members" (Washington, DC: National Center for Nonprofit Boards, 1991), 11.

7. Ronald R. Kovener, "Aiding Your Auditor" *Executive Update*, 23 (April 1990): 29.

8. Kovener, 27–28.

9. Dalsimer, 13–14.

10. Dalsimer, 15.

11. "Questions Which Board Members Should Ask About the Financial Condition of Their Organization," *Chronicle of Philanthropy*, 2 (March 21, 1990): 23.

12. "Facing Bad News," *Nonprofit Management Strategies*, 2 (November 1990): 5.

13. The Boston Consulting Group's four-fold analysis of products is summarized in Richard L. Daft, *Organization Theory and Design* (New York: West Publishing Company, 1989), 495–496.

14. "Facing Bad News," 5.

Chapter 7
Human Resources Management: Building an Accomplished Staff

Management ... pertains to every human effort that brings together in one organization people of diverse knowledge and skills.
—*Peter Drucker*

EXECUTIVE SUMMARY

Written on the Berlin Wall before it was torn down was a slogan which read: "Belief becomes reality." It is a sentiment worthy of adoption by nonprofit managers: if you believe in the mission of the organization, believe in yourselves, and believe in those with whom you work, you can make it happen. This chapter is about the last of those: believing in the capabilities of others and finding ways to realize that belief.

After a review of seven principles of management, this chapter tackles a management bugaboo—performance management and how to make it work in the nonprofit. It continues with the art of delegating (both when and how) and motivating (including the relationship of motivation to morale). Next, managerial styles; a discussion of "manage or lead"; and, finally, characteristics of the effective manager of the 1990s.

WHAT IS MANAGEMENT: SEVEN PRINCIPLES

In *The New Realities* (1989), Peter Drucker lists seven "essential principles" of management:

1. Management concerns itself with human beings. Working with people, encouraging their joint efforts, is what management is all about.

2. Because management seeks to involve people in joint ventures, for it to be successful it must understand and be involved in matters of organizational culture. Management that matches culture is most likely to succeed.

3. Common goals and shared values are essential. Without them, "there is no enterprise, there is only a mob."[1]

4. Management must be responsive to the changing needs of its employees and the changing nature of the environment in which the organization functions.

5. Because organizations comprise diverse backgrounds, knowledge, and skills, good communication is vital.

6. The organization that measures its accomplishments solely by the bottom line is using inadequate measures. Among other criteria are the cultivation of its people, its innovativeness, and the quality of its products and services.

7. The most important measure of management's achievement is this: Are the customers, however they are defined, satisfied?[2]

A number of the points raised by Drucker are addressed at some length in this book: mission (common values and goals), planning, communication, marketing (the satisfaction of customers). This chapter concentrates on critical management functions—performance management, dealing with change, working with difficult employees, and more.

HOW TO MAKE PERFORMANCE MANAGEMENT WORK

Ask any ten employees of an organization what they think of the company's or institution's performance management program, and you are likely to get some very negative responses from half:

*   "It's management's way of keeping people from getting a decent raise."
*   "I think it's unfair. You get singled out for what you did wrong and little credit for what you did right."
*   "Performance management is punitive. If anything, it makes people feel worse, not better."

Why Performance Management Has Such a Bad Reputation

One reason for the bad "rap" has to do with the name; unfortunately, performance management smacks of control—controlling what people do, and how. It sounds manipulative. Therein lies the crux of the challenge of management; in a very real sense, management is about control. A poorly managed organization means, to many, one that is "out of control." To be an efficacious manager, it is necessary to exercise some control over the allocation and disbursement of resources, human resources included. The question becomes how to meet the overarching goal of management (i.e., control) within an atmosphere that encourages trust, shared vision, and excitement about goals. Said another way, the challenge of management is how to mesh the individual, disparate interests of employees with operational and organizational goals. How do you get employees to accomplish the objectives set for the organization and feel good about it?

Don't expect any easy answers—or, better said, any easy solutions. But an analogy to marketing might provide some clues.

Applying Marketing Principles to Performance Management

For marketing to "work," it must identify the needs, interests, and wants of its constituencies, and match those against the capabilities and product or service line of the organization. If the customer doesn't perceive some benefit in the product or service being offered, he or she is unlikely to purchase it at whatever cost. Similarly, if a member of the organization's staff does not feel part of the vision, the mission, the goals of the organization, it becomes difficult for that person to see "what's in it for me?" Saying that salary—getting paid—is what's in it for that person is insufficient. More than one study has demonstrated that, while salary is a motivator, it is not the only motivator, and rarely is it the number one motivator (at least not for long).

Marketing seeks to make the hard sell unnecessary by understanding the wants and interests of the buyer and relating those interests to the product or service being offered. Broadly speaking, the same is true for management/employee relations. Employees who see value in what they are doing, who have an interest in buying into the organization, do not require the hard sell of a taskmaster. To be sure, one will never obtain that level of interest in the organization on the part of all staff, but neither will marketing ever replace the need for direct sales. In both instances, that doesn't negate the value of the goal.

Effective performance management is thus, in marketing terms, a process of exchange in which both parties feel they have benefited. It's helping people to succeed; it's helping them to win.

Performance Management: Guiding Principles

Principle One: Performance management should be conducted in an atmosphere that is positive, nurturing, and mature.

As one company views it, there are three assumptions that underlie this win-win view of performance management:

1. The process should not be focused on just measuring results, but rather should provide a chance for employee and supervisor to build on their relationship.

2. The fact that one party in the transaction is management and one is not should not imply some sort of class system.

   This is not the time (if there ever is a time) for one party to assume a dominating role over another.

3. Performance management should foster and encourage teamwork.

   Results should not be measured solely in terms of individual achievement.[3]

Principle Two: Performance management is not a once a year or twice a year activity.

According to management author Ken Blanchard, the performance management system has three components which are collectively ongoing throughout the year:

1. Performance planning.
2. Day to day coaching (helping people to win).
3. Performance evaluation.[4]

Blanchard decries what we calls the "seagull school of management," which describes the manager who appears on the scene only occasionally, and then only to make a lot of noise and dump on his or her staff before flying off. Performance management that works, in Blanchard's view, begins with an agreement on goals between employee and supervisor. In this initial meeting, the two, working together, agree on goals that the employee wants to achieve and on the ways in which both will know if the employee is doing a good job.

Performance implies outcomes. While Blanchard is rather vehemently against forced numerical performance management systems, he does point out that some means of measuring progress needs to be established; employee and supervisor might include indications of:

- Quality (with an indication of how that will be judged and by whom)
- Quantity

- Timeliness
- Amount of change[5]

Once both parties have agreed on what constitutes meritable performance, the goals for the year should be written down and then re-read to be sure they mean what was intended. They then need to be revisited, both formally and informally, throughout the year.

Which leads to **Principle Three: The goals need to be kept visible**.

In many organizations, the goals are written and then filed away until performance review time approaches. For performance management to work, the goals must manage the behavior, not the calendar or the clock. It may be helpful for the employees to tape them into the front of notebooks, list them periodically on their calendars, jot them down on 3 x 5 cards.

Principle Four: Both parties need to understand their responsibilities.

Managers have the responsibility to:

- Coach and encourage their employees;
- Challenge those reporting to them to not only meet their goals but take some risks;
- Provide positive feedback for encouragement;
- Provide accurate and candid feedback on shortcomings.

Employees have their own responsibilities relative to performance management:

- Set goals that are realistic, doable, but not a "cakewalk";
- See that their principal activities are achieving the agreed upon goals;
- Conduct realistic self-assessments;
- Talk with their managers about any problems that arise;
- Listen to feedback, and make use of it.

Principle Five: Performance management demands candor.

Why is performance appraisal time greeted with so much dread? Why do all involved try to get through it with all the speed that can be mustered? One reason is because it can involve confrontation, and most people will go out of their way to avoid confrontation. Computers have been a boon to civilization in many ways, but they have also provided a management crutch, allowing memos or electronic mail messages to be sent in lieu of face-to-face interaction. And try as one might, it is difficult to achieve candor by mail.

The truth of this principle having been recognized, it is incumbent on nonprofit managers to incorporate that fact into performance management planning—at the front end. Manager and employee should acknowledge in the goal-setting that there may be times when they will disagree, when they will have differing perceptions of what has been accomplished and on how they will deal with this disagreement. It is of consequence to consider how dissonance will be handled early on, and not wait until a problem arises.

The understandable concern over the possibility of conflict can be ameliorated as well by carefully planning how the performance appraisal itself should proceed. In the heat of the daily workload, it is not difficult to underestimate how important it is to plan this meeting so that both parties leave it with memories that foster continued good relations.

Here is what one nonprofit manager suggests:

> Prepare an opening that sets an appropriate tone for the session. For example, he or she might say, "The [organization] has had a good year, and your performance has contributed significantly to that. I realized as I prepared for this review how much I depend on you and how much I enjoy working with you."[6]

Mentally lay out the points that need to be covered, highlighting those elements of the performance management appraisal form that reflect the key tone and the direction you wish to take. During the meeting, center the discussion on behavior—what was or was not achieved—and not on attitudes (unless attitude change was an agreed upon objective).

Where a problem exists, both parties must acknowledge it, preferably aloud, before a solution can be constructed. Verbalizing it will reveal many of the underlying perceptions and emotions. It is the supervisor's role to state the problem as a behavior that lends itself to modification.

Once the problem has been stated, the plan to correct can be outlined. Asking questions may help frame this part of the appraisal meeting:

- "What might the desired behavior look like? How will we know when the problem has been resolved?"
- "What are the alternative courses of action? What are the probable outcomes of each?"
- "Of these courses of action, which seem to be the most productive?"
- "When should we meet again to see how we're doing? What checkpoints should be put in place?"[7]

THE ART OF DELEGATING

Delegation assumes that there is a distinction between supervision and accountability. It is possible for a manager to have several staff members reporting to her or him with varying degrees of supervision. Yet the manager is accountable in the overall scheme for their individual success or lack of it.

The fear that delegation may come back to haunt you—that delegation does not reduce accountability—is one of several reasons why managers sometimes find it so difficult to delegate. Some other reasons:

- It takes time up front.
- There is little point in giving a subordinate an assignment if one cannot be sure that person understands what is required.
- It requires ongoing communication to be sure the job is being done, and done satisfactorily.
- It sometimes feels easier just to do the job oneself, especially if it's a job that the manager can do well.

The challenges to delegation are behind what management professor Henry Mintzberg calls the "dilemma of delegation":

> Tasks involving only one specialist function are easily delegated . . . . But what of tasks that cut across specialties or that involve the manager's special information? The manager, as nerve center, has the best command of the relevant factual and value information . . . . Yet he cannot do everything. Some of these tasks must be delegated.[8]

As a consequence, managers feel caught in a kind of "Catch-22" situation. As repositories of knowledge, they may well be the best persons to complete the task, or at least stay thoroughly on top of it. And yet if they don't delegate, not only are they solid candidates for duodenal ulcers, they're also not performing their jobs as managers.

The bottom line, then, is that delegation is not only necessary, it is desirable for the growth of the organization and the growth of those who work for it. Here are some thoughts on how to make the process work:

1. **Make delegation a part of the performance management system.**

   If you want to cultivate your employees' ability to take on work, present that as a goal. Agree on milestones—e.g., "In the next quarter, Wilberforce will take over responsibility for all accounts receivable."

2. **Don't delegate responsibility without authority.**

One of the quickest ways to drive your staff crazy is to instill in them a sense of the responsibility which they bear without giving them the tools to carry out the tasks. If they are taking over certain areas, make sure those involved are apprised of that move. And don't encourage others to bypass the supervisor (do an end-around) in order to keep you in the decision-making.

3. **Expect mistakes and deal with them fairly.**

Martin Stone, head of Monogram Inc., says that in his company "we don't punish mistakes unless they're repeated. I figure that out of ten things you do, six will be mediocre, one will be lousy, and, if you're lucky, three will be great."[9] Three out of ten "hits" is not so bad; major league baseball players are delighted to achieve it.

4. **Delegation should reflect the individual differences among staff.**

As is addressed elsewhere in this book, effective management is based on a comprehension of "situational leadership." Some employees will embrace the opportunity to take on more responsibility; others will shun it. Some are ready to do so; others may wrongly perceive their readiness.

5. **There are times when delegation is right and when it is not.**

The right time to delegate responsibility to another is when sufficient time can be committed to be sure that the person fully comprehends the job and what is expected in terms of accomplishment. That includes an understanding of the range of tasks to be performed and a time frame in which they need to be completed.

The wrong time to delegate is when you have a job you would rather not do yourself.[10]

6. **Delegation means accepting that yours is not the only way to get the job done.**

While it is true that, as the supervisor, you do not relinquish ultimate responsibility when you delegate work to another, it is no less true that you must give the person enough room to exercise his or her own responsibility. To the degree that you can be comfortable doing so, you must let go. Live with approximations of the ideal. And don't insist that work accomplished be a clone of what you would have done.

7. **Even when you have the time to delegate, know when it is best not to do so.**

Some circumstances favor opting not to delegate:

- When the issue is sensitive;
- When the stakes are highest;
- When other key players are involved.

HOW TO MOTIVATE STAFF

In his classic article on the topic of motivation, Frederick Herzberg argues that much of what we call "motivation" is really just getting the employee to move, i.e., to act. We have affected a change in behavior, but not in attitude. The real motivators, argues Herzberg, are:

- Achievement;
- Recognition of that achievement;
- The work itself;
- A sense of responsibility;
- Opportunity for individual's growth and advancement.[11]

Address the job itself and not the accoutrements when motivating an employee. While the importance of other factors cannot be denied—salary, work setting, positive interactions with other staff—these cannot change a job that in and of itself does not provide an incentive.

American industry came to much the same conclusion after years of trial and error. In the desire for efficiency, industry created the assembly line, in which one worker was responsible for one part or one function, often with little if any understanding of how that part or that function fit into the larger whole. Unions pushed for higher wages, better benefits packages, shorter hours, longer breaks. And yet none of these in the last analysis resulted in more motivated workers. Workers who realized the gains provided by union strength, but whose jobs were not in themselves restructured to make them more interesting or more challenging, found themselves increasingly frustrated. The result is all too familiar: vehicles and other products of less than superior quality, heightened tension between worker and management, diminished productivity.

In the name of motivation, what we had done was to pit work (a "sacrifice to one's leisure") with wages ("a kind of compensation for that sacrifice.")[12]

What have we learned: that we need to distinguish between factors that have the short-term effect of getting the job done (such as standing over someone's shoulder) and factors that change the attitude and hence the behavior of the employee. Herzberg's studies found that the way to motivate the employee on the job was to change the content of the job to make it more motivating:

- Reduce controls placed on the employee;
- Increase the accountability of the employee for the job performed;
- Structure the work so that it has meaning in itself (ideally, so that there is some sense of completion and accomplishment);
- Extend the employee's span of control—giving him or her freedom in how to accomplish the work;
- Upgrade the job from time to time with additional tasks;
- Design the work so that individuals can become expert in some facet of what they do.[13]

In sum, motivating staff, requires looking with scrutiny at the work that is being accomplished—not only the quality and quantity of the work, but the nature of the work.

Implicit in this theory of motivation is that a positive reinforcement strategy works best. Fear and punishment in the form of threats and coercion may keep people in line; and a disciplined work environment may be requisite. But in addition to the negative psychological implications, fear and punishment tend to be short-term. Applying a fear tactic to an employee who has "screwed up" does not teach that employee how to do the job effectively; nor does it have anything to do with an inner-driven sense of motivation. More subtly, what fear and punishment may mask is the anger and frustration of the manager who at some level acknowledges his or her ineffectiveness.

Said another way, motivation ought to be based on the assumption that most people, if given the choice, would prefer to achieve and indeed to excel.

MOTIVATION AND MORALE

Morale is the first cousin to motivation. If motivation is intrinsic to the job, morale is conditioned by the work environment. Here are ways to build morale. Some are easier to list than to implement; that is what makes management a challenging profession.

1. Establish an atmosphere of trust.

Simpler said than done. Many of us give lip service to this goal. When we say we applaud candor, we mean candor up to a point. If you had a spot on your blouse or tie, would your staff feel comfortable telling you? If you could benefit from a breath mint? If you were simply being wrongheaded about a new project you badly wanted to establish?

Establishing an atmosphere of trust means permitting, nay even encouraging, staff to express sentiments openly; being honest about your own shortcomings; and being careful not to "shoot the messenger."

2. Listen attentively.

Active listening means putting down the report in hand when someone comes into the office, making eye contact, and then hearing what is being said. It means as well allowing the other party to speak before formulating a response. Again, easier said than done. But if you do not appear to listen, and in fact if it is clear that you miss important points in others' comments, you are sending a very powerful message.

3. Be willing to ask hard questions.

In many colleges and universities, end of semester evaluations of the professor are conducted in strict confidence. The professor passes out the evaluation forms, which have been designed by the department, so that they are now skewed to a particular professor's strengths; filled out independently; and then collected and returned to the department by a fellow student. The professor sees only the summary tallies and unattributed commentary.

Nonprofit managers who want to learn how their staffs truly feel in order to build morale need to do no less. If your staff are reluctant to speak candidly, either in your presence or in small groups, about the organization's strengths and weaknesses, you have a morale problem. To improve the situation, it will be necessary to hear some unpleasant news.

3. Engage the staff in the process of building morale.

There is a tendency sometimes to assume that morale can be improved by instituting some change—in-house newsletter, improved medical benefit, staff get-together off hours, flexible work hours—without asking the staff themselves what they would like. By asking staff, management is not only learning what really will make a difference, but also sending the message that the staff's opinion counts.

This message, of giving people a chance to say what is on their minds, is fundamental to morale. It is as old as the famous Hawthorne studies, which found that worker morale and productivity increased in direct relation to the opportunity provided to them to speak up, to vent.

4. Communicate.

"Nobody tells us anything." "By the time we hear about it, it's usually too late." "We're like the proverbial mushroom—kept in the dark, up to our cap in manure."

Communication is such an important topic that it is addressed in its own chapter in this text. Suffice it to say that there is a direct correlation between morale and the opinion of staff that there is a genuine flow of communication, vertically and horizontally.

5. Maintain an atmosphere that is fair and supportive.[14]

Nothing undermines morale more quickly than a climate of negativism. Question to consider: Are new ideas generally greeted with enthusiasm or cynicism? Do the department heads evince respect for one another? Are senior staff meetings characterized by positive comments about others' suggestions and activities, or subtle (and not so subtle) backbiting?

Top management must set the tone and the expectations. It may be necessary to meet in private with one or more of the senior staff to remind them that the organization is looking to build teams, not turfdoms.

MANAGERIAL STYLES

Managers, like leaders, are made, not born. Management is a set of skills which can be acquired over time and with effort. While it may be true that some individuals possess characteristics that lead to being effective managers, it is also true that all managers improve in their jobs by working at them.

One way of working at becoming a better manager is to understand some of the different managerial styles. Listed below are a sampling of those styles.

Theory X/Theory Y

Advanced by Douglas M. McGregor, Theory X and Theory Y represent contrasting points of view on the nature of workers and management. Theory X is rooted in the following assumptions:

- The typical employee has an inborn dislike of work and will avoid it when possible. It is human nature to be lazy.
- On average, most people are more interested in their own needs, not in the needs of the organization for which they work.

- Because of the employees' natural tendency to avoid hard work, it is the responsibility of management to coerce, motivate, punish, reward, control, induce, direct.
- Management is responsible for seeing that the work gets done through the proper utilization of human and other resources.[15]

The Theory X manager is thus at the center of the organization. Without him or her, the organization would not begin to reach its objectives.

Theory Y takes into account the research done by Maslow and others on motivation. It acknowledges that individuals have a hierarchy of needs, beginning with the most basic (food, safety), and progressing through to needs for self-fulfillment. In this context, the roles of worker and manager are rather dramatically recast:

- Work is not necessarily something which most people avoid. To the contrary, it is a natural and desirable part of life.
- Most people, if given the opportunity, welcome challenge and responsibility.
- Control and punishment are not the sole means for meeting organizational objectives. If the worker believes in the job, is committed to it, he or she will not require that kind of external control.
- It is the task of management to understand what truly motivates people in order to foster an environment in which personal goals mesh with organizational.[16]

It should be remembered that Theory X and Theory Y represent extremes. It is probably fair to say that, while not all employees are indolent, neither are all of them in pursuit of higher goals of self-realization and self-actualization. Just as the school system cannot be considered a failure if some students do not succeed for reasons beyond the boundaries of the school, so, too, it is unnecessarily critical of management to maintain that, if employees fail, it is because management has failed.

At the same time, Theory Y treats workers as complex human beings, with their own wants and needs; organizational success is linked to the degree that human needs and organizational needs can be joined.

Organic or Mechanistic

The terms "organic" and "mechanistic" are somewhat akin to Theories X and Y in that they represent end points of managerial control, as shown in Table 8.[17]

Table 8.
Organic vs Mechanistic Organizations

Organic	*Mechanistic*
Loose managerial control	Tight managerial control
Top-down structure and flow of communication	Less hierarchical structure; more lateral communication
Extensive rules, written documentation	Few written or expressed rules
High degree of standardization	High degree of flexibility

As with Theory X and Theory Y, neither the mechanistic nor the organic approach is right for all occasions and all people. Depending on one's view of human nature, one or the other will have appeal. What is imperative is to recognize that not every individual will achieve the optimum level of competence within the same system. The inner-motivated, educated health care professional who wants to make a name for herself in her professional association will not require the same kind of mechanistic structure that might be appropriate for the housekeeping staff. Using mechanistic and organic controls as extreme ordinates, we need to ask ourselves about the job at hand and the persons charged with completing that job:

- Does the job lend itself to a high degree of standardization? Can standards for how it should be completed be developed with a high factor of reliability?
- Is the typical person working on this job likely to have extensive knowledge about his or her field?
- From past experience, what seems to motivate the individuals involved?
- What are the long-term implications? Is this a job that will encourage growth and maturity, or is it so routine that the most important factor is assuring that it is done right each time?

MBWA

MBWA—Management by Walking Around—is explained as follows by a former corporate executive:

> Probably the most important principle of MBWA is really a philosophy—a philosophy that says that the boss's job is to make sure of three things: first, that [the] staff understands what they are doing; second, that [the] staff has the tools they think they need to do the job; and last, that the boss lets the staff know he [or she] has an appreciation of what the employee is doing. . . In my book, the best reason for a boss's open door is so he [or she] can go out the door and walk around.[18]

Implicit in the principles behind MBWA is the realization that effectual management is contingent on information. In a very real sense, MBWA is a return to a much earlier management approach, but with a twist. Some of the first management theorists (Frederick Taylor, Frank and Lillian Gilbreth) were able to effect sizable increases in production by carefully analyzing the task in order to discern what tools and what methods would make the task more efficacious. MBWA goes a step further by asking the employee what he or she thinks would lead to improvement—thus learning from the most informed person and at the same time sending the message to that person that his or her opinion has value.

MBWA depicts manager as learner, as information-gatherer. It is not necessary for the MBWA manager to appear as omniscient. Nor does the MBWA manager leave his or her door open and wait for employees to come in with complaints or ideas; the MBWA goes to the staff—which is another message in itself.

The Dimensional Model of Management[19]

The dimensional model looks at managerial behavior along two axes: control and regard for others. The control axis has "dominance " at once extreme and "submission" at the other. Hence, the control measure describes the extent to which a manager is in charge, exercises control, directs the task.

The second axis examines the manager's relationship with others: from "hostility" at one pole to "warmth" at the other.

According to the dimensional model, a manager can be described as one of four types:

1. Dominant-Hostile: The dominant-hostile supervisor represents the "keep-them-running-scared"[20] school, which assumes—a la Theory X—that a tight rein works best. The dominant-hostile manager makes decisions unilaterally, on the assumption that he or she knows best what is needed and how to get it done. The bottom line is the bottom line.

2. Submissive-Hostile: The submissive-hostile manager is afraid to take a stand. Whereas the dominant-hostile manager uses top-down communication ("Here's how we're going to do this"), the submissive-hostile manager avoids communication whenever possible. He or she prefers the security of doing things as they have been done.

3. Submissive-Warm: The submissive-warm manager represents the immoderate embodiment of the human relations school. Getting along with staff is more important than setting direction. There is much interaction, but little real communication. In the desire to foster morale, the submissive-warm manager goes out of the way to avoid conflict.

4. Dominant-Warm: The dominant warm manager engages his or her staff in decision-making and planning. The needs and interests of the employee are linked to the goals of the organization. This is a participatory style of management that would not find MBWA to be a foreign idea.

The dimension system is clearly biased in favor of the fourth model, the dominant-warm. The name implies that the manager is in control but shares that control with subordinates within an ambience of trust. It assumes that employees want to be part of the planning and decision making, and that employees who are part of those processes will perform better. In all probability, those are safe assumptions.

Situational Leadership

Early management theory was clearly in the dominant camp: the manager should know best how to get the job done and impart that knowledge to his or her subordinates. More recent theory looked at management from the vantage point of the employee and his or her needs. Situational leadership attempts to bridge the two. Unlike Theory X, situational leadership assumes that some staff are motivated and want to achieve; they need to be given room to do so. Unlike Theory Y, situational leadership assumes that not all people are so motivated, and some will need direction and follow-up.

As depicted by one of its creators, Paul Hershey, situational leadership is comprised of four management types; these represent a gradient from the most to the least directive:

1. Telling: precise instructions, followed by close and regular observation of performance; appropriate for staff deemed unprepared or unwilling to take on responsibility.

2. Selling: the manager is still directive, but the staff person feels some sense of ownership over the task by virtue of the manager's explaining its importance and allowing the employee to ask for clarification.

3. Participating: used with staff who are motivated and capable but who need some counsel; the manager plays a supportive role, is less directive than the selling manager.

4. Delegating: as the name implies, the responsibility and authority to get the job done are invested in the staff person, who is judged both capable and motivated.

Situational leadership makes an implicit separation of supervision from accountability. It is possible to have staff who are held accountable with varying levels of supervision. The staff person who functions within the delegating mode and the person within the telling mode are both held accountable for their actions and accomplishments, However one receives a greater amount of supervision.[21]

Situational leadership is something of a misnomer; it is closer to situational management, for what is being considered is the nature of the interplay between supervisor and supervised. The main tenet of situational leadership is that the competent manager must read each situation to determine what managerial style is required. Some staff may always require a high degree of direction and indeed find that most comfortable. Others bristle at being told how to do the job and having their work monitored. Nonetheless, even the most capable and motivated staff may need direction in some circumstances—e.g., when given a new assignment or trying out a new set of skills.

Situational leadership (or management) puts demands on the manager, who must:

*   Be capable of modifying his or her management style to fit the occasion.
*   Assess each situation to determine which style will facilitate completion of the task in a timely and efficient manner.
*   Be cognizant of each employee's strengths, experiences, motivators.
*   Correctly ascertain not only if direction is needed but the amount of direction that is needed.

Considered earlier in this chapter was the question: "Under what conditions is it appropriate to delegate to others?" To the list provided, situational leadership would add: Delegate when the situation calls for it and not otherwise. The key determinant in situational leadership is not whether the manager has time to explain the task before delegating; it is whether delegating at all is the correct style to use.

MANAGE OR LEAD

In describing situational leadership, the distinction between leadership and management was alluded to. The aphorism commonly recounted to describe the distinction is this: *Managers do things right. Leaders do the right thing.*[22]

Simply stated, what this means is that managers are concerned with efficiency—with seeing that the product or service meets requirements, that the input (staff, equipment, money, other resources) results in the maximum output. Managers use human resources to meet the goals of the organization. By contrast, leadership "is any attempt to influence the behavior of another individual or group."[23] If managers are concerned with efficiency, leaders are focused on effectiveness—on making a difference.

The distinction does not stand up to rigorous scrutiny. Virtually all of management is an attempt to influence the behavior of another. For most organizations to meet their objectives and operational goals, it is incumbent on managers to get others to agree to work. To a varying degree, that means having some influence over the actions (i.e., behavior) of another human being. If that is leadership, it is also elemental to management.

The discrimination becomes even fuzzier with management consultant Peter Drucker's description of management as "the organ of leadership, direction and decision . . . ."[24] The distinction between leadership and management, however muddied it has become, is nonetheless worth making. It is possible to be a leader of people without being their manager. Whether it is possible to be a competent manager without being a leader is another question. The designers of the dimension model of management discussed earlier would (one can assume) argue that to succeed the manager needs to establish some direction and influence others to follow; that is implicit in the favored, Dominant-Warm model (otherwise it would be Submissive-Warm or at best Neutral-Warm).

"Doing the right thing" is thus insufficient. The manager who carries out organizational goals through the deployment of staff is arguably doing the right thing. Is he or she a leader by virtue of this achievement? Not necessarily.

A more useful definition is that provided by John Gardner in *On Leadership*. "Leadership is the process of persuasion or example by which an individual (or leadership team) induces a group to pursue objectives held by the leader or shared by the leader and his or her followers."[25] What makes Gardner's notion of leadership distinguishable from management are the "objectives held by the leader." Many persons in management positions do a creditable job of seeing that the staff assigned to them meet the objectives which those staff or the organization has set. They monitor, follow-up, discuss, exercise some control.

But they do not lead. They do not have goals of their own to which they induce others to ascribe. They do not have a vision. As Gardner notes:

> The individual with a gift for building a leadership team may successfully delegate . . . tasks to other members of the team. One function that cannot be delegated entirely is the envisioning of goals. Unless the leader knows where the whole venture is headed, it will not be possible to delegate . . . the other functions.[26]

There is one further way to isolate leadership from management. The leader, as contrasted with manager, is an embodiment of the goals and the vision which he or she seeks to achieve. When we think of those goals, we picture that individual—just as when we think of civil rights we see Martin Luther King in our mind's eye.

An elderly chairman of the board of a major Japanese company was once asked what his job was. His answer captures the image of leader as symbol: "I am the soul of this company," he said. "Through me the values pass."[27]

What does all this have to do with managing people, with cultivating an accomplished staff? There are three somewhat disparate implications:

1. **The chief staff person of the nonprofit organization needs to be a leader as well as a manager.**

It is not enough to assume that the leadership will come from the volunteer component of the organization. While volunteer leadership is an absolute requirement, it alone will not make for an outstanding organization. Instead, it can result in a disjuncture between board and CEO. If the board is capable of seeing and articulating a larger picture—a vision—and the CEO is not, the volunteer leadership may perceive a vacuum and move to fill it.

Said another way, for the organization to realize its overarching goals, the chief staff need to be able to perform some of the functions of leadership, inducing the staff, by persuasion or example, to buy into the larger picture.

The nonprofit CEO needs to be a leader within and among the volunteer leadership as well. Volunteers come and go; staff provide continuity. For the vision to postdate the current leadership, it is vital to have a CEO who can infuse excitement into new board members.

2. The nonprofit CEO needs to be a leader but not necessarily *the* leader.

Being CEO requires the ability to be politically apolitical. If the volunteer leadership sees the CEO as being too much the symbol of the organization and its goals, they may take one of two actions:

- Withdraw from active involvement;
- Attempt to diminish the role played by the CEO, even if that means replacing him or her.

3. The role of other senior staff must be considered in terms of leadership.

The nonprofit executive director should give careful thought to the type of staff which he or she wants in key management positions. Assuming the CEO has leadership qualities, he or she needs to ask if those same elements ought to be present in other senior staff. The advantages of hiring staff with leadership qualities are evident:

- They motivate those who report to them.
- They are often the source of new ideas, new strategies, new sources of funding.
- They make the organization an exciting place to work.

The disadvantages of having leaders among senior staff are equally apparent:

- They might compete with one another.
- They may prove threatening to boards and committees, especially those with a dearth of leadership.
- They may be difficult to manage, because they will have their own goals and ideas on how the organization should be run.

Shared leadership is an admirable concept. The nonprofit CEO will want to give serious thought to his or her ability and willingness to hire staff who will want a share.

TASKS FOR THE EFFECTIVE MANAGER IN THE '90s

Managing a nonprofit organization into the year 2000 will demand a blend of qualities. Listed below are an even dozen tasks for the effective manager:

Instill a Sense of Teamwork

The nonprofit CEO will need to instill an enthusiasm for teamwork not only among staff, but between staff and volunteers. In order to be responsive to potential threats and opportunities, the organization will be required to form teams across departments, between board and staff, between CEO and staff or volunteers. For the teams to work, the performance management system must reward team players.

Delegate

As nonprofits grow and become more complex, their CEOs must be on the lookout for staff with specialized skills. It is neither possible nor desirable for the chief staff person to be expert in all areas. He or she will be more of a generalist who hires capable personnel and then gives them the room to get the job done.

Empower

Empowering goes beyond delegation. The CEO who empowers his or her staff not only gives them responsibility for the completion of tasks, but also nurtures their aptitude. This will mean building the job around the person rather than the reverse.

Lead

The nonprofit CEO needs to have a vision for what the organization can become and the ability to share that vision with both volunteers and staff. There will be a delicate balance to be maintained—serving as a leader without being seen as too powerful by the volunteer board.

As a leader, the CEO serves as a mentor to others with less experience and seniority and is, both publicly and behind the scenes, an agent for change.

Communicate

Possessing good communication skills is such an important ability of the executive manager that it has its own chapter in this text. The nonprofit CEO must be able to interact positively with staff, volunteers, and the organization's publics. Communication implies active listening and a willingness to hear other points of view.

Manage a Diverse Workforce

The workforce will be older, browner, more female. The CEO of a nonprofit should embrace the diversity by modeling appropriate attitude and behavior, hiring and providing career ladders for the workforce of the year 2000.

The diverse workforce will also include the knowledgable worker: highly educated, well trained, and mobile. Traditional management styles may result in high turnover among such individuals.

Communication, leadership, empowerment will all come into play in finding, attracting, cultivating, and keeping top notch volunteers. So, too, will the capacity to express appreciation for time given to the organization.

Set the Standard for Quality

Within the for-profit business community, quality is already the byword; the nonprofit sector is close behind. Whether he or she employs an encompassing system such as Total Quality Management (TQM), quality circles, or other methods, the nonprofit CEO will be looked to as the standard setter and bearer of quality. Attracting top volunteers and sufficient resources will demand it.

Know the Market

While the chief staff person may not need an MBA in marketing, he or she will have to be conversant with marketing terminology and appreciate the differences, large and small, among various constituencies.

Assure the Organization's Financial Viability

The ability to garner sufficient contributions and other sources of funding, coupled with the wisdom to administer those funds prudently, will characterize the "marketable" nonprofit CEO of the '90s. As with marketing, the chief of staff will not necessarily be expected to be a certified fund raiser or accountant, but he or she must be cognizant of both fields and able to manage employees skilled in them.

Being able to convince the volunteer leadership of the importance of fund raising and sound fiscal management will be no less valued.

Juggle Multiple Priorities

Envision the circus juggler spinning plates on sticks. The nonprofit CEO will need equal facility in moving between priorities. Skills in planning, organization, and time management will be invaluable.

Act Ethically

Ethics and the bottom line have not always seen much of one another. In the decade ahead, however, ethics will be one measure of the bottom line. As with quality, it will be up to the nonprofit CEO to set the standard in both word and deed.

Be a Futurist

The CEO should read widely, ask questions, and be capable of synthesizing information from numerous sources. It will be imperative to see trends as they emerge, staying far enough ahead of the curve to be able to recognize and respond to opportunity and threat.

NOTES

1. Peter F. Drucker, *The New Realities: In Government and Politics, in Economics and Business, in Society and World View* (New York: Harper & Row, Publishers, 1989), 229.

2. Drucker, 228–230.

3. Tom Peters, "Herman Miller's Performance Reviews Are as Unique as Its Furniture," *Tom Peters on Achieving Excellence*, 3 (July 1988): 2.

4. Kenneth Blanchard, speaking at the first Future Leaders conference, sponsored by the American Society of Association Executives (ASAE), June 1988.

5. Blanchard, ASAE Future Leaders conference.

6. Janet G. Crane, "Getting the Performance You Want," *Association Management*, 43 (February 1991): 27.

7. Crane, 27–29.

8. Henry Mintzberg, *The Nature of Management Work* (New York: Harper & Row, 1973), 79.

9. Tom Peters, "How Stone Delegates 'Total Authority'," *Tom Peters on Achieving Excellence*, 3 (August 1988): 6.

10. Day-timers, Inc., "The Art of Effective Delegation," *Chats*, no volume (1990): 5.

11. Frederick Herzberg, "One More Time: How Do You Motivate Employees." In *The Great Writings in Management and Organizational Behavior*, 2d ed., Louis E. Boone and Donald D. Bowen, eds. (New York: McGraw-Hill, 1987), 174–176.

12. E. F. Schumacher, "Buddhist Economics." In *Technology and the Future*, 5th ed., Albert H. Teich, ed. (New York: St. Martin's Press, 1990), 224.

13. Herzberg, 177–182.

14. Gary M. Stern, "Ten Steps to Help Raise Staff Morale," *Communication Briefings*, 8 (August 1989): 8a–8b. Some of the ideas for the section on morale building were inspired by this article.

15. Donald McGregor, *The Human Side of Enterprise* (New York: McGraw-Hill, 1960), 33–35.

16. McGregor, 47–49.

17. Richard L. Daft, *Organizational Theory and Design*, 3rd ed. (New York: West Publishing Company, 1989), 60–61.

18. James H. Lavenson, "How to Earn an MBWA Degree," *Vital Speeches of the Day*, 42 (April 15, 1976): 412.

19. Robert E. Lefton, V. R. Buzzotta, Manuel Sherberg, and Dean L. Karraker, *Effective Motivation through Performance Appraisal*. (New York: John Wiley & Sons, 1977), 16–21.

20. Lefton et al., 18.

21. Paul Hershey, *The Situational Leader* (New York: Warner Books, Inc., 1984), 62–71.

22. Warren Bennis and Bert Nanus, *Leaders: The Strategies for Taking Charge* (New York: Harper & Row, 1985), 21.

23. Hershey, 16.

24. Peter F. Drucker, *Management: Tasks, Responsibilities, Practices* (New York: Harper & Row, 1974), 17.

25. John W. Gardner, *On Leadership* (New York: The Free Press, 1990), 1.

26. John W. Gardner, "Leadership: An Overview," No. 12 in the series of *Leadership Papers* (Washington, DC: Independent Sector, 1988), 6.

27. Blanchard, ASAE Future Leaders conference.

Chapter 8
Communication:
Creating a Knowledge
Industry in Your
Organization

EXECUTIVE SUMMARY

This separate chapter on communications has been prepared because this topic is extremely important to the nonprofit. The following subjects are covered within: Understanding why effective communication is so difficult; listening, a test of listening skills, and listening strategies; establishing a climate for communication; learning how to overcome the anxiety of public speaking and the skills needed to speak effectively before a group.

Ask the employees of almost any organization—multinational corporation, federal agency, state association, local hospital—to describe a recurrent problem within their organization, and poor communication will be on virtually everyone's short list. They may not describe it exactly in those terms—they may say, instead:

- "Decisions are made in a vacuum."
- "Top management went ahead with the new performance management system, only to find out that everyone hated it. We could have told them that, if they'd taken the time to ask."
- "The only time we hear from the boss is when he (she) has something negative to say."
- "Nobody says what's really on their minds, because they know what'll happen if they do."

Why is it so difficult to maintain good communication among staff? The following apocryphal story, entitled "Operation Halley's Comet," provides some clues:

A colonel issues the following directive to his executive officer: Tomorrow evening at approximately 2000 hours Halley's Comet will be visible in this area—an event that occurs only once every 75 years. Have the troops assemble on the parade ground in fatigues, and I will explain this rare phenomenon to them. If it rains, we will not be able to see it. Instead, assemble the men in the gymnasium and I will show them a film of it.

The executive officer, in turn, to the company commander: By order of the colonel, tomorrow at 2000 hours, Halley's Comet will appear above the parade grounds. If it rains, have the troops assemble in fatigues and proceed to the theater, where this rare phenomenon will take place, something that occurs only once every 75 years.

The company commander then speaks to his lieutenant: By order of the colonel, at 2000 hours tomorrow evening the phenomenal Halley's Comet will appear in the theater. If it rains in the parade grounds, the colonel will give another order, something that occurs only once every 75 years.

Says the lieutenant to his first sergeant: Tomorrow at 2000 hours, the colonel will appear in fatigues in the theater with Halley's Comet, something that occurs every 75 years. If it rains, the colonel will order the Comet into the parade grounds.

Sergeant in turn to his squad: When it rains tomorrow at 2000 hours by order of the colonel, the phenomenal 75-year-old General Halley, accompanied by the colonel, will drive his Comet through the parade grounds theater in fatigues.[1]

The point of this somewhat whimsical story is that communication, however well intended, can easily go awry.

GOOD COMMUNICATION IS HARD WORK

Why does it seem to be so difficult to create a situation of continual communication flow?

Infoglut

Part of the problem in any organization has to do with the sheer volume. Consider these statistics:

* Children graduating in the Information Age will already be exposed to more information than their grandparents were in their lifetimes.
* We are seeing a change of values and relationships within one lifetime that might once have taken 500 years.
* There is more information in one weekday edition of *The New York Times* than the average person was likely to have encountered in an entire lifetime in the seventeenth century.

- There are some 7,000 scientific articles written in the United States *every day*.
- According to futurist Marvin Cetron, the body of knowledge will double four times between 1988 and the year 2000.[2]

All of us suffer from this infoglut. Even if our intentions are good, we simply cannot keep up with the information that we feel we need, much less share it with others on our staff and within the organization.

Power

If information overload contributes to the difficulty in maintaining the communication flow, so, too, does the fact that information is power. That's what makes rumor mills so powerful; they are a source of presumably reliable information. The director wields power in his or her dealings with the board because he or she knows so much about the organization's inner workings. [3]

Departments become "silos of private information." Department directors hold power because of the information which they obtain at the weekly meetings with the director. And so on.

Why do we sometimes feel so powerless when we sit on the runway waiting interminably for the plane to taxi and take off?

Why do we get so frustrated when we sit in the waiting room of a hospital reading old copies of *Women's Day*, not knowing whether we'll be there for ten minutes or an hour and ten minutes?

Why do we feel so childish dealing with specialists in any field, be it medicine or auto mechanics, who use terminology to explain something about which we have no comprehension? Because they—the airline pilot, the hospital staff, the specialist—have information that we don't have and we feel they're lording it over us.

Some employees understand this better than others. They realize that if they are in the pipeline, they have a real, if intangible, advantage over others even on their level within the organization.

Lack of Useful Strategies

One of the consistent reasons why organizations suffer from a lack of good internal communication is that they have not established workable communication channels and strategies:

"I just can't understand it," says the CEO. "We hold regular meetings with the senior staff. We've got an in-house newsletter that goes to all employees. We encourage staff to comment, anonymously if they wish, in our suggestion box. And all I hear is people saying they don't know what's going on."

No two organizations are exactly alike. What works for one may or may not work for another. Not everyone reads, and what we read we may retain only if we link the information in some way—if the information has value for us. We have read that the annual goals and objectives are being submitted to the board at its February meeting, but if we didn't make the connection—that our department's objectives must be written by year-end in order to make the February deadline—what we read would pass like sand through a sieve.

WHAT VALUE DOES COMMUNICATION SERVE?

It is worth taking a minute to remind ourselves of the reasons why good communication is important. There are at least three cogent reasons:

1. **Communication increases the chances of making good decisions.**

   The number one value of information may be that it improves decision-making. Nothing is more frustrating to your staff than to see a decision made, say, at the board level, with partial information. It's often a bad decision as a result. And the staff is understandably frustrated over not having been asked to provide input.

   The essence of success in an organization is the ability to plan. And the process of planning is little more than gathering information and then using that information to chart a course of action.

2. **Information is basic to completing most jobs well.**

   In virtually every position within an organization, there is a body of information that is crucial to performing that job well. For the secretarial pool it may be knowing not only how to use the word processing software, but what expectations the director has in terms of style and format. For the professional staff it is both a thorough grounding in an individual discipline and an up-to-date grasp on the issues and trends affecting it. For a board it is a clear understanding of the organization's purpose and mission, familiarity with the bylaws and related policies, and a shared sense of what the organization can become.

   For all, staff and volunteers alike, it is a stated agreement on expectations, so that there exists a yardstick on which to measure performance. How many times have problems been created because those involved were operating under a different set of assumptions of what constituted satisfactory achievement? This discovery is often made only after the damage is done.

3. Information provides a sense of belonging.

Too much emphasis is put on who needs to know and not enough about who wants to know. The person driving the van may not need to know the long-range plan of the organization inside and out, but understanding the reason why the organization exists and the value that it has for society and for him personally—can only make him a better employee.

The donors to a new pediatric wing may not need to know about the award that the cardiac unit just won, but the more they learn about what is being accomplished, the more they will feel part of the family; and the more they feel part of the family, the greater the organization's chance to share of their largess.

Instead of asking "Who needs to know?," one would be better off asking: "Is there any reason why everyone shouldn't know this information?" If not, why not share it? Let those receiving the information tell you when they're overloaded.

CULTIVATING THE ART OF LISTENING

People are, to put it bluntly, lousy listeners. They fiddle with papers while talking on the phone. They watch TV with one eye and read the paper with the other. They are constantly saying to others (spouse, friend, coworker), "Don't you remember that we talked about . . . ." "I thought we agreed that we'd meet on Tuesday about that." "Don't you remember—tonight's the night I have to work late because the committee's going out to dinner."

Listening may begin with hearing, but it doesn't end there. To be an effective listener, one has to—

- Interpret the message;
- Evaluate its contents, filtering what has been heard, linking the message to other, relevant pieces of data; and
- Respond.

Being a good listener is not a native skill. Babies listen well, to everything they hear. Their attentiveness to sounds, to the spoken word, is part of what makes them so charming. But they lack the contextual cues to make sense of very much of what they hear. They cannot evaluate the content.

Unfortunately, as they mature and can interpret what is being said, they begin to hone the skill (if it can be called that) of hearing but not listening, a skill that they master as they reach their teenage years if not before.

Why are people such poor listeners?

- Frankly, they're egoists.

  They tend to think the document they're working on is more important than the staff person who interrupts with a problem.

  The result is that they sort of half-listen, sneaking glances at the page in front of them, muttering occasional "Uh huhs."

- They have not practiced the art of good listening.

  They are just coming to realize how poorly they listen. And admitting they have a problem is a necessary first step.

- They are, in John Naisbett's phrase, drowning in a sea of information.

  Precisely because there is so much information all around—and so much NOISE—managers need to cultivate new ways of listening if they are going to manage effectively in the 1990s.

HOW GOOD A LISTENER ARE YOU?

Give yourself the self-test in Figure 6.[4] For each statement, choose from 1 (almost never) to 5 (almost all the time):

Figure 6. Are You a Good Listener?

Listening Behavior	*Rank*
I am frequently uninterested in the material that I am hearing.	1 2 3 4 5
I find that I am often mentally evaluating the speaker while he or she is talking.	1 2 3 4 5
I tend to interrupt other persons, especially in a one-to-one conversation.	1 2 3 4 5
I find that I miss the main argument or point being made because I have concentrated on the specific details.	1 2 3 4 5
My body is often in a slumped (slouched) position when I am listening to someone talk.	1 2 3 4 5
I am easily distracted while in conversation with others.	1 2 3 4 5
I tend to look at material on my desk from time to time in a conversation, even if it does not relate to the topic being discussed.	1 2 3 4 5
I do other work while talking on the telephone.	1 2 3 4 5

Find yourself circling a lot of "5's"? You may have—excuse me!—you may have a listening problem.

LISTENING STRATEGIES

Here are five ways that you can become a better listener immediately.

1. **Consciously put aside what you are doing.**

   Look at the person(s) with whom you are talking. Close the notebook in front of you. Sit up. Pay attention. Body language and metalanguage convey messages as powerful as the apparent spoken word.

   Do you value the person with whom you are speaking? Then show it by giving him or her your full attention. There is no higher form of flattery.

2. **Ask questions or make statements from time to time to be sure that you are capturing the main thrust of others' comments.**

   "Let's see if I hear you correctly." "Let me try to summarize what I think we've agreed to." "Would it be fair to say that where we have come is the opinion that . . . ." "I sense we have decided to . . . . Is that correct?"

3. **"When it comes to listening, the mind is like a parachute. It only functions when it's open."** [5]

   Translation: you can't be a good listener if you've already decided the person speaking has nothing to say. Communication requires at least two players—sender and receiver. If you're not willing to receive the information being sent, process it, interpret it, consider it, and then respond, you're not listening.

4. **Don't dominate the conversation.**

   That doesn't mean you have to sit and let the other party drone on. You can be an effective listener by asking questions that direct the discussion. And don't rush the person speaking or attempt to finish his or her sentences.

   But test yourself. The next time you're meeting with someone, especially someone reporting to you, keep a running mental log on who's doing the talking.

5. **Build trust.**

   Recall the story of "The Emperor's New Clothes"? What the new clothes actually amounted to was the emperor's "birthday suit." But no one in the kingdom had the courage to tell him that he was parading in the altogether for fear of reprisal.

Building trust is easier said than done. You're going to have to be capable of hearing unpleasant news without shooting the messenger. That doesn't mean you have to subject yourself to gripe sessions in which discontented staff dump indiscriminately on the organization and its leadership. But it does mean that the organization has an atmosphere of trust, wherein employees feel safe in speaking honestly and openly about what they believe to be important issues.

If all that's in the suggestion box are ways to improve the lunch room, examine the climate of trust—or fear—that has been fostered.

SIX STEPS TO ESTABLISHING A CLIMATE FOR COMMUNICATION

Assume you perceive that the communication climate in your organization is less than attractive. There are six sequential but interrelated steps which you can take.

Step One: Determine The Goals

What do you (plural) want to accomplish? What would constitute, in your estimation and that of your staff, a climate supportive of real communication?

You may want to use one of the group process techniques addressed in Chapter 7 to come to some agreement on what an atmosphere of effective communication might look like.

Step Two: Identify the Problem(s)

What factors inhibit your organization's creating the desired climate? Are the causes structural? Attitudinal? Do they come from the top? From the department directors?

Is there agreement as to what ought to be communicated and to whom?

Step Three: Define the Parameters

Four areas might be addressed as you define the parameters within which to create and measure effective communication flow within your organization:

Skills necessary

For example, will it be necessary for everyone on staff to learn to use electronic mail? How about teaching some basics of memo writing, or interpersonal and conflict management skills?

Standards

What are the minimal expectations? For example:

- "Every department director should meet with his or her staff for information-sharing at least twice a month."
- "Information to be included in Board of Directors meetings should be in the director's hands no later than two weeks in advance of each board meeting."

Resources

In order to achieve a minimal level of communication, will it be necessary to:

- Reserve the conference room for an all-staff, no-holds-barred meeting once a month?
- Create an ombuds position on staff with whom employees can speak freely, who will serve as an advocate to the senior management?
- Provide computer access to all staff in order to have everyone on electronic mail?
- Budget for a once a year retreat?

Rewards and punishments

In addition to the obvious rewards—improved morale, better productivity—what kinds of specific rewards might be provided? Some ideas:

- Dinner for two for the person coming up with the best suggestion on how to improve communication;
- A "Communicator of the Month" award;
- Recognition at a board meeting for the department director receiving the highest rating on a communications effectiveness audit.

The nonprofit CEO needs to consider negative consequences as well. What (if anything) should befall the individual or the unit that fails to improve its communication? While the term "punishment" sounds a bit harsh ("Put him on the rack!"), that is in effect what ought to be considered. In other words, what degree of uncooperative behavior is tolerable? No overt punishment may be necessary. Publish the results of the communications effectiveness audit; seeing his or her department at the bottom of the list may be disincentive enough.

Step Four: Describe an Implementation Plan

Lay out the specific strategies and the timelines for their implementation. What are the forces that might work for or against achieving the objectives; what strategies might be developed either to capture the forces in favor or to negate those against?

The plan should be a staff-wide product. Don't get a communications effectiveness plan off on the wrong foot by failing to communicate with everyone who will be affected.

Step Five: Implement

Give the institution enough time—perhaps a year, in which to get the new communications systems into place. And don't forget to include funding in the next budget cycle. [6]

Step Six: Evaluate and Revise

SPEAKING IN PUBLIC

For many executives in both the for-profit and nonprofit world, the prospect of having to make a speech elicits a fear normally reserved for walking through minefields. The 1977 *Book of Lists* rated public speaking as our number one fear. Dying came in sixth.

That is unfortunate, to say the least. This is an age of information. Communication skills will be among the highest valued commodities of nonprofit executives in the year 2000. Being able to speak for the organization, to convince others of its worth, to invite others to become part of its mission—these abilities may prove essential to the viability of the nonprofit organization in the next decade.

Getting Past the Fear

So the question is not "How can I avoid having to make a speech in public?, but "How can I learn to overcome my terror of doing so?" Here are three tips that practiced speakers find useful:

1. **Practice. Practice. Practice.**

   Evading speech-making opportunities only heightens the tension of those times when we simply cannot get out of a talk. If there is a Toastmasters Club in your community, you may want to join it—or start one of your own. Toastmasters is designed to help people get over the anxiety; members provide a supportive setting for each other's talks.

Practicing the speech before a mirror can be useful. Make eye contact with yourself. Be sure you're standing erect and not fussing with your jacket or twisting your hair. Practice from notes until you need to refer to them only occasionally as a prompt. If you have a camcorder, have someone tape your presentation; then review in the safety of your own office or home.

2. **Yawn.**

It's nearly impossible to keep your face tense and yawn at the same time. Whistling can work as well.

3. **Practice relaxation techniques.**

There are several techniques that can be used—visioning (picturing yourself speaking competently and confidently in front of a crowd); deep breathing; meditation; anchoring (in which the desired feeling of confidence is anchored—i.e., linked—with some physical manifestation, such as a thumbs-up signal).

4. **Remove the distance between yourself and the audience.**

If you are making a presentation as part of a conference, make it a point to get to know others in attendance so that you will have some friendly faces to rely on. Before your session starts, introduce yourself to people in the audience. Find out something about them—where they work, what brought them to the conference. If the numbers allow, you may want to have members of the audience introduce themselves to one another.

Get out from behind the podium. Return to it from time to time to remind yourself of your next point, if necessary, but don't hide behind it. That will only increase your feeling of being the only person in the room who is talking.

Speaking with Effect

What orators lack in depth, they make up to you in length.
                                        —*Charles de Montesquieu*

If there is one thing worse in public speaking than speakers who are nervous and underprepared, it is speakers who are convinced that they are a font of wisdom. They pontificate, insulting the audience both in terms of its intelligence and the value of its time.

Assuming it is likely that you are going to be called upon to make a speech from time to time or better that you have made the commitment to become more visible in order to make your organization more visible, you will need to garner some tools. Listed below are ten tools for the effective public speaker.

Develop a Speech File

Get in the habit of clipping articles, statistics, cartoons, graphs that might be of use in making a talk. File by probable speech topics.

Supplement the file with a ready-reference library—*Bartlett's Familiar Quotations*, books of aphorisms, sources of anecdotes.

Know Your Audience

When you agree to a talk, make it a point to learn what you can about the probable audience. What is the age range? What is their level of knowledge of the topic about which you will be speaking? And their level of interest?

What expectations will the audience have? Are you essentially an after dinner space filler, a keynote who should get participants enthused, an imparter of knowledge? Would the audience be most comfortable with a formal presentation, or would an interactive talk that involves the audience be more appropriate? What level of documentation will be required? Will the audience want verification of key points?

Determine Your Focus

What the speech should achieve is as important as the words themselves. Purpose should dictate content. What do you want to accomplish: a better understanding of the topic, a shift in attitude, a willingness to modify behavior? And are you seeking to confirm what the audience may already believe, challenging it to rethink its assumptions, or changing them in some way?

The confirming speech is basically a "feel good" talk. The audience goes away refreshed, feeling positive about themselves. An example: speaking before a group of volunteers, whom you want to reward for service rendered.

The challenging talk is designed to stir things up a bit. The fact that you are presenting a challenge is not necessarily confrontational; you may challenge assumptions that have caused some anxiety. Or you may be offering novel paths to traditional goals.[7]

Talks designed to effect change can be the most difficult to achieve—especially if what you propose is potentially threatening.

Write It Down

Accomplished speakers will tell you not to read the speech. It will come across as read, and the audience will wonder why you didn't just pass it out and let them go home.

However, it may be helpful, especially if you are unaccustomed to public speaking or unfamiliar with the topic, to write out at least a detailed outline of what you will say. There are a number of useful software packages that can be used to prepare outlines; they allow the user to move material from one heading to another, collapse the outline or expand it, and even provide a table of contents.

Writing out the speech offers two other benefits:

1. It will mitigate anxiety.

    The "I don't know what I'm going to say" phobia can be significantly lessened when what you are going to say is in print. Having the speech written out provides a psychological safety net; "I can always read it if I have to." That is rarely the way it plays out, but it is comforting to know that the possibility exists.

2. You will have a clearer sense of timing.

    The speaker who has been allotted 45 minutes and finds that he or she is going to be finished in 25 minutes can literally feel the ulcers forming in his or her duodenum. Conversely, the speaker who tells his or her audience he or she had a lot more to cover but that "time has gotten away from us" is asking for an on-the-spot lynching. Writing out the speech helps to avoid either fate.

Know Who Is Making the Speech

Simply put, are you being invited as a spokesperson for your organization or as an individual? And if as an individual, will it be perceived by some as if you are speaking for the organization?

As a corollary: what implicit (unstated) goal do you hope to achieve? Are you seeking to better position your organization? To be seen as a gifted orator? As a compassionate nonprofit executive? Answering these questions will help to determine what persona you assume. That is not to say that your speech is an act; rather, that you are capable of filling a number of roles. Speaking is not merely talking. You may not feel comfortable making a dramatic presentation but remember that you are there at least in part to entertain as well as to inform.

Provide a Visual Accompaniment

Statistics vary, but generally speaking a person recalls only about 10 percent of what he or she reads, 20 percent of what is heard, 30 percent of what is seen, and 50 percent of what is heard and seen. That argues cogently for the use of overhead projections, slides, charts, animation, simulation, and handout material.

Don't provide the audience with everything. If you are using slides or overheads or a handout, use them to reinforce key points. The handout can be an open outline of your presentation, with space for the participants to fill in as you talk. Colored pictorial slides, cartoons, and graphic displays can all augment the points you wish to make. If you do use slides or overhead projections to display salient facts, keep these pointers in mind:

- Make the visual readable to the person in the last row.

    Be sure the typeface is large and bold. If you are speaking before a group of 20 make the overhead visible to an audience of 40.
- Keep the material uncluttered.

    An overhead or slide should have no more than about six lines of copy. There is nothing more frustrating than trying to follow a speaker who is referring to an overhead projection that looks vaguely like a map of the Paris sewer system.
- Use the medium sparingly.

    Whether it be slide or overhead or computerized projection, after 45 minutes any visual medium becomes a visual tedium. Visual material should complement and reinforce the presentation, not be the presentation.

Give the Listener Some Cues

Written language offers the reader organizational cues: topic headings, capitalization and bold face print, new paragraphs. Cues alert the reader to a movement in the train of thought.

Oral language needs to provide similar kinds of cues. They can be overt: "I'd like to talk with you for a few minutes about [topic to be discussed]." They can be verbal clues: "However . . ." "Maybe. And maybe not . . ."

And they can be nonverbal cues. For example pausing before making a main point or gesturing to signify: "Beats me," "Why?," "Victory," "Power."

Use Conversational Speech

While then Vice President Spiro T. Agnew may have snared headlines with his use of "nattering nabobs of negativity," he also came across as something of a buffoon who was reciting the words of a speechwriter. That is not to say that for a speech to be effective it must be in plain vanilla language. To the contrary ringing phrases are often the hallmarks of a memorable speech. But the speech needs to fit the speaker. It was difficult to believe that Agnew used words such as "nabob," and one wondered if he understood their meaning. William F. Buckley possesses a large vocabulary; for him to avoid using it would be equally incongruous.

Some of the most noteworthy speakers in recent time have perfected the speech patterns and vocabulary of their origins and cultivated those as their milieus. Senator Sam Ervin created the pose of a country lawyer. Martin Luther King employed the stirring manner of a black Baptist minister.

In the instances just mentioned, the successful speakers have been those who cultivated the best of their abilities: building on their backgrounds and experiences, refining the language and vocabulary with which they were accustomed into an art form.

Speak from the Heart

Not every speech is—or should be—designed to evoke emotion, but even rather abstract concepts can be made more clear by personal example. If you are representing your organization and cannot impart the excitement and the enthusiasm of its mission, there is either something wrong with the mission or with you as its spokesperson. Use examples from personal experience. They will shorten the distance between you and your audience.

Take Some Risks

Shakespeare, in *Measure for Measure*, wrote that "Our doubts are traitors/And make us lose the good we oft might win/By fearing to attempt." In their professional lives, many have achieved goals that loomed large before they set out to accomplish them, which then seemed relatively small in retrospect. There is no way to become even a competent public speaker, much less a skilled presenter, without speaking in public.

PARTING THOUGHTS

For the organization to thrive, it must have shared values, and shared goals. If values and goals are the organization's lifeblood, communication channels, both formal and informal, are its vessels. Communication has always been a valued skill. In the Information Age, it is a critical one.

NOTES

1. Appreciation is expressed to Frederick Spahr and Irma Brosseau for bringing to the author's attention the story of "Operation Halley's Comet."

2. Terrence Cannings, "Visions for the 90's," *CUE Newsletter*, 12 (March/April 1990): 1.

3. Glenn E. Hayes, "Quality and Productivity: Challenges for Management." In *Readings in Management*, Philip B. DuBose, ed. (Englewood Cliffs, NJ: Prentice-Hall, Inc., 1988): 17.

4. The listening inventory is loosely based on one developed by Arthur K. Robertson, consultant and teacher of effective listening skills.

5. Richard Koonce, "Listening 101, Part Two," *Executive Update*, no volume (March 1990): 63.

6. David W. Miller. "Staff Communication Networks." A workshop conducted for the Greater Washington Society of Association Executives, Washington, DC, 1989.

7. Alan M. Perlman, "Effective Speechwriting: Ten Mega-Tips." Speech before the International Association of Business Communicators, March 8, 1989.

Chapter 9
How to Run a
Productive Meeting

Even the best meeting becomes unproductive after an hour and a half.
—*Old Jungle Saying*

EXECUTIVE SUMMARY

Which of the following statements is more accurate: (a) Meetings are the way an organization does business. Without meetings there would be no planning and no communication. (b) Meetings are the reason that nothing gets done in the organization.

There is truth to both. The solution is not to abandon all meetings, although it is healthy to question the need for them on an individual basis. The solution is to make them productive. This chapter describes the roles that those convening or facilitating the meeting should play, as well as some of the roles that other meeting participants often play within meetings; group process techniques; and practical tips for making the meeting productive and keeping it on track.

Picture this scene: Monday morning, 11:00 am. You have been sitting in a regular, weekly staff meeting since 9:00 and the agenda still has three more items which will need to be postponed until the following week. Of the ten senior staff who are supposed to be part of these weekly meetings, seven are present. About average.

There is a palpable air of tension in the room. There has already been one run-in between the director of accounting and the head of the development office over who's responsible for accurate maintenance of donor records—a discussion of only passing interest to the rest of the group.

You had hoped to devote a fair portion of the meeting to an initial consideration of the goals and objectives for the next year, but the tenor of the meeting does not lend itself to the kind of upbeat discussion that you were hoping for.

Some of the reasons why this meeting and others like it are less than productive are probably larger than what's wrong with the meeting itself—conflicting personalities, time pressures, uneven commitment to the overall organizational goals. But there is much that can be done to make the time spent in meetings not only more productive, but more amicable as well.

KEY ROLES AND BEHAVIORS

In order to conduct a more fruitful meeting, it is helpful to understand the different roles that people play in meetings. Below are some roles for those charged with the meetings' success:

Meeting Convener (Leader)

The pivotal role in the meeting, of course, is that of the convener, who is typically also the individual who conducts the meeting. The meeting convener is responsible for planning the meeting, conducting it, and evaluating its outcomes. Specifically, the meeting convener *sets the agenda*—making it clear what the purposes of the meeting will be (preferably when the date for the meeting is established) and laying out the objectives that will be accomplished.

In order to fulfill this agenda-setting role, the convener:

1. Informs all participants of the meeting's time and place.

2. Prepares and distributes a written agenda.

3. Opens the meeting, reviewing the agenda, so that each participant knows by what measures the meeting will by judged to have concluded successfully.

4. Concludes the meeting with a summary of what was discussed, highlighting tasks which were agreed upon, timeframes, and dates for future meetings.

This is not to say that the meeting convener dictates. Everyone participating in the meeting should have an opportunity to suggest items for the agenda (or future agendas, if the list becomes too extensive). Attending a meeting that fulfills only the objectives of the convener is doomed from its start; frankly, there are more important ways to spend time. Having to attend a meeting that seems to fulfill the interests of only the person in charge doesn't suggest that the convener values the time of others. The other role of the meeting convener is to *encourage participation by the full membership of the group*—showing respect for the opinions of others, accepting their comments.

Encouraging participation does not translate into letting one person dominate; to the contrary, that tends to discourage full participation. The convener needs to tactfully keep the meeting on task, balancing the need to give everyone a chance to speak his or her piece with the concomitant need to keep the meeting from turning into a diatribe or wandering down someone's personal emotional tour.

This implies an ability on the part of the convener to address problems that arise during the meeting. "It's clear that this is an issue that is laden with a lot of emotion for several of us. I'm wondering if we might discuss it in a smaller meeting where we can concentrate on it alone, and in the interest of time move on to the next item on the agenda."

Facilitator

In most of the instances in which organization members participate in a meeting, the role of facilitator is played by the meeting convener. Technically, a facilitator is an objective, disinterested party whose sole function is to see that the meeting meets its objectives, without actually participating in the discussion itself. While the typical organization may rarely use a formal facilitator, it is useful to incorporate the tasks that the facilitator should play into the conduct of the meeting. These include:

- Keeping the discussion to the point, on time, and of interest to the majority
- Posing questions that serve the purposes of the meeting

Some examples of the kinds of questions which the facilitator might pose include:

1. To initiate the discussion—"Does anyone have a thought on how we might address this issue?" or "Let's take a couple of minutes to brainstorm on some new ways to address the issue of morale."

2. To hear from members who have not spoken—"Is there someone who's not had a chance to express his or her idea?" or (Name,) "I don't think we've given you a chance to say anything on this topic . . . ."

3. To reduce the domination of the meeting by a minority viewpoint— "Thanks, (name of dominating person), for some good ideas. Who else has something to contribute on this point?" or (Name,) "I don't want to lose your thought. Let's hear from some others in the group and then pick up on it again as time allows."

4. To focus the discussion—"Let's look again at the goals of this meeting to be sure we're on track. As you'll recall from the first chart ....!" or "I wonder if it would be useful to summarize the discussion to this point to be sure we're on track."

5. To keep the group discussion moving along: "I'm mindful of the hour. Perhaps we should move on to another topic in order to be sure we complete the objectives of this meeting." or "Is there an aspect of this issue that we've neglected?"

   If yes, go to it; if not, move on to some other agenda item.

6. To help the group evaluate its progress—"It feels as though we may be getting a little bogged down. Any ideas on how we might avoid doing so for the rest of the meeting?" or "Let's conclude the meeting by taking a couple of minutes to suggest some ways in which we might improve the operations of our next meeting."

7. To help bring the group to a decision—"I sense that we're coming to consensus on this. Is that right?" or "Let's review briefly what we've agreed upon to this point."

Some Other Roles People Play in Meetings (Both Negative and Positive) [1]

In any meeting, one or more of the following role "types" may appear. Recognizing them makes the job of running the meeting easier.

Silent Observer

As contrasted with the outside observer, who can play a legitimate role in helping to evaluate the meeting, the silent observer sees it as his or her role to say little or nothing. Why? Perhaps because he or she truly has little to offer; but more likely, because by not saying anything, the silent observer is not vested in the outcome.

While they do not contribute to the discussion, silent observers provide a warning light. Ask yourself why some are not participating. Is it because they fear the outcome of the meeting (perhaps some change which they perceive is coming)? Is it because of the way the meeting is being conducted? Is the behavior consistent with their behavior in other contexts?

Middle Child

Students of birth order have observed that the middle child in a family (the second of three, the third of five) often plays a conciliating, mediating role. He or she attempts to give others the benefit of the doubt, may intervene in conflict situations in order to make peace, and generally operates by the dictum of Thumper in the movie "Bambi": "If you can't say anything nice, don't say anything at all."

The middle child can be a helpful member of the group by ameliorating any conflict, but he or she can prove a detriment if that behavior keeps the group from grappling with thorny issues that need to be aired.

The Willow

As the name implies, the willow bends in the direction in which the wind blows. The willow may be a conformist, who by nature fears taking a position that might prove controversial; "brown nose," who says whatever he or she thinks will please the boss; or a yes man, cousin to the brown noses, who agrees first with one and then another point-of-view.

There are ways to draw out the true opinions of willows, if that is important; employ a strategy of the Nominal Group Technique, asking each member of the group to jot down a few ideas and then offering one in turn that has not been mentioned.

The Leading Lady (Leading Man)

This meeting participant likes to hear herself or himself talk and monopolizes the discussion, sometimes trying to convince others of his or her opinion. They may suggest that they sense themselves to be "speaking for the group."

It is essential to a productive meeting that this individual not dominate the discussion; otherwise the meeting will neither elicit the full range of ideas possible nor leave everyone with a positive feeling about what was accomplished. The roles just described should prove useful to the facilitator.

EFFECTIVE GROUP PROCESS TECHNIQUES

There are several proven techniques to facilitate group discussion and group consensus. Each has its own pluses and minuses. None should be used in every meeting. In addition to some techniques already described (future wheel, Normal Group Technique), here are two more.

Brainstorming

Brainstorming encourages maximal input on a problem—literally, a storm of ideas from which to make a decision. Brainstorming provides the group with a wide range of options, each of which at least initially is received with equal value by the group.

Underpinning the concept of brainstorming are these points:

- Many ideas are preferable to a few ideas.

  Out of the generation of a lot of ideas, a few gems will emerge.

- If you (singular or plural) criticize one member's ideas, you may inhibit that person and probably others as well from making any additional comments.

  The facilitator or convener who says he or she wants an open discussion and then is critical of every idea presented need not be surprised if the meeting fails to generate much information.

- Ideas beget ideas.

  A certain synergy occurs in brainstorming, with the totality of the ideas proposed being greater than the sum of the parts.

How Brainstorming Works:

1. The facilitator explains the purpose of the session, reviewing what is hoped will be accomplished, and by what means. The issue or problem at hand is briefly described.

2. The groundrules are reviewed:

   - Every idea has value and will be recorded;
   - Members of the group should refrain from commenting on the ideas of others either affirmatively or negatively;
   - Variations on an idea are encouraged and will be recorded as new ideas;
   - There will be no attempt to group ideas as they are being presented.

3. Ideas are captured visually as presented by members of the group until all ideas have been elicited.

   Each idea should be recorded as stated by the author. Avoid numbering the ideas or in any way creating a list that suggests that some ideas are more valued than others.

   Do not be alarmed by silence. Good ideas require thought.

4. When it appears that all ideas have been presented, ask if any item needs clarification.

5. Discuss.

Storyboarding

Sometimes referred to as compression planning, storyboarding is a process to draw out the ideas of each person in the group and focus on the best of them in order to establish a course of action. The term is analogous to storyboards used in creative media such as film making, in which highlights of the story to be filmed are captured on large storyboards as a means of organizing the production.

Storyboarding begins with a brainstorming activity. Each person in the group is given a set of 3 x 5 cards of a single color, a second set of smaller cards of a different color, and a large marking pen. The moderator explains the topic for discussion and asks for ideas, indicating that all ideas are welcomed. For example, suppose the group was meeting to consider a new personnel manual for the nonprofit. The moderator might begin by asking "What are some of the topic areas that we want to include in the manual. Any ideas?"

As ideas are proposed, the moderator asks the person making the suggestion to write down the idea on one of the 3 x 5 cards, which the moderator then affixes to the storyboard (a large board that can accept push pins). The moderator may briefly restate the idea, so that it is clear to all what the abbreviated message means. The moderator also, from time to time, offers some reinforcement: "We're getting some good ideas down. Let's keep it going."

The moderator also reminds group members that in this first phase there is no commenting on individual ideas, either positively or negatively.

Some suggestions will spawn others. These are written on the smaller cards and are "hitchhiked" (i.e., attached so as to overlap) onto the card to which they relate.

The moderator needs to keep the flow of ideas moving, being sure that everyone has a chance to contribute. In order to keep the process interesting, the moderator must also be ready to move onto the next stage when it seems that the well of ideas is drying up.

In the next stage of the process, the moderator invites the group to look at all of the cards on the storyboard to see if any grouping can occur. For example, in this hypothetical group there may be several cards having to do with earning and using vacation or sick leave. The moderator and group may identify this clustering and move the cards of like topic together. It is helpful here to create some headings, using larger cards (e.g., 5 x 7) at the top of the storyboard. During this clustering stage, it may be helpful as well to ask for some amplification or clarification.

Once the grouping of ideas has been achieved, it is time to vote. Each member of the group is given a number of colored dots or circles and invited to vote for his or her choices by affixing the colored votes to the desired cards. Members can scatter their votes across several cards or put all of them on one or two. By using this visual means of voting, the group can readily see which ideas have been given priority.

(*Note*: See Chapter 2 for another method of facilitating group discussion, the Nominal Group Technique.)

SOME PRACTICAL TIPS FOR MAKING THE MEETING PRODUCTIVE

Consider these points as a means to making virtually any meeting you run a success:

1. **Prepare a specific agenda.**

   It should be clear in advance of the meeting to anyone reviewing the agenda what will be accomplished, what materials need to be brought to the meeting, about how long it will run, and at least in general terms who will participate.

2. **Vary the type and place of meeting.**

   Don't meet every Wednesday in the conference room. What other sites either within the building or without lend themselves to an occasional meeting?

   Use reports from the members for some of the meetings (but not all). Employ different group processes—Nominal Group Technique, storyboarding, visioning, etc.

3. **Make use of visual aids.**

   Use overhead projections—sometimes; or provide handout material to guide the discussion. Show a short (no more than 10–15 minutes) film.

4. **Adhere to the time.**

   If you've promised that the meeting will take 1 1/2 hours, be sure that it doesn't wander on past that time. Better yet, end a little early from time to time. Use the clock as an ally to keep the discussion moving.

   Start the meeting on time—thereby rewarding those who show up on time.

5. **Don't just end the meeting; bring it to a close.**

   Summarize what was accomplished. Review assignments. Let the group feel good about what was accomplished; let the members know that you do, too. Thank members individually as they leave. If necessary, and only if necessary, prepare a written summary of the meeting. (Chapter 11 contains a sample meeting summary which is both short and purposeful.)

6. **Provide a treat.**

On occasion, bring bagels or donuts. Be sure there are liquid refreshments appropriate for the time of day. But avoid heavy foods, sticky buns, loud food.

7. **Be sensitive to when is the best time to hold the meeting.**

Not everyone likes morning meetings. Right after lunch is deadly. Poll the group. If you can do so without losing participation, vary the time to accommodate needs (e.g., those with young children, those who have a long commute, those taking an evening course).

PARTING THOUGHTS

This chapter has provided practical information on how to make the most out of organizational meetings. There may be wisdom in conducting an inservice program on the topic of productive meetings. The organization may also want to develop some written guidelines, complete with specific examples of how to make the time spent in meetings justifiable.

NOTE

1. Appreciation is expressed to Trudy Snope for some of the ideas on the various roles which individuals play in a meeting.

Chapter 10
Board and Staff:
Toward a Partnership

EXECUTIVE SUMMARY

One of the recurring issues for nonprofits is how to work out an acceptable equilibrium between the roles of staff and board. Both are vital to the organization. This chapter addresses: Characteristics of weak and strong boards; roles and responsibilities, including job descriptions for trustees, board chair, executive director; criteria for board selection; how the board should go about hiring and evaluating the chief staff person of the organization; getting the board to fund raise, four key steps and detailed suggestions for educating the board about them; questions prospective board members should ask about the organization before joining it; and how to institute a board orientation program.

PICTURE THIS

Case Study

Ann O'Farrell has been executive director of the Lakewood Community Center for two and a half years. While her background is in European history, she found the idea of running a nonprofit community service organization challenging and was pleasantly surprised when she was not only invited to interview but was offered the position of executive director. The previous executive director, it turned out, had helped found the organization and had moved into a staff position after having been a volunteer for several years.

As executive director, O'Farrell oversaw a staff of ten professionally trained and six support staff, most of whom were fairly new to the Center. At the volunteer level, she had a board of governors, as it was called, that comprised nearly 35 members of the greater Lakewood community. Most of the board had served in this capacity for over five years, many for nearly ten. They knew each other well, making it easy to make decisions without a great deal of discussion.

After she had been with Lakewood for about a year, O'Farrell approached the board president, a local attorney, with the idea of an ambitious expansion to the programs and services which Lakewood provided. "What we should do," she proposed, "is to create a committee of the board of governors who would work with me to develop a five-year plan, laying out new programs for the center, together with timelines and projected costs. On the basis of this plan," she reasoned, "the board could then launch what would be a major fund raising campaign."

The board president, not wanting to dampen the enthusiasm of the relatively new executive director, suggested she go ahead with the idea, choosing two or three "senior" board members with whom to work. He suggested that this planning committee should lay out a plan, and that he would hold off telling the rest of the board until it was complete, so that there would be something concrete to show the other members.

Because the members of the committee whom O'Farrell selected to work with her were all fairly prominent members of the community, with interests in addition to Lakewood, the planning process took the better part of a year, even though she did most of the work between meetings. The plan, called "Lakewood Tomorrow," was presented at a quarterly meeting of the board of governors.

There was little discussion, although what did take place generally focused on the question of why board members should be expected to fund raise. After all, one member reminded her colleagues, that was why the board hired professional staff. The item was concluded on the agenda by a motion to accept the report and refer it to staff for possible implementation.

ABOUT BOARDS AND STAFF: AN INTRODUCTION

Ann O'Farrell's experience is hardly unique. Planning, fund raising, and working with volunteer boards are all challenges which directors of nonprofit organizations face. They are in many ways intertwined issues; for the sake of study we separate them, concentrating our attention in this chapter on working with volunteer boards— without which neither planning nor fund raising is likely to have lasting impact.

O'Farrell is dealing with a board that knows what its role is; unfortunately, it's the wrong role. The board is well entrenched, with little change occurring or desired. As we look at some specific recommendations regarding working with a board, it might be useful to give thought to how the principles apply to O'Farrell's situation—and to your own.

WHAT MAKES A GOOD BOARD "GOOD"?

The makeup and to some degree the responsibilities of the governing board will vary according to the vagaries of each nonprofit. However, there are certain characteristics which appertain generally.

Boards that are weak either fail to live up to their charge, to their fiduciary responsibility, or concentrate more on management than issues of organizational policy and planning. Some characteristics:

- The board is regularly involved in the management of the organization. Formal and informal discussions of the board revolve around decisions best left to staff.
- Similarly, most board discussions center on the day-to-day, with little debate on where the organization ought to be headed and the issues that it will face.
- The board asserts its control over the actions and activities of organization staff.
- There is a lack of commitment to personal giving to the organization.
- As a corollary, there is a lack of commitment on the part of the board to planning and engaging in fund raising.
- It appears that some members of the board give little thought to the organization outside the actual board meetings.

By contrast, the strong board will evince most of the following:

- Discussions, which grow out of and help to shape the policy of the organization.
- Understanding of its overarching, fiduciary role as reflected in its decisions.
- Meetings and the execution of individual assignments reflect an enthusiasm for the mission of the organization and its potential.
- Appreciation of the fact that it plays an essential role not only in shepherding the organization's resources but also in garnering them—that is, in fund raising (even if not exactly thrilled with the prospect).
- Respect for staff, for their capabilities, and allowing staff the latitude to manage the organization within stated policies.[1]

With some idea of the characteristics of weak and strong boards as background, what is it that makes for a good board? For starters, the good board is not necessarily one that is always easy to please. Like a good teacher, a good board sets high expectations, provides the support as needed, and gives the staff room to carry them out. The analogy of teacher works if the term "teacher" is actually used in the sense of a graduate instructor—providing the overall guidance, being responsible for the success of the class, but functioning in a collegial environment in which there are distinct responsibilities for all participants.

ROLES AND RESPONSIBILITIES

There has been much said and written about the role and responsibilities of governing boards. Below is a sampling of some of the best thinking:

1. **The board has both legal and fiduciary responsibilities.**

   Regardless of the nature of the organization, the board is legally accountable. The genesis of an organization's charter, which stipulates not only what its general purposes will be but who will administer those purposes, "entrusts" (hence the name "trustee") the organization to the trustee. And it is on the basis of the charter that an organization receives its incorporation within a state, and its tax status from the Internal Revenue Service (IRS).

   Typically, the charter's broad statements are refined in bylaws which stipulate something like "the affairs of the organization shall be vested with a board of trustees . . . ." As the legally constituted body, the board, according to the standards established by the National Charities Information Bureau, "should be an independent, volunteer body. It is responsible for policy setting, fiscal guidance, and ongoing governance."

   Fiduciary responsibility refers to the fact that the board is entrusted (hence the name "trustees") with the well-being of the organization. Organizations gain their legitimacy by virtue of their charter. They thrive based on public trust. Securing and maintaining both formal and social legitimacy is the core responsibility of the board.

   That is a primary reason why it is so important for boards to understand their responsibility and accountability. If they are spending their meeting time on administrative matters, it is unlikely that they are giving proper attention to the role of ensuring the accountability and viability of the organization entrusted to them.

2. **The board governs.**

   Governance is a tricky word. The concept of governing encompasses at least these actions: holding in check, controlling, restraining, guiding, requiring, directing, regulating, having predominate influence. Boards at one time or another may do any or all of these things; to a greater or lesser degree, so, too, might staff.

The origin of the word "governance" comes from the Latin word for "to govern" meaning "to steer" (a ship). By analogy, those who govern set the course and make sure that it is maintained.

3. **The board sets policy.**

Here, too, the language is a little murky. It is fair to assume that boards and staffs of equal good will sometimes come into conflict one with the other because they hold differing opinions on what is and is not "policy."

Selected members of the Association of Governing Boards of Universities and Colleges were surveyed as to whether a series of issues constituted policy or management. Here are some of the questions on which the university CEO differed from the governing board concerning whether specified policy required board action:

- Should the president authorize dispensing birth control devices without board approval?
- Should the board close a "pornographic" art exhibit when the president does not wish to do so?
- Should the board be involved in various stages of the budget process?
- Should the board retain outside consultants on direction for the institution without concurrence of the president?[2]

What's the course of action? CEO and board need to come to agreement on what constitutes policy and what constitutes management—not item by item, but in a set of operating principles. It may be necessary to revisit these from time to time, and it would probably be helpful as well to have a mechanism in place to resolve "grey areas" (perhaps a subcommittee comprised of two board members plus the executive director).

On another plane, it is important to recognize that, while boards establish policy, staff members certainly are involved—and they should be—in its formulation. Board and staff members should work together to develop both overriding and specific statements of policy. The distinction then comes when these are presented to the full board, where only a board member actually has a vote.

The issue often comes up not so much in the context of "What is policy" as in "What is management?" If the board wants to frustrate its chief operating officer, it can find no better way than to instill in him or her a sense of responsibility but no authority to carry out that responsibility. Here, too, some operating definitions, jointly prepared by members of the board and staff, can be of help.

4. The board has overall fiscal responsibility for the organization.

The fiscal responsibility is twofold:

- The financial health and security of the organization rests ultimately in the hands of the trustees.
- The task of raising funds for the organization cannot be simply delegated to staff.

Fiscal accountability does not mean that the board must develop the budget, although it should approve it and receive periodic financial reports. If it is helpful, the board chair might want to establish a financial planning committee (whose members need not involve members of the board) with oversight responsibility; the financial planning committee should report in an advisory capacity on what it observes of the organization's financial health and make recommendations on adoption of the budget, change in investment policy, and requirements for reserves.

Having a financial planning committee does not mean the board abdicates that obligation; rather, that its role is facilitated by the advice of a volunteer-driven committee. Nor does it mean that the preparation of the budget should be removed from the hands of staff hired for that purpose.

The issue of fund raising will be addressed subsequently.

SOME ADDITIONAL ROLES

The above listing of board roles is meant to be more illustrative than exhaustive. Here are some further examples, supplied by Independent Sector, the membership organization for both grantmaking and grantseeking organizations:

- Appoint the chief staff officer;
- Support the chief staff officer;
- Monitor the performance of the chief staff officer;
- Clarify the mission of the organization;
- Approve long-range plans (to which might be added, and participate in their creation);
- Oversee the programs of the organization;
- Preserve the organization's independence;
- Serve as intermediary between organization and community;
- Assess board performance.[3]

BOARD SELECTION: ESTABLISHING CRITERIA

When it's time to replace a member of the board, on what basis are decisions made as to whom to recommend? It can be valuable to have individuals proposed who are known to current board members; to some degree, they are staking their own reputation as board members by suggesting someone whom they know. But the selection process need not stop there. Before contact is actually made with a prospective board member, it can be very enlightening to match the individual's credentials against predetermined criteria.

The following are some sample criteria which you might want to suggest to your own nominating committee:

- Reflects the cultural diversity of the organization and its constituencies;
- Has the potential to raise funds for the organization;
- Demonstrates qualities of leadership in related contexts;
- Appears to be interested in the mission and purposes of the organization;
- Exhibits sound communication and interpersonal skills;
- Should make a contribution to the goals of the organization and the work of the board.

Each candidate can be rated according to these or other criteria using a Likert scale (SA = strongly agree, A = agree, NO = no opinion, D = disagree, DS = disagree strongly). In this way, it is possible both to objectify the process and come to some rank ordering of candidates proposed.

The next step in the process is the statement of expectations. Candidates who are to be considered should be measured with these qualifications in mind as well. Those who are finally recommended should then be contacted to inquire if (1) they are interested; (2) they agree that they meet the criteria; and (3) they believe they will be able to fulfill the expectations.

Here are some examples of expectations:

- Willingness to participate actively in at least <fill in the number> of board meetings per year;
- Ability to commit to at least a <fill in> year term;
- Willingness to participate actively in the organization's fund raising programs;
- Willingness to participate on at least one committee.

BOARD ORIENTATION

It is commonly observed that new board members may take a year to become familiar with the organization and the board: understanding procedures and precedents, observing and absorbing the culture, grasping the politics. While it is wise for a new board member to perceive the lay of the land, it is no less true that nonprofits can ill afford to have members spend one-third of their term (assuming a typical three-year post) on the board in a learning mode.

Board orientation can speed up the process considerably. The orientation should occur well in advance of the first regularly scheduled board meeting to allow time for the information to be digested. New board members should be given the opportunity to meet either one-to-one or in small groups with at least the following:

- The board president.
- The organization's CEO.
- Key board and committee members.

  For example, if the new board member is going to be assigned to the planning committee, it makes sense to schedule some time with the chair of that committee.

- Senior staff—especially the head of the development office.
- Consumers of the organization's services (students, parents, clients).

The board chair and CEO should set the tone for these meetings: they should be open, candid, and focused on the organization's potential. This is not the time to air the organization's dirty laundry or to establish political alliances (although the new board members would be well served to learn the political nuances of the organization). It is the time to make it clear that board membership implies high standards of conduct and achievement.[4]

Board Handbook

Providing written information in the form of a board handbook reinforces the orientation and provides a ready reference for future use. The handbook might contain the following:

- A board calendar, complete with meeting dates, and dates that are important to the organization's history and functioning (e.g., deadlines for submission of material to be included on a meeting agenda);
- Names, addresses, and telephone and FAX numbers for board members and for key staff;

- Job descriptions—for the board chair, board members, chief staff person;
- Committee charges for those committees with which the board member will interact
- Mission statement and strategic plan for the organization;
- Bylaws;
- Recent annual reports and annual audited financial statements;
- Minutes of board meetings for the past 12 months;
- Brief summaries of major programs and staff responsible for them;
- Important statistics (e.g., number of persons served);
- An organization chart;
- Fund raising and public relations literature;
- A copy of the organization's case statement, if one has been prepared.[5]

QUESTIONS PROSPECTIVE BOARD MEMBERS SHOULD ASK ABOUT THE INSTITUTION

When approached to join the board of directors (trustees) of a nonprofit organization, the candidate should be sure he or she fully understands what is involved before saying yes. Deciding to become a board member is (and ought to be) a serious commitment.

The internal questioning that a candidate goes through will of course vary according to the individual and the situation, but there are some questions that ought not to be overlooked:

1. Do I believe in—and care about—the purposes of this organization?

There is an understandable temptation to say yes to board membership because of the status of being on a board. Boards set policy. Boards make decisions. Boards are comprised of leaders. But the candidate would be wise to ask if the mission and purpose of the organization are consonant with his or her own values and beliefs: Does the organization make a contribution to the well-being of society? (Does it at least have the potential to do so?) Are there other organizations whose mission is more of interest?

Serving on a nonprofit board provides both reward and frustration. For there to be a favorable tilt toward reward, the candidate needs a reservoir of good will about the organization's raison d'être.

2. What is the nature of board membership?

- Is the board comprised of prominent members of the community? Are the typical board members individuals who have enjoyed successful careers, or is the board more of a stepping stone for persons on the way up?
- Are the board members active? Do they regularly attend meetings, work on committees, represent the organization? Or is the board comprised of persons who are merely lending their name?
- What is the demographic composition of the board? What's the average age? Is there diversity in race, ethnicity, and gender?

3. What expectations does the organization have of its board members?"

How many meetings are held during the year? About how many hours/week does the typical board member spend on organizational responsibilities?

Are most board members responsible for monitoring the work of committees? If so, what level of involvement does that responsibility entail?

4. What has been the board's role in fund raising?

- Are all board members expected to raise funds?
- What have been the results of board fund raising? Were goals met?
- Are there any plans for a major fund raising campaign? If so, is the organization going to evaluate the campaign's potential by means of a feasibility study?

5. What is the relationship between board and staff?

The effective nonprofit organization depends on a partnership between volunteers and paid staff. Board candidates may want to inquire about the way board and staff interrelate. How do most board members view the staff? Are the staff seen as helpful, supportive, and informed; or is there clearly mistrust between the two bodies?

Is the CEO regarded highly by the board? What is the likelihood that the CEO will remain in his or her position?

Is interaction between board and staff encouraged? Through what channels of communication does most such interaction occur?

6. Is the organization fiscally sound?

- Has the organization ended its last five years in the black?

- Do the audited statements suggest that the auditors were concerned about the organization's financial health?
- What are the prospects for financial growth? Is the organization overly reliant on a few funding streams which could dry up?

7. To what extent can board members be held liable?

As a general rule, board members are liable for what occurs within the organization.[6] Candidates should seek clarification of the extent to which they might be liable, ask whether there is any history of litigation, and be sure that the organization carries sufficient liability insurance.

USING POSITION DESCRIPTIONS TO DESCRIBE BOARD ROLES AND RESPONSIBILITIES

Position descriptions are commonly prepared for staff positions. One way to both clarify distinctions between the responsibilities of staff and board, while establishing some assessment criteria, is to develop position descriptions for members of the board. Two examples are presented in Figures 7 and 8.

Figure 7. Position Description: Board of Trustees

Ultimate responsibility for <name of organization> resides with the board of trustees, as recognized by both state and federal statute. The board is the "primary force pressing <name of organization> to the realization of its opportunities for service and the fulfillment of its obligations to all its constituencies."[7]
Duties:

1. Annually assess the external environment and develop new initiatives in response as warranted.

2. Approve and evaluate major programs of the organization.

3. Review and approve the operating budget.

4. Establish policies and guidelines for the conduct of the organization.

5. Hire, support, and evaluate the performance of the chief operating officer.

6. Approve the fund raising plan of the organization and participate in its execution.

7. Establish financial objectives and monitor their accomplishment.

Figure 8. Position Description: Board Chair

The board chair serves as chief elected officer of the organization, representing and interacting with its constituencies. The chair directs other members of the board and presides over board actions.

Duties:

1. Preside at all meetings of the board of trustees.

2. Keep other board members and appropriate committees informed regarding the organization and its activities and conditions affecting it.

3. Coordinate the activities of the board in formulating or modifying policies and major programs of the organization.

4. Conduct or designate the undertaking of a periodic review of the organization.

5. Coordinate the evaluation of the performance of the executive director.

6. Participate as a spokesperson for the organization.

7. Schedule meetings of the board.

8. Work with other board members and staff and the executive director in identifying, selecting, and orienting capable board membership.

To make the distinction clear, it's a good idea to write (or rewrite as necessary) the position description of the chief staff person (see Figure 9).

By developing such position descriptions, the organization accomplishes three things: (1) clearly articulates board roles and responsibilities; (2) fosters a feeling of partnership between elected leadership and staff in pursuit of common goals; and (3) avoids some very unpleasant confusion that often follows lack of clarity on roles and expectations (see position description for the CEO later in this chapter).

GETTING THE BOARD TO FUND RAISE

Most people find fund raising—specifically, having to ask people for money—to be, at best, unpalatable. They just cannot get up the energy to pick up the phone, make an appointment, ask for support. Members of nonprofit boards are no exception. That notwithstanding, their involvement in fund raising—their direct involvement in fund raising—is essential.

The board's role vis-à-vis raising funds used to be captured in the phrase: Give, get, or get off.

Give a contribution, get others to contribute, or get off the board to make way for someone who will. Today, that maxim is expanded: Give *and* get, or get off. For the organization to succeed, it needs volunteers who can and will fund raise; and to be effective, they need to be contributors themselves.

There are *four steps* that can be taken to increase the probability that your board will become actively involved in raising funds:

1. Top Leadership Must Set the Example

If your board president is unwilling to ask his or her own contacts for support of the organization, he or she will be hard pressed to convince others. What this translates to is that the CEO should spend time and effort on helping the board president with fund rasing efforts. The CEO can help arrange appointments, draft correspondence, provide moral support. And be sure that the first time the board president makes a call on a potential donor, the prospect has been identified as being as close to a sure thing as can be found.

2. Make Fund Raising and Personal Giving Expectations of Board Membership

Having solicited someone for a contribution, hopefully with success, and having made some contribution himself or herself, the board president will be in a position to set some expectations of others. Those expectations need to be written into the criteria used to select and evaluate board membership.

3. Fund Raising Should Be a Natural Consequence of the Writing of a Strategic Plan

President Eisenhower is credited with having observed that it was not the plan that was important but the planning. One of the principal reasons for embarking on a plan is that it heightens the feeling of ownership among those involved. If your board members are active participants in the planning process, they will feel that sense of ownership over the goals and objectives that have been established. It is a logical follow-up to build on that sentiment by encouraging the board members to take the steps necessary to bring the plan to fruition— notably, seeing that it is sufficiently funded.

4. Give the Board the Tools They Need

Here are some strategies to help board members become efficacious spokespersons for the organization.

Teach the board to fund raise.

It is worth the expense to bring in outside fund raising or board development counsel to assist in teaching your board how to raise money. That training should explain that people give to people, and especially to people whom they know. It should encourage board members to speak in the first person: "I need and invite your support of . . . ."

Consider sending one volunteer on his or her first fund raising to someone whom you do not think will give.

It was suggested earlier that it is important to be sure that the first time your board president asks someone for money, the odds are more than good that he or she will succeed. A rather different strategy is to allow a volunteer to fail. Why? Because that person can then practice the approach he or she will use with relative impunity. If no gift is forthcoming, nothing has been lost, since one wasn't expected. If, with luck, the prospect proves better than anticipated (or the board member does a particularly cogent job of convincing the prospect), so much the better. Either way, the volunteer gains invaluable experience without risking a prospect who was counted on for support.

Focus on One Board Member

Assume that the board president has made it clear that board members are expected to participate fully in attracting and asking for money. Select one board member on whom to concentrate training. Then set up a series of fund raising visits for him or her. The odds are that one in three will result in some kind of positive response. When the successful board member reports his or her success, the feeling of excitement—and of wanting to similarly succeed—will be infectious.

Set Lower Goals Than You Think the Board Will Achieve

If your development office staff have estimated that the board can raise $1.8 million, set a goal of $1 million. Let them enjoy the thrill of going over the top.

Encourage the Board to Dream

What do they imagine could be accomplished? What would they do if funds were unlimited? Scholarships, new staff, a new building? An endowment fund? An endowed chair? The reason for fostering this visioning is to infuse enthusiasm. From the long list generated, have the board then pare down to the goals that they think can really be funded and accomplished.

Remind the Board If They Get Only Three Hits Out Of Ten, They're Batting .333

Limit the Time Individual Members Need to Spend

In a well-organized development approach, each board member probably will not need to dedicate more than the equivalent of about five days in one year. Much of the preparatory and follow-up work should be the responsibility of staff. Said another way, don't waste the time of people you've deemed important enough to lead your organization. Show them you value their time with a solidly organized development effort.

Make the Point: Fund Raising Is Not Begging

Begging is negative, and there is no room in fund raising for the negative. One board president used to regularly refer to his fund raising efforts as "tin cupping," a reference to a bum holding out a tin cup and hoping for a few meager coins. That kind of attitude gets what it deserves—small change.

By contrast, the potent development system offers potential donors the opportunity to invest in the future of the organization and the community. Note the pivotal words:

- Opportunity
- Invest

- Future
- Community

Find Out All You Can About Board Members

Virtually everyone knows someone who could be deemed important or famous, and who might be a prospect for funds or a lead to funding. Knowing where your board members went to school, the clubs to which they belong, their religious affiliations, will expand your development office's vista of prospects dramatically and increase the board's success rate at the same time.

Everyone on the Board Must Give Something

At least at first, the amount that each member of the board contributes is less important than the fact that 100 percent of the board believes in the organization enough to invest in it themselves.

Visits to Funding Prospect Should be a Team Affair

The best team combination is a member of the board and a member of the staff, both of whom are well versed in the script and know how much they can realistically ask for. Unless the board member is especially good at asking for funds, he or she should be primarily employed in setting the stage, talking from the heart about the organization and why it represents such a good investment. As a rule, specific questions should be fielded by the staff person.[8]

Prepare "Board Fund Raising Policy" to Detail Roles and Responsibilities[9]

There is something official about putting what has been agreed into print. The policy document may or may not be referred to once it has been written, but it will have an effect either way.

HIRING AND EVALUATING THE CHIEF STAFF OFFICER (THE CEO)

One of the critical functions for the board is to hire and evaluate the chief executive officer. Typically, he or she is the only staff person who reports directly to the board. The chief operating officer is usually the principal liaison to the board and is a nonvoting member. The relationship between board and staff and the way in which the two bodies work together to carry out the organization's mission is in the hands of the chief operating officer.

Hiring the CEO

For all the reasons noted above, it is imperative that the board exercise care both in choosing the chief staff person and communicating about his or her achievements and any areas needing improvement. In addition to the specifics spelled out in the position description, the board may want to consider other factors in its search for a CEO (some of which have been suggested by Independent Sector, a national organization of funders and nonprofit organizations):[10]

- Commitment to public service;
- Sociability and ability to interact well with others;
- Willingness to subordinate personal "agendas" for the goals of the organization;
- High patience threshold;
- Maturity;
- Willingness to work hard and ability to work efficiently.

Evaluating the CEO

Evaluating the work of the nonprofit organization's chief staff person should be as integral to the activities as program planning. For indeed that is in large part what it is. Done properly, the CEO evaluation becomes an opportunity for both the CEO and the board to jointly assess the organization's strengths and weaknesses, as well as its progress.

There are three vehicles that lend themselves to an evaluation of the CEO:

1. The CEO's formal contract;
2. Annual operating plans;
3. Standards of performance appraisal.[11]

In a growing number of nonprofit organizations, the CEO is hired and functions under the terms of a contract with the board. The contract may describe salary and benefits, expectations (what the board expects will be accomplished,) and conditions (for example, that the CEO position is contingent on successful completion of annual goals).

The annual operating plan (or annual goals and objectives) provides a second vehicle. The CEO and board may delineate a number of goals which the CEO will seek to accomplish; these can be drawn from the organization's overall strategic plan or written to reflect specific, desired goals. As an example of the latter, the board and the CEO may agree on a goal of improving the managerial capabilities of the organization's senior staff. Where possible, the means by which the CEO will be evaluated should be stated in measurable outcomes.

Under certain conditions, the board may feel that behavioral performance standards (sometimes referred to as behaviorally anchored rating scales, or BARs) ought to be used in the evaluation. There are two steps to developing such standards:

1. **Define what behavior is to be evaluated.**

   The board may come up with a list of 10–15 behaviors or activities which in its collective opinion represent the ideal for a CEO. After some discussion, it may be possible to pare these down and even prioritize them.

2. **Determine exemplars of acceptable or nonacceptable behavior.[12]**

   The second step is to ask: What would the desired behaviors look like? What kinds of activities would someone exemplifying the desired behaviors be doing? Conversely, what behaviors would seem inappropriate for the goals in mind?

The term "behaviors" need not be negative. Basically, the behavioral approach is no more than a way to describe the actions and attitudes characteristic of the ideal nonprofit CEO.

As would be the case with any evaluation program, it is essential that the CEO and the board mutually agree to the process employed and the expectations by which the CEO will be judged. Most CEOs want to know how they are doing and to be sure that they and the board are of like minds as to how they are doing. But, as with any staff, they want assurances that the evaluation will be fair and objective.

What are some of the criteria by which the CEO might be evaluated?

- Managerial skill (the ability to manage others, bringing out the best in other staff);
- Leadership (recognized as a leader in the community; ability to inspire);
- Organizational skills (capable of juggling numerous deadlines and priorities);
- Communication skills (both oral and written);
- Interpersonal qualities (ability to work with a wide range of personalities, among both staff and volunteers);
- Demonstrated knowledge of the field in which the organization operates (as evidenced by professional presentations or papers);
- Skill in fund raising;
- Knowledge of emerging technology that may affect the organization or make its work more efficient;
- An ability to grasp, relate, and articulate trends and issues that may affect the organization.

The position description for the CEO clarifies responsibilities and provides assessment criteria for that position (see Figure 9).

Figure 9. Position Description: CEO

The executive director is the chief executive officer of <name of organization>. The executive director both reports to and is a nonvoting member of the board of trustees. In cooperation with the board, the executive director establishes major direction for the organization and articulates the mission and goals of the organization to its constituencies.

Duties:

1. Facilitate the work of the board and its committees "in its efforts to fulfill its accountability."[13]

> 2. Hire, train, and be responsible for all staff of the organization, and perform the role of liaison with the board of trustees.
>
> 3. Prepare the annual budget of the organization and present it to the board.
>
> 4. Together with the board, represent the organization to its various constituencies.
>
> 5. In cooperation with the board chair, recommend members of the board and coordinate their orientation to the organization and board.

PARTING THOUGHTS

It is difficult to imagine a nonprofit being successful in the 1990s without an active, committed, and capable board. Developing such a board does not come without effort and without compromise.

Management theorist Mary Parker Follett, some 70 years ago, pointed out that leaders and followers both follow the invisible leader whose name is common purpose. The same might be said of the successful balance between staff and board.[14]

NOTES

1. "Characteristics of Strong and Weak Boards," *The Digest of Non-profit Management*, 4 (March/April 1990): 3.

2. Robert E. Cleary, "Who's in Charge Here?", *AGB Reports*, 21 (November/December 1979): 21–24.

3. Brian O'Connell, "The Role of the Board and Board Members." *Nonprofit Management Series* (Washington, DC: Independent Sector, 1988), 7.

4. Andrew Swanson, "Learning the Ropes: Orienting New Members." *Nonprofit World*, 7 (March 1990): 34.

5. Some of the items suggested for the board orientation handbook were from Carol Strauch, "Getting Oriented," *Foundation News*, 31 (September/October 1990): 31.

6. George D. Webster, "What Your Board Can Do," *Association Management*, 42 (September 1990): 73.

7. Kenneth N. Dayton, "Define Your Roles," *Foundation News*, 26 (May/June 1985): 69.

8. Barry Nickelsberg, "Getting Your Board to Fund Raise." Speech before the Association Foundation Group, Washington, DC, April 10, 1990.

9. Julia Bonem, "Build Relationships: Funding Will Follow," *NSFRE News*, (April 1990): 1

10. Brian O'Connell, "The Board's Biggest Decision," *Foundation News*, 31 (January/February 1990): 48–51.

11. Mark Michaels, "CEO Evaluation: The Board's Second Most Crucial Duty," *The Nonprofit World*, 8 (May/June 1990): 30.

12. Michaels, 30.

13. Brian O'Connell, "The Roles and Relationships of the Chief Volunteer and Chief Staff Officers." *Nonprofit Management Series* (Washington, DC: Independent Sector, 1988), 24.

14. Mary Parker Follett, "The Essentials of Leadership," *Classics in Management*, Harwood F. Merrill, ed. (New York: American Management Association, 1960), 331.

Chapter 11
Volunteers

EXECUTIVE SUMMARY

One of the distinguishing characteristics of the nonprofit organization is its ability to attract and use the talents of volunteers. With changing demographics, changing values, and demands on time, the ability to attract top volunteers takes on particular importance. This chapter addresses: The volunteer marketplace, including the roles that volunteers say they would like to play; what motivates people to volunteer, and what trends tell us about volunteering in the 1990s; rethinking the role of volunteering and how to identify future leadership.

The chapter also describes how to create committees that work, including the following suggestions for successful committees: how to orient and train volunteers, and staff to work with volunteers; how to establish expectations for volunteers and evaluate their achievements; how to understand the respective roles of volunteer and staff on committees, replete with job descriptions. Also covered is information on getting useful committee reports; working toward a partnership; and, finally, recognition of volunteer service.

THE VOLUNTEER "MARKET"

As is the case with any other constituent body, volunteers comprise a market that needs to be understood for the unique qualities that it represents. Referring to volunteers as a market in no way diminishes the vital role that they play in society in general and in nonprofit organizations specifically. To the contrary, by applying marketing techniques to the volunteer program, a better match will result between the interests of the organization and those of this essential element of the nonprofit world.

Segmenting the Volunteer Market

Typically, the volunteer market might be segmented along these dimensions:

- Demographic lines (age, gender);
- Geographic dimensions (location within the city, which in turn may reflect certain societal segmentation);
- Ethnography (race, culture).

Applying these modes, the organization might look for certain demographic factors—e.g., age—when recruiting for a foster grandparents program, which pairs infants abandoned by their parents with older persons who provide care and affection. One might apply geographic characteristics in a search for volunteers to work in the new outreach center located in the outskirts of town. Or the organization might employ ethnographic factors in addressing the needs of minority children in the early intervention program.

VOLUNTEER ROLES

For the purpose of recruiting, there is an additional dimension that can be considered which has to do with how volunteers envision the role they would like to play in the organization. Katheryn Weidman Heidrich[1] has suggested that there are four types of roles that volunteers see themselves filling. In any given organization, different kinds of involvement will hold attraction to different personalities and to different needs and interests. The organization that matches up volunteer perceptions of where they might serve best with available volunteer functions will result in the smoothest running volunteer program.

The four types of volunteer roles suggested by Heidrich are the following:

Leadership

Somewhat surprisingly, the study found a majority of those polled said they would like to serve in a leadership capacity. This tends to run counter to one trend that has been observed—the difficulty in getting volunteers with the interest and ability to fill leadership positions.

It is consistent, however, with two other trends:

- As will be discussed in greater detail later, volunteers have, on average, less time than might have been the case a few years ago. As a consequence, they are less likely to opt for mindless tasks, preferring instead to see that what they are doing makes a difference.

- Leadership positions, as has been noted, are being filled by less senior individuals—those on the way up the corporate or other ladder, who view volunteer service in part as a means to further career goals.

   According to Heidrich, there are several areas in which volunteers might be interested in taking on a leadership role, including officer, board member, committee chair, committee member, project leader, and fund raiser.

Direct Service

The direct service role appeals to individuals who are not looking for a leadership role as volunteers, but rather are seeking ways in which to work directly with other human beings and, in that way, to make a difference. The businessperson who volunteers to read for someone who is blind and the lawyer who spends an evening a week caring for crack babies falls into this second category. So, too, do scout troop leaders, home companions, and coaches.

General Support

Some individuals are most comfortable with a volunteer role that does not require either leadership or direct service. Among the projects that these volunteers might be engaged in are telephoning, typing correspondence, running errands, cleaning, maintaining buildings and grounds.

Member-at-Large

The member-at-large does not want an ongoing assignment, but is willing to fill in, take on occasional tasks, and help out from time to time.

MOTIVATION TO VOLUNTEER

There is also some literature suggesting what motivates persons to volunteer. One study, conducted by SRI International, identified three different types of persons in the context of what types of volunteers they would make.

The first type is the *need-driven*. These are individuals who are living marginally. Virtually every effort expended goes toward survival. Obviously, this type is not a good candidate for volunteering.

Type two is the *outer-directed* individual, who is motivated by what he or she perceives to be widely shared values. Outer-directed persons may be either those who volunteer out of a sense of belonging or those who volunteer in order to accomplish some goal.

The third category addressed in the study is the *inner-directed* person whose volunteer efforts are the result of his or her own inner sense of values and priorities. Younger inner-directed individuals may view volunteering as a path to inner growth. Older inner-directeds bring a balance and inner security to their volunteerism and may prove to be the best source of volunteer talent by virtue of their high degree of dedication to a cause or belief.[2]

VOLUNTEERISM: A LOOK AT SOME TRENDS

In order to effectively attract, cultivate, and utilize volunteers— particularly as we approach the year 2000—we will need to be cognizant of several major trends. We alluded to two—limited time and the changing nature of volunteer leadership—above.

1. **The good news: most people say that they value volunteering.**

    Several studies recently have revealed that the majority of persons in the United States place a value on volunteering. A study commissioned by Chevas Regal and conducted by Research & Forecasts, for example, found that nearly six in ten Americans would be willing to volunteer for a cause in which they believe.[3]

    Of course, you say. Who wouldn't see the importance of volunteering? The answer: potentially many. It was not that long ago that we were talking about the "me" generation, whose ranks were filled with persons mostly interested in getting ahead, making vice president, buying the BMW. Free time was spent dashing off to Club Med destinations. "Volunteering? Giving up my free time? For a charity?"

    Whether the me generation ever truly existed or was media-manufactured, it does appear that even among those we once called Yuppies (young, urban professionals) there is a trend toward giving something back. Society is starting to pay heed to the notions that contentment cannot be found by chasing after it, that it may be a function of something more than business success, and that how we use our time is what brings satisfaction. Rabbi Harold Kushner, author of *When All You've Ever Wanted Isn't Enough*, puts it this way:

    > The happiest people you know are probably not the richest or most famous, probably not the ones who work hardest at being happy by reading the articles and buying the books and latching on to the latest

fads. I suspect that the happiest people you know are the ones who work at being kind, helpful, and reliable, and happiness sneaks into their lives while they are busy doing those things.[4]

There is anecdotal evidence to back up the polls on volunteering. Articles in the popular media show single, male Wall Street executives who spend a night a week feeding "boarder babies," who have been abandoned by their mothers and are often born drug-dependent; or depict families from wealthy suburbs who donate time and resources to shelters for the homeless.

What does this mean in terms of attracting volunteers? Simply that we need to think of the nonprofit organization in a human context. It's easy in the day-to-day hurly-burly to forget why an organization was created in the first place. Those involved with nonprofits need to be reminded, so that they can point out to others the enriching experiences that volunteering can provide to persons who are looking for something more out of life than making more money.

2. **The majority of volunteers will come from the maturing baby boom generation.**

By the year 2000, the first of the baby boomers will be 55 years of age; the youngest, 35. As an age cohort, this "pig in the python," as it is sometimes graphically described, will be in its peak earning years. We need to recognize what makes this large segment of our population tick. Some characteristics of baby boomers as a class are:

- Well educated;
- Accustomed to getting attention (their sheer numbers have made them a force to be reckoned with since they were children;
- Less willing to accept authority by virtue of title or position—respect is earned, not deserved.

The typical baby boomers will probably be married, with both spouses working outside of the home; or be divorced and single parents. They will view job changing, and indeed career changing, as commonplace. They may be caring for an aged parent; this will be especially true for female baby boomers.

As they age, baby boomers will likely find that the path to the top becomes ever more narrow. Even some of the brightest and most capable will lose out in corporate or organizational musical chairs, which may offer a new pool of volunteers.

Retirees may also be a substantial source of volunteers. The American Association of Retired Persons, which is the fastest growing association in the United States, estimates that about 30 percent of persons aged 55 or older do some volunteer work on a regular basis.[5] Many such volunteers bring a lifetime of skills that can be tapped. The Service Corps of Retired Executives (SCORE), for example, is composed of over 12,000 retired executives willing to advise and consult with nonprofit organizations and businesses.

3. Volunteering needs to be meaningful.

It was suggested earlier in this chapter that the days are gone when volunteers were willing to spend three afternoons a week stuffing envelopes, addressing invitations, maintaining office files. As a rule, volunteers will want to do something that makes a difference. Nonprofit managers may need to rethink entire staffing patterns, hiring staff for the more menial tasks for which volunteers cannot be attracted, and engaging volunteers in what have traditionally been considered the domain of professional staff.

This is not to say that the public information program is going to be turned over to volunteers simply on the basis of their expressing an interest in public relations activities. But nonprofit managers may want to examine the range of activities in public relations and the skills needed to carry them out, to see if new matches can be made between volunteer interests and organizational needs.

This will, for many managers, be a radical departure. They are accustomed to thinking that they are the experts and they know what is best for those to whom the organization provides service. They need to learn the ways of participatory management in order to recruit and retain volunteers with desired knowledge and skill.[6]

4. Time is at a premium.

It is not enough to keep in mind that volunteers may have less time than their counterparts did 30 years ago. Interesting capable individuals in becoming volunteers will require at least three other things:

- Make it possible to volunteer beyond the hours of 9:00 to 5:00.

  To attract persons who have something to contribute, nonprofits may have to extend hours to be available some evenings, weekends, and holidays.

- Keep current with technology.

  Augment both the contributions and interest of volunteers with full-time jobs by making it possible for them to communicate and participate via FAX, conference call, Electronic Mail, Voice Mail, and computerized bulletin boards.

- Do the homework up front.

  Meetings should be held only when necessary, and should be well planned and efficient. The nonprofit staff should keep a mental if not a data-based inventory of volunteer interests and backgrounds so that they can match new activities with the right volunteers.

5. **Volunteers will reflect the diversity of the population at large.**

   Extraordinary changes are taking place in the demographics of society, as discussed in Chapter 2 on planning. As we become an older, more racially and ethnically diverse population, nonprofit organizations will be both serving individuals from a wider cultural diversity and needing to attract volunteers who reflect those same characteristics.

RETHINKING THE ROLE OF THE VOLUNTEER[7]

It is clear that the very nature of whom nonprofits serve and the nature of the volunteers are undergoing dramatic change. It is not inappropriate in such an environment to ask, Why do we want and need volunteers?

- Get certain basic jobs done within the organization?
- Encourage commitment to the organization, which might translate into other kinds of support?
- Foster the growth of future leadership?

To Get the Job Done

Assume that the organization decides that the primary purpose of having volunteers is to accomplish certain ongoing activities. It then needs to step back and ask: "Do we need this job in the first place? Is it essential, or have we merely grown used to it?"

If it is essential, are there ways in which it can be restructured, broken into manageable units, modified so that it can be done by several volunteers, or staff, or both?

To Nurture Commitment

Volunteering is a proven way of bringing individuals into the organizational family. The ownership that volunteers begin to feel about the projects in which they are involved can be broadened into a commitment to the organization in general. However, other ways of stimulating that sense of commitment may need to be considered: including a volunteer member on a task force that rewrites the personnel policies; creating a volunteer-driven product market group; turning over the planning of a new wing to volunteers with expertise in building design. Risky stuff, to be sure. But this level of imaginative involvement may be necessary if the goal is to nurture commitment.

To Identify Future Leadership

It makes sense to have a leadership ladder, with members of the board coming from a larger, proven leadership pool. However, as change occurs both in who the volunteers are and what they do, some structure will need to be given to what has been an informal, evolutionary process. Specifically, when jobs are identified which volunteers can fill, which also meet the interests of the volunteer marketplace, two additional factors should be considered:

1. What kind and amount of training will be necessary to be sure that volunteers are being asked to do a job for which they are qualified?

2. Against what standards will the work of the volunteer be measured?

"Measured? We're going to evaluate the work of volunteers?"

Absolutely. Volunteers play an integral role in the organization. They have a right to know how well they are performing, and the organization has an obligation to see that they are in fact meeting minimal standards.

CREATING COMMITTEES THAT WORK

The value of volunteer committees has probably been debated since the first organizations were created. Here's what author John Galsworthy had to say about them:

> In an age governed almost exclusively by Committees, Michael knew fairly well what Committees were governed by. A Committee must not meet too soon after food, for then the Committeemen would sleep; nor too soon before food, because then the Committeemen would be excitable. The Committeemen should be allowed to say what they liked, without direction, until each was tiring of hearing the others say it. But there must be someone present, preferably the Chairman, who said little, thought more, and could be relied on to be awake when the moment was reached, whereupon a middle policy voiced by him to exhausted receivers, would probably be adopted.[8]

A bit harsh, to be sure, but many nonprofit organization executives have stories not wholly unlike it. Which leads to the question: Why have a committee?

1. To assist the organization in getting the work done.

Estimates are that some 90 million people in the United States work as volunteers in nonprofit organizations, most in addition to their paying jobs. Collectively, they contribute 7.5 million full-time work years—a savings amounting to $150 billion each year.[9]

2. To involve constituencies, thereby increasing their feelings of ownership.

If you want to make a friend of someone, ask him or her to do something for you. There is probably no better way to bring potential donors into the fold than to offer them a chance to work for the organization. Everyone asks them for money. The organization that gets them involved will get it. It's hard not to support a new project when your committee came up with the idea.

3. To identify, recruit, and cultivate leadership.

Committees are living laboratories for leadership development. Watch a committee at work: it becomes clear very quickly which members are most willing to work, which ones are always coming up with an idea, which ones the others listen to.

Individual committee assignments provide another way to find potential leaders. Not every leader is an orator; some of the best leaders are hesitant to speak up at a meeting, especially a large one. But given an assignment to complete, they can know some success, which may in turn give them the confidence to take on additional responsibility.

4. To get fresh ideas and a wider perspective.

It is dangerously easy for "Groupthink" to set in within any organization. Staff interact with one another as much as they interact with their own families. They start to dress alike, think alike, go to the same hangouts, watch the same television shows. Ironically, Groupthink can be an indication that the staff members get along well.

Which is not to say that the role of committee members is to stimulate disharmony. Rather, bringing in volunteers is a way of hearing a new point-of-view, especially if the volunteer pool is large (so that the same cadre of volunteers are not being continually recycled) and committee members are encouraged to believe that no question is stupid.

Some organizations make the mistake of drawing their volunteers from backgrounds virtually indistinguishable from those of the staff. While an interest in the mission of the organization is imperative, a personal reflection of it is not. Don't be afraid to involve volunteers who have little knowledge about the professional issues; if they are competent, they will learn—as will the staff who come into contact with them.

Orienting and Training Volunteers

Nonprofits are coming to realize that giving volunteers an orientation to the organization is beneficial to both parties: the volunteers better understand the organization and the role that they are playing within it; and the nonprofit has an informed volunteer workforce that can spread the word about the organization to others.

The orientation session or sessions ought to address at least the following:

- The mission and purposes of the nonprofit;
- A brief history and description of the persons served;
- A reminder of the meaningful role that volunteers play in furthering the organization's purpose;
- An overview of the governance structure—which in itself points out other areas in which volunteers serve;
- An organization chart, including names of contact persons (e.g., whom to call if someone is interested in making a donation);
- A description of the role that the volunteer will play and how it fits into the plans and purposes of the nonprofit;
- Any do's and don'ts.

Much of the information can be captured in writing. That does not suggest that the orientation ought to be simply handing out printed material—any more than one would orient a new staff person by giving him or her a manual to read.

The training portion of the orientation and training may occur at two points:

1. At the outset.

   For example, a nonprofit serving children with disabilities might want to have the education and medical directors explain something about the disabilities represented.

2. Periodically thereafter.

Increasing the skills and knowledge of the volunteer workforce will pay dividends; providing training to volunteers is no less than offering leadership development.

Orienting and Training Staff to work with Volunteers[10]

Orienting and training volunteer leadership and committee members is only half of the job. Staff assigned as liaisons to committees also need training in how to work with a volunteer body. Here are ten points to cover in staff orientation:

The Role of a Committee

Staff need to be clear, in general, about what committees in general are expected to accomplish; how they relate to the overall governance structure; and how they relate to staff. Training should provide information on standing committees, ad hocs, task forces—and the differences among these. The role of the committee chair—and the critical relationship between the chair and the staff liaison—need to be stressed. If the chair/staff duo works well, if there is accord on what the committee can accomplish and how to do so, the committee's chances for success are increased. The staff liaison should meet with the chair prior to the first committee meeting to establish a relationship and an understanding of roles and goals.

Staff also need to grasp the importance of "no surprises." Failing to forewarn the committee chair of a possible problem is a sure way to lose his or her cooperation and respect.

Group Dynamics

If staff have had little experience in committee work, they may be unprepared for the job. A primer on how groups interact (the roles that group members assume, models of decision-making, organizational theory) can prove invaluable.

It is important for staff to understand the 50/50 principle: in any meeting, half of what is accomplished is content, half is process. Groups need to bond, and what may appear as peripheral to getting the work done may in fact be necessary to forging the relationships that will allow for positive group dynamics.

Group Process

The staff liaison can be a resource to the chair if he or she knows several group process techniques, so that the committee does not become mired in discussion with little hope for consensus. Some of these techniques are described in Chapter 9.

Organizational History

Not every member of the committee will be familiar with the organization or with the work of the committee or other bodies, which impinges on the committee's own charge. Helping the committee members (and the chair as well) to understand the organization's history, culture, and purpose will put the work of the committee into context. It may be that the committee chair prefers to provide this information, with behind-the-scenes assistance by the staff liaison.

Organizational Mission

If the staff person does not display enthusiasm about the organization, he or she may inadvertently set the tone for the committee. No organization is without its faults; complaining about them is counterproductive to the work of the volunteer body. Enthusiasm about the organization and its contributions to society is equally infectious.

Organizational Policies and Procedures

The staff person needs to be the reservoir of information about organizational policies and procedures. Are formal reports required? Is it necessary to have a resolution prepared in order for the committee to request action by the board of trustees? Can the chair of the committee attend a board meeting or contact another committee directly? What approvals need to be secured before a meeting can be held? Who should be kept informed of committee actions?

Budget and Finance

Staff need to know the parameters within which committees operate: Does each committee have a budget? What sign-offs are needed? If the committee wishes to develop a product that will require outside printing, what approvals must be obtained? Can committee members be reimbursed if the committee meets over lunch at a downtown restaurant?

Meeting Logistics

Even the most exciting agenda can be jeopardized by holding the meeting in a room that is too small, too hot, without flipcharts. Committee members traveling from out of town, whose travel arrangements were fouled up, are going to bring frustration to the table which has nothing to do with the work at hand. So, too, will members who failed to receive sufficient advance notice or background information.

Respect

Staff members who are young and lacking in experience in working with volunteers can be intimidated by the prospect of trying to facilitate committee work when the members comprise persons with considerably more status. The CEO and other experienced staff members can share tips (do's and don'ts), introduce new staff members to the volunteers, and be a resource both before and during the meeting. It may prove wise to have the new staff person serve in an assisting capacity on a committee at first, gradually taking over more responsibility.

Follow-up

There is an understandable tendency, once a committee meeting is concluded, to think, "Whew, that's over." To the contrary, the competent staff liaison will communicate with the chair upon conclusion of the meeting to discuss what went well (and where improvement is in order), assignments which were made, and next steps. Volunteers leave the meeting and return to their other life—typically, the one that pays their salary. The staff needs to be sure that any work agreed upon is not forgotten.

Establishing Expectations for Committees

The organization of the 1990s will look at volunteers less as charitable helpers and more as staff and leaders who serve without financial compensation. The stereotypical volunteer assignments of the 1960s revolved around charity balls, benefits, and home tours. Volunteers were the wives of the wealthy, socially prominent (or wishing to become so), with time on their hands. It was difficult for the organization to which they were donating their time to direct or monitor their efforts, to say the least. They had a great deal of latitude, owing both to social position and to the fact that they often knew best how to coordinate the activity for which they were volunteering.

While major fund raising special events continue and are likely to do so, the work of most volunteers today and into the next century will be in less glamorous activities which further the goals of the organization: planning, marketing, public relations, policymaking, consumer advice. Thus, members of committees and committees themselves need clear delineation of their responsibilities and a means by which their efforts can be evaluated.

Expectations for Committee Membership

Here are some expectations for individual committee members:

- Become familiar with the specific charge to the committee. Be sure that you understand what the committee responsibilities will be and what your role will be in meeting those responsibilities.
- Attend at least two-thirds of all regularly scheduled committee meetings.
- Complete tasks assigned to the committee or to you as a member of the committee.
- Inform yourself about the overall purposes and goals of the organization, so that you can speak for it when the opportunity arises.
- If you have concerns about the progress of the committee, share them candidly with the committee chair or the staff liaison.
- Set the example for teamwork.
- Consider the staff liaison as an integral part of the committee and not as a record-keeper. Share the duties of taking minutes, making coffee, etc.

Expectations for the Committee

The committee itself should adhere to certain expectations. In addition to those listed above for committee members, the committee should:

- Stay within the charge to the committee. If there are matters which ought to be addressed but are outside the purview of your committee, bring them to the attention of the board member assigned to interface with your committee, or to the staff liaison or executive director.
- Remember that none of us is as smart as all of us. The strength of committees is their synergy.
- Keep other bodies within the organization informed. If you are developing recommendations which may affect the work of another body, be sure that your recommendations don't come as a surprise; use the channels of communication to both inform and obtain feedback.

Staff and Committees: Understanding Respective Roles

There are times when getting it in writing makes eminently good sense. Clarifying the roles of staff and volunteers on committees is one of those times. If your organization does not have a written description of how committees should function, seize the opportunity. Set the right tone by involving members of the volunteer leadership and staff jointly in the effort.

Role of the Staff Person on a Committee

The bylaws of some organizations stipulate that the chief staff person is automatically a member of all committees and other similar bodies created by the organization. The CEO can in turn delegate that responsibility to a member of the staff.

The role of the staff person on a committee might be described as shown in Figure 10.

Figure 10.
Role of the Staff Liaison

Staff liaisons serve as full members of committees and related bodies, although without vote. They are selected for committee assignment on the basis of their ability to contribute to the work of the committee in a substantive way. As such, they share the functions and responsibilities of other committee members, participating in discussions within a collegial context with other members of the committee.

Staff members can be expected to bring to the committee relevant organizational history, background on the issues involved, and an understanding of organizational policies, procedures, and practices. They thus facilitate the work of the committee in both content and process.

On occasion, the staff member serving on a committee may be assisted by staff persons who possess particular knowledge or experience. The involvement of additional staff can be requested by the committee chair and arranged by the staff liaison.

Information relating to committee activities should be fully shared among the committee chair, the staff liaison, and the member of the board of directors assigned to monitor the committee. It is the joint responsibility of the committee chair and staff person to assure that meetings are planned effectively and that appropriate parties are kept informed.

Figure 11 describes the role of the committee chair.

Figure 11.
Role of the Committee Chair

Committee chairs are selected based on their ability to coordinate the work of a committee. Desired characteristics of committee chairs include: understanding of the issues to be addressed; a high degree of communication and interpersonal skills; experience in group dynamics; respect within the organization and among its constituencies.

The committee chair is entrusted with fulfilling the charge of the committee, working with the staff liaison and any board members assigned to the committee. He or she sets the tone of the meeting, participating as a discussant while at the same time assuring that all members of the committee have an opportunity to have their views heard.

Specifically, the chair prepares meeting agendas, works with the staff liaison in distributing advance materials, writes and distributes meeting minutes, and keeps the board liaison informed.

In cooperation with the board liaison and staff liaison, the committee chair recommends the incoming slate of committee nominees.

The role of committee chair should not be taken lightly. Effective committees not only further the goals of the organization, they also are an excellent way to identify and cultivate future leadership. The committee chair needs to see beyond the bounds of his or her committee charge:

- What is the relationship of the committee to the organization's long-range plan?

  What elements of the plan are being addressed in the committee's charge?

- How does the committee fit into the formal organizational chart and the informal organizational culture?

Are there other bodies within the organization or other individuals who should be kept informed? And if so, what are the accepted avenues of communication? How will the work of the committee affect key staff? Should they be invited to participate in some of the committee's ruminations?

The committee chair also has the responsibility, which may or may not be captured in writing, to communicate individually with other members of the committee who have been dominating discussions, failing to complete agreed upon assignments, or providing exceptional service.

The committee chair and staff liaison should be committed to communication between committee meetings to discuss the committee's progress, consider any midcourse corrections which need to be taken both in terms of objectives and committee member assignments, and consider future committee composition.

An important distinction is contained within the description of both the staff liaison and committee chair: it should not be the role of staff to take notes and compile meeting minutes. That is the responsibility of the committee chair. He or she may ask the staff liaison to keep a running record, which will facilitate the completion of minutes. But assigning the staff person to the role of notetaker sends an unfortunate message; the staff person becomes a scribe rather than an equal partner in the deliberations. That shortchanges the committee. It deserves better—a staff person who can bring knowledge and experience to the committee.

This sometimes raises a dilemma: how can the chair keep a record of what occurred and exercise the leadership role assigned? There are at least three options:

1. Rotate the minute-taking responsibility among members of the committee.

2. Set aside 10 to 15 minutes at the conclusion of each meeting for the committee to summarize what transpired.

   Ask one member of the committee to use a flipchart, chalkboard or other device to capture key points: what was discussed, what was decided or agreed upon, what assignments were made.

3. Audiotape the meeting or portions thereof.

The third key element to successful committee work is, of course, the members of the committee themselves. The committee's role is described in Figure 12.

Figure 12. Role of the Committee

A committee plays an essential function within the organization. It allows for careful deliberation on issues and facilitates the organization's planning and programs. Committees are appointed by the Board of Trustees to fulfill a specific charge, and typically members of the Board are assigned to work with them. Committees are thus advisory to the Board.

Committee members are selected on their perceived comprehension of the issue at hand with consideration given to the diverse constituencies of the organization. Committee members are from time to time given specific individual assignments and share the overall responsibility of completing the committee's work in a timely and efficacious manner.

Committee members should be prepared to attend at least two-thirds of all committee meetings and to participate fully in committee discussions.

Understanding the Difference: Committee, Board, Ad Hoc, Task Force, Council

The terms "committee," "board," "ad hoc," "task force," and "council" are not interchangeable, although the distinction among them is often blurred. The board may be called a board of directors, board of trustees, or board of governors. By definition, a board of trustees is the body to which the organization is *entrusted*; it holds the fiduciary responsibility and its composition may be included in the organizational charter. The overall well-being of the organization, including its finances, is entrusted in the board of trustees.

Some organizations refer to this body as a board of directors. A board of governors, by comparison, is often a larger body that is more advisory in nature. It does not truly govern but does have some say in deciding policy, or at least recommending it. Some nonprofits have an operating board of trustees, which sets policy; and a larger, more loosely formed board of governors, whose members may include persons who have made substantial contributions to the organization and who represent certain constituencies.

A committee is advisory to the policymaking board. It may be a standing committee whose role is described within the bylaws (e.g., a nominating or finance committee), or a committee with certain ongoing functions—fund raising, public relations, budget. Ad hoc committees, as their name implies, are created for a special purpose; once their work is completed, they are disbanded. Using an ad hoc committee structure allows the organization to address issues or complete work without creating a committee whose term is indefinite.

Task forces operate somewhat similarly to ad hoc bodies in that they are assigned to complete a specific task—e.g., come up with recommendations for employee family day care. In some organizations, task forces are headed by staff who have knowledge of the topic under consideration, whereas ad hoc committees are chaired by volunteers.

Councils may be either advisory or have a policymaking function. Advisory councils are often created by elected officials to obtain input on a sensitive topic, or at least present the appearance of doing so. These citizen advisory councils do not have decision-making power, although they can become influential.

Some nonprofits use the term "council" (or assemblies) for a legislative body that is charged with overall policy setting. This is true particularly among professional and trade associations.

Toward a Partnership Between Staff and Volunteers

The descriptions noted above will help to clarify the roles of staff and volunteer—and hopefully the expectations that one has of the other. Fostering the growth of a volunteer/staff partnership involves some intangibles as well. Here are some additional points worth considering.

What the committee should expect from staff:

- Coordination of meeting logistics—mailings, room set-up, provision of background and backup information;

- Timely response to requests for assistance;
- Suggestions for alternatives and options and not merely posing problems or roadblocks;
- Knowledge of the subject at hand or access to such knowledge;
- A spirit of cooperation;
- Reinforcement for work well done.

Staff, in turn, might expect the following from committees to which they are assigned:

- Evidence of commitment to the goals of the organization and to the objectives of the committee;
- Timely completion of tasks;
- Treatment as colleagues;
- Willingness to "roll up one's sleeves"—as contrasted with a "leave it for staff" attitude;
- A spirit of cooperation;
- Reinforcement for work well done.

Staff should recognize that the following are likely to lead to friction between them and the committees with which they are working:

- Lack of communication from staff—communication in a less than timely fashion;
- Being pulled into office politics, asked to "take sides";
- Lack of responsiveness;
- Apparent undervaluing of the worth of committee activity;
- Insufficient orientation to the organization, to the background of the committee, and to its charge;
- Consistently being presented with reasons why something cannot be done (the "We already tried that" or "That'll never work" mentality).

Committees, on the other hand, need to recognize that the following will hardly endear them to the staff:

- Failing to keep staff involved and informed about actions or plans;
- Going around the staff person to his or her supervisor or to someone else on staff without prior consultation;
- Apparent lack of appreciation for the efforts that staff expend;
- Being drawn into committee politics;

- Committee members who use the committee as a soap box or platform to advance their political aspirations;
- Failure of volunteers to complete work to which they have agreed.

Committee Reports

Committee reports are not detailed minutes of what has occurred. There is little value in a report when the majority reads something like this:

> The committee meeting was called to order by Chair Lester Ferguson at 9:14 am. . . . Committee member Doris McJabber reported on the plans for the upcoming flea market. It seems that the county is requiring organizations to get a permit and she wanted to know how she should proceed.
>
> There was a discussion about the need to reschedule the time of committee meetings. One committee member maintained that 8:00 am was too early. After some considerable discussion, it was agreed that future meetings would be held at 9:00 am . . . .

A bit farcical, perhaps, but not remote from what appears in the reports of too many committees. So what should the committee report include?

- Place/date/time of the meeting and persons in attendance;
- Issues addressed (in summary form; list, if possible);
- Decisions reached;
- Actions taken;
- Assignments;
- Other recommendations/miscellaneous;
- Details regarding next meeting;
- Name of person submitting report;
- Distribution (to whom the report should be circulated—other committees, board of trustees, selected members of the staff);
- Information that may be pertinent to an in-house article or external news release.

Evaluating the Work of the Committee

Evaluation should be both formative (ongoing) and summative (conclusive). The evaluation asks three questions:

1. Is the committee meeting its charge? (Is it accomplishing the objectives for which it was established?)

2. Are there problems that can be forestalled?
3. Is the committee working well together? (Do the group dynamics contribute to an "upbeat," positive meeting tone? Do members feel safe to speak their minds freely?)

The agenda should allow for a brief review at the end of each meeting, at which time the chair can invite observation. What have we accomplished? Do we seem to be on track? Are there any concerns that should be addressed? Any problems which loom ahead?

The chair may want to contact members individually. "Linda, I sensed that you were feeling frustrated at our last meeting. I'm wondering if it would be helpful to get together to talk about where we might make some improvements. You're a vital member of the committee and I value your opinion." Or: "Don, I need to ask you candidly if your workload will allow you to continue as an active member of our committee. We have a lot of work ahead of us, and I want to give you a chance to evaluate your own potential to continue as a contributing member. Either way, we'll of course respect your decision and appreciate the work that you've put in thus far."

Evaluation of the committee's work is not unlike staff performance management; in both, ongoing evaluation is made easier when the clear objectives have been established and agreed upon. It may be relatively simple to evaluate objectives based on committee products—e.g., the writing of a report. Evaluating the quality of the work is always more difficult.

Some of the ongoing evaluation will occur off-the-record between staff and committee chair. Both should feel comfortable being forthright about the progress being made by the committee and its individual members.

The summative evaluation—conducted once the committee has completed its work—provides an opportunity for members to feel good about themselves (the spilloff being that they will also feel good about the organization). The summative evaluation can also be used to ask "Where next?" questions. Are there issues that surfaced that the committee believes should be considered by some other body? Were trends noted that should be brought to the attention of the strategic planning committee? Are any changes in the governance structure in order?

Finally, the summative evaluation ought to include a confidential appraisal of committee members, so that those evincing leadership potential can be targeted in the future.

The Meeting Management Record: A Tool for Evaluation

The meeting minutes (as described above) can provide a useful tool to monitor and evaluate the work of a committee. Another tool is the Meeting Management Record.[11] It may include items such as:

- Task/activity (what did the committee agree to?);
- Agent (who is responsible?);
- Cost/income (what are the direct cost implications; will any income be realized?);
- Timeframe (start and completion dates);
- Policy/procedures (relationship to long-range plan or other policies or written procedures);
- Status (as of a certain date).

RECOGNIZING THE WORK OF VOLUNTEERS

The importance of recognizing volunteers is so rudimentary, so ingrained in the whole concept of volunteering and voluntarism, that we tend to take it for granted. We treat it routinely: once a year, the president of the board signs a bunch of plaques, thanking <Fill In Name Here> for his or her free-will work for the organization.

This is not to demean the use of plaques. They are a proper way to thank persons for their volunteer work. But they are by no means the only way. Just as performance management needs to be integrated into the behavior of the organization, so, too, recognition of the volunteer needs to be incorporated into the daily operations.

1. **Attitude is recognition.**

   How do your staff feel about volunteers? Are they considered part of the team? Are they looked at as professionals? Or are they considered a necessary nuisance? Do volunteers ever sit in on staff meetings, perhaps as a liaison to the volunteer body? Do they dress as other staff, or are they expected to wear uniforms which brand them as "aides"?

   If you have a volunteer auxiliary, does its head interact with a senior member of the staff?

2. **Recognition should reflect achievement.**

   Giving the same plaque to everyone who has in some way volunteered for the organization in the past year may be overdoing it for some and diminishing the attention deserved by others. Imagine yourself as volunteer; you've chaired a committee that has worked with staff to entirely revise the budget for the organization. Your committee spent upwards of 100 hours on this task, the result of which will be that the organization will be able to track expenditures and bill for services with greater speed and accuracy. For your efforts, you get a plaque, identical to one given to volunteers from the local high school who helped out with spring clean-up.

Recognition need not be expensive, although at times (say, to recognize someone retiring after 20 years of volunteer service) an expensive gift or ceremony is requisite. Some alternatives to the more traditional plaque? How about acknowledging outstanding service by getting an article placed in the local press or in the alumni magazine of the volunteer being recognized? Planting a tree? Getting a letter of commendation from the mayor, governor, even U.S. president?

Some other ideas:

- Dedicate a publication in honor of the work of a volunteer.
- If your organization serves young children, have them make drawings or cards which say thank you.
- Provide levels of recognition according to years of service (certificate for one year, pin for three, glass serving bowl for five, etc.).

Even if it is only a letter, the recognition should make it clear to the receiver that the organization knows what he or she has contributed. Specific elements of the letter of appreciation might include:

- Mention of the project(s) on which the volunteer has worked.
- A description of the difference that the volunteer's efforts made (e.g., "With your help, we were able to raise over $25,000 at our annual golf tournament");
- Language which reminds the volunteer that you welcome her or his continued involvement.
- Signature by someone whose name (or title) has meaning to the volunteer.[12]

Not every letter need be signed by the executive director or board chair. There are times when having someone with either of those titles sign the letter will have special meaning; at other times, it may be most appropriate for a member of the staff or another volunteer who has worked directly with the volunteer to sign the correspondence.

Regardless of the form that the recognition takes, it should accomplish four things:

1. Help the volunteer to feel that his or her work is valued.
2. Invite the volunteer to maintain, if not upgrade, his or her level of participation.
3. Attract others to contribute their time through the means of recognizing the work of a volunteer.
4. Present the organization in a positive light.

PARTING THOUGHTS

In a baccalaureate address at Princeton, Woodrow Wilson said this about volunteering:

> Nothing but what you volunteer has the essence of life, the springs of pleasure in it. . . . The more you are stimulated to do such action the more clearly does it appear that you are a sovereign spirit, put into the world, not to wear harness, but to work eagerly without it.[13]

Managers of nonprofits have the opportunity and the responsibility to inculcate that spirit of volunteering. In the decade before us, the roles of volunteer and staff may become intermingled, making it difficult to tell where one begins and the other leaves off. All the more reason to keep in mind that volunteers do what they do without financial remuneration and to look for ways to enrich the jobs that they perform.

NOTES

1. Katheryn Wiedman Heidrich, "Volunteers: Life Styles: Market Sigmentation Based on Volunteers' Role Choices," *Nonprofit and Voluntary Sector Quarterly*, 19 (Spring 1990): 21–31.

2. "Study Consumer Actions to Recruit Volunteers, *"The Taft Nonprofit Executive*, 18 (August 1989): 10.

3. Research & Forecasts, *The Chevas Regal Report on Working Americans: Emerging Values for the 1990s* (New York: The House of Seagram, 1989), xvi.

4. Harold Kushner, *When All You've Ever Wanted Isn't Enough: The Search for a Life That Matters* (New York: Simon & Schuster, 1986), 23.

5. The statistics gathered by the American Association of Retired Persons were reported in *Nonprofit Management Strategies*, 2 (September 1990): 18.

6. Joan Carolyn Kuyper, "Volunteer Management into the 21st Century," *A Sharing of Expertise & Experience*, Vol. 7 (Washington, DC: American Society of Association Executives, 1988), 72.

7. The section on rethinking volunteer roles draws on Henry Ernstthal, "A Marketing Approach to Voluntary Involvement." Spring Meeting, Council of State Speech-Language-Hearing Association Presidents, Baltimore, MD, May 1990.

8. John Galsworthy, *The Forsyte Saga* (New York: Charles Scribner's Sons, 1948), 577.

9. Peter Drucker, *The New Realities: In Government and Politics / In Economics and Business / In Society and World View* (New York: Harper & Row Publishers, 1989), 197.

10. Some of thinking for the section on orienting staff on how to work with committees was drawn from Anette E. Petrick, "Orient Your Staff," *Association Management*, 43 (February 1991): 41–45.

11. The Meeting Management Record draws on the work of Charles Rumbarger and his presentation before the Association Foundation Group, March 12, 1991.

12. Rebecca F. Brillhart, ed. *Accent on Recognition: Saying Thank You to Donors and Volunteers* (Washington, DC: Philanthropic Service for Institutions, Adventist World Headquarters, 1988), 9.

13. The quotation from Woodrow Wilson was found in Harold J. Seymour, *Designs for Fund Raising, Second Edition* (Ambler, PA: Fund-Raising Institute, 1988), 198.

Chapter 12
Maintaining the Edge:
What You Don't Learn
in Management School

EXECUTIVE SUMMARY

Although this is not primarily a text on personal development for the nonprofit executive, it is worth remembering that the success of the organization is inextricably related to the capabilities of its chief staff person. This chapter briefly reviews the nonprofit career: how to develop a career ladder; how to recognize and deal with burnout; and management of self.

BUILDING A CAREER LADDER

Those in nonprofit organizations don't know much about career ladders when compared with executives from the business world, academia, or the military. Even today, most nonprofit executives have come from some other field to nonprofit management; a relatively small percent have received formal schooling in how to manage the nonprofit enterprise.

To some degree that is an advantage: it allows for some creativity.

Education

A growing number of colleges and universities in the United States, Canada, and Great Britain are offering courses, if not full programs, in the nonprofit sector. That is a trend worth watching, and may be of interest to the individual looking for a way to enrich his or her career. In addition, some of the more traditional programs in business administration are offering opportunities to specialize in the nonprofit area.

Opportunities for continuing education are vast; because they do a good job of marketing themselves it is not necessary to take up space in the chapter listing them. (Information on upcoming workshops can be found in periodicals geared to nonprofits, such as *The Chronicle of Philanthropy.)* One thought: there is benefit to taking courses that are not geared to the nonprofit executive—to American Management Association courses, for example, and institutes in leadership development or management courses in a college or university. One risk in the proliferation of educational opportunities aimed at nonprofits is that those taking them may become too narrow in their thinking. Hearing from the for-profit sector helps maintain perspective.

A third option is to become certified as a professional in some field relating to nonprofit management—fund raising, public relations, accounting, association management. (This list is illustrative rather than exhaustive.) Becoming certified allows the nonprofit executive to extend his or her name a bit with initials denoting achievement (for fund raising, CFRE; for public relations, APR; for accounting, CPA; for association management, CAE). The initials signify that the individual has a firm grasp of the knowledge base in that area and has been recognized as an informed practitioner by a national body. There is some indication that certified executives tend to earn higher salaries; whether that is a result of certification or an indication of the type of person who seeks it has not been proven.

OPPORTUNITIES FOR GROWTH

The nonprofit world offers neither the salary nor the upwardly mobile potential of large corporations, as anyone in the nonprofit sector knows well. But it does offer wide ranging opportunities for growth:

Advancement to a larger organization.

There is wide variance between the executive director of a three-person, local agency with a budget of $250,000 and the chief staff person for a nonprofit with a budget of several million dollars and a staff of over 100. While the title may not change, the challenges and chances for growth surely do.

Involvement in an association.

The majority of adult Americans belong to at least one special interest group for reasons relating to professional interests, politics, business, personal growth, or ideology.[1] Membership in an association offers opportunities in education, networking, and personal leadership development.

Sharing information with others.

Information-sharing might take the form of presenting on convention or workshop programs, writing an article, or serving as a mentor.

Becoming a volunteer.

Volunteering is a win-win-win. The organization benefits from nonpaid help. There is personal satisfaction for the volunteer. And if he or she is a nonprofit executive, the experience enriches his or her understanding of the needs and capabilities of volunteers.

DEALING WITH BURNOUT

The first step in dealing with burnout is to recognize some of the signs:

- Forgetfulness;
- Change in sleep patterns;
- Daydreaming on the job;
- An atypical willingness to be critical about the organization;
- Reluctance to go to work on a Monday morning;
- Overindulgence—overeating, drinking to excess, candy "binges," etc.;
- Frequent frustration with staff or colleagues;
- General impatience—with offspring, spouse, traffic, lines;
- Frequent colds or other minor illnesses.

A "yes" vote to more than half (i.e., five) of the items above may indicate a need to rethink the nature of work. If it seems probable that burnout has arrived—as it will for nearly everyone at some time—there are several courses of action. Some, in the nature of horizontal change, have been already suggested—further education, involvement in an association, volunteering—as has considering a move to another facility. Later in this chapter consideration will be given to looking at life goals, which is another means to addressing burnout.

Within the organization, here are some additional suggestions for combatting burnout:

- Keep a long view.

  It is easy to get so mired in the day-to-day that one loses sight of bigger goals.

- Prioritize the workload: Essential, Important, Other.

  Skip the "other" if at all possible (although it is tempting to do otherwise; the essentials are often also the most challenging). Spend time where it counts.

- Focus on what you can do well; capitalize on that.

- Correct for deficiencies.

  If you are better at problem-solving than detail, be sure to have someone on staff who is both good at and likes detail.

- Know what you can live with in terms of others' work.

  Some of the work which you assign will not meet with the expectations that you would have had of yourself. Decide when it is important to step in, when to give staff a chance to learn from failure, and when less-than-perfect is acceptable.

- Remember that progress comes slowly.

THINKING ABOUT LIFE GOALS

People are often better at advising others about their careers than at thinking about their own. A jumping-off point for thinking about the future is to examine what has real meaning for you. Rank the items on the following list (Figure 13) in order of personal value. Resist the temptation to group items or give more than one the same numerical rating; rank each separately.

Figure 13. Ranking Goal Areas

Rank	Item	Description
	Expertness	Becoming a recognized expert in some area
	Knowledge	Being well-informed about many topics
	Wisdom	Ability to interpret, to see "bigger picture"
	Love	Unqualified affection from another
	Respect	Looked up to by staff, peers, others
	Power	Ability to exercise control
	Spirituality	At one with a higher order of being
	Wealth	Earning a large income
	Pleasure	Enjoying life day to day
	Happiness	Contentment; peace of mind
	Security	Holding a job which is secure
	Achievement	Self-actualization; achieving personal goals
	Family	Being a spouse or parent (or both)
	Service	Commitment to others[2]

Once you have ranked the list, give thought to how well it matches up with your day-to-day activities. Are you doing something on a regular basis to reach the goals which you placed in the top five?

Ten Years from Today

Another way of asking the question of yourself regarding long-range goals is to imagine it is ten years from today. Based on the goals which you set for yourself, you rethought your own personal and professional life and have made certain changes to achieve those goals. Assume that you have had some success in reaching those goals. Ask yourself:

- Where are you living?
- Whom are you living with?
- Imagine it is a Friday. What will you be doing, hour by hour?
- How do you feel about yourself and what you are doing?[3]

William Glasser argues that we need in our lives some "positive addictions"—"positive because they strengthen us and make our lives more satisfying."[4] Reaching even a portion of the goals embodied in the vision of where you would like to be ten years from today may require some positive addictions. Said another way: If the goals are as important as you would like to think they are, being somewhat compulsive about achieving them can be quite healthy.

If becoming the CEO of a major organization is your goal, you need to be addicted to the idea in the sense that Glasser uses that term. Positive addictions are driving forces; they compel people to take risks. They ask you to reach beyond self.

PARTING THOUGHTS

In a commencement address, Jesuit priest William S. Byron echoes the idea of "positive addiction":

> Every one of you has a healthy appetite for the highs this life has to offer you through legitimate pleasure and honest achievement. . . .
>
> Those of us who have gone before you in the practice of life are not necessarily ahead of you. We have, for the most part, confused the easy way with the happy life. . . .
>
> Do not be taken in by the big lie our culture of consumerism perpetuates. Do not believe that to have is to be, that to have more is to be fully human, and, worst lie of all, to live easily is to live happily."[5]

Those who manage nonprofits in the 1990s will understand the speaker's sentiments: there is more to life than acquiring and consuming. What gives life meaning is doing something that makes a difference. That's a pretty good definition of the nonprofit organization.

NOTES

1. James J. Dunlop, *Leading the Association: Striking the Right Balance Between Staff and Volunteers* (Washington, DC: American Society of Association Executives, 1989), 1.

2. The table regarding life choices benefited from the work of George A. Ford and Gordon L. Lippitt, *Planning Your Future* (San Diego, CA: University Associates, 1976), 7.

3. Appreciation is expressed to Ken Blanchard for the questions in "Ten Years from Today."

4. William Glasser, *Positive Addiction* (New York: Harper & Row, 1976), 2.

5. William J. Byron, S. J., commencement address, St. Thomas University, Miami, May 14, 1989; quoted in *The Executive Speaker*, 10 (August 1989): 10.

Index

by Linda Webster